Money Matters

To our respective parents

Money Matters

A KEYNESIAN APPROACH TO
MONETARY ECONOMICS

SHEILA C. DOW   PETER E. EARL

Barnes & Noble Books
Totowa · New Jersey

First published in the USA in 1982 by
Barnes & Noble Books
81 Adams Drive,
Totowa, New Jersey 07512

Library of Congress Cataloging in Publication Data

Dow, Sheila.
  Money matters.

  1. Money.   2. Monetary policy.   3. Keynesian economics.   I. Earl, Peter. II. Title.
HG221.D65 1982   332.4′01   82-11380
ISBN 0-389-20323-8

Printed and bound in Great Britain.

Contents

Contents

viii Contents

Acknowledgements

The overall approach to monetary economics presented here reflects the influence of a wide variety of people who have helped form our 'world-views'. While the sources of these influences are too numerous to list, they have contributed most to the way in which we understand and present the working of monetary economics.

We would like to make particular mention, however, of those who have contributed directly to the specific arguments put forward within this broad approach. Through the generosity of the Esmee Fairbairn Institute of Finance and Investment Fund, we were able to duplicate an early draft of the book and circulate it widely for comments. The following provided helpful suggestions and constructive criticism on the basis of this early draft: S. G. Checkland; V. Chick; A. B. Cramp; A. S. Eichner; D. W. Laidler; H. P. Minsky; C. Munn; L. White and an anonymous referee; and our colleagues at Stirling: P. J. W. N. Bird, A. C. Dow, K. W. Glaister, P. Hare, R. Shone and N. Zouvelos. We do of course accept full responsibility for all remaining errors.

We are grateful to Garry Mackenzie for allowing us to use material he had researched on the 1970s bank failures. *The Times* has kindly allowed us to reproduce their 'League of Bank Losses' table from their Europa section, p. X, 7 January 1975. Finally, we are grateful to Mrs E. Bruce and Mrs A. Cowie for the efficiency and patience with which they typed successive drafts of the manuscript.

Introduction

This book is designed primarily for intermediate and final-year under-graduates, but it would be of interest to all economists looking for a comprehensive exposition of monetary theory from a Post Keynesian standpoint.

We perceive a need for such a book, when there are already so many books on monetary theory, because of the tendency for monetary theory to be shunted off into its own siding, while core macro-economic theory courses give it only peripheral importance. (Core microeconomic theory courses generally have no monetary content at all.) Certainly monetarist economists give money a central role in macroeconomic theory, but only as something which confuses under-lying economic relationships in the short run, and of minimal 'real' importance in the long run.

The essence of Post Keynesian monetary theory, which we attempt to convey in this book, is that, in a monetary economy, money is central to all economic relationships. The fact that in many chapters we discuss issues conventionally discussed not only in macroeconomic theory, but also in microeconomic theory, is quite deliberate.

It is not surprising that many economists can conduct their analysis purely in real terms, without reference to finance, when we operate in an academic environment where monetary theory is generally taught as a subject quite distinct from the theory core. We attempt here to show how it may be integrated into economic theory, from a Post Keynesian standpoint.

Clearly, this approach has been influenced fundamentally by Keynes' work. The reinterpretation of Keynesian economics in the last two decades has attempted in various ways to reinstate money to the central position given it by Keynes. Of the interpreters, the greatest influences have been Cramp, Davidson, Minsky and Shackle.

The ideas in the book are expressed mainly in words, with minimal recourse to mathematical shorthand. While the book starts, in chapter 1, with a discussion of the issues dealt with by monetary theory expressed in terms of the IS–LM diagram, this framework is not used again, except where we show how it can be a misleading tool. It is employed here simply to form a bridge between students' existing understanding of macroeconomic issues, which has usually been acquired by means of IS–LM analysis, and the analysis in the rest of the book. The scant use of mathematics does not reflect any reservations about the value of mathematical economics. Rather, it is necessary if a 'new view' of economic relationships is to be acquired. The broad understanding of institutional arrangements and economic inter-dependencies, which is assumed when mathematical shorthand is used, is precisely the area we wish to discuss here.

The general outline of the book is as follows. The introductory chapter is designed to clarify the major issues with which monetary theory is concerned, using IS–LM analysis with which students should already be familiar. Bearing these general questions in mind, the student should then be able to understand the significance of the detailed discussions in the rest of the book.

Chapters 2–4 consider the supply of money in the long run, looking at how and why financial institutions develop. The Scottish banking system, the first to introduce many banking innovations, is used as a case study. Differences in financial structure also apply to contemporary economies at different stages of development, similar to those for one economy over the long run. The implications for the pattern of economic development of interactions between different economies' financial systems are then discussed, in chapter 4.

Chapters 5–7 consider money supply in the short run, as analysed by the multiplier approach and the portfolio approach. The degree of supply endogeneity and the policy implications of each approach are then considered. The analysis of money supply in the Eurocurrency market is used as a case study. The role of Non-Bank Financial Intermediaries, which resembles that of the Eurocurrency market, is then considered with respect to monetary (macroeconomic) and pru-dential controls.

With the previous chapters having examined the development of the money supplies of both developed and developing countries chapters 8–16 attempt to examine the factors affecting the demand for mone-tary assets and the consequences of portfolio choices thus made for the stability of prices and output. This is an area fraught with controversy and in the middle of this part of the book (chapter 13) there is an examination of some questions of methodology and the central tenets of the major schools of thought in monetary economics. This chapter may at first seem rather oddly located but it follows a series of chapters where important features have largely been examined in cold institutional terms to avoid controversy as far as possible. By examining the mechanics of the system, the factors that a rational speculator has to consider in making her choices and the actual causes of particular bank failures, we provide the student with a body of material which she can use in analysing the controversies in chapters 14–16. The case study analysis of Minsky's theory of financial instability is put before the chapter on method, to awaken the student to the complexities of appraising a theory derived by pushing institutional facts of life to their logical limits and seeing what disastrous consequences might thus potentially be in store for a monetary economy.

Chapters 14–16 should be seen as a series of case studies of controversies that need to be solved before sensible policy-making is possible: how does money affect the price level, the level of output and the balance of payments? Having studied these chapters the student is then well placed to get the maximum benefit from the final part of the book, the discussion of monetary policy. The strong methodological emphasis of the middle section of the book, in particular its concentration on the problems of identification and the interlinked nature of theories (research programmes) should make it of wider interest than conventional treatments of 'Monetarist versus Keynesian' debates.

Chapter 17 brings together the policy discussions incorporated in earlier chapters. It discusses the purposes of monetary control, the means of control, and the trade-offs involved. These trade-offs refer particularly to the financing of fiscal deficits, distributional and inefficiency side-effects of controls and the interrelationships with prudential control. Chapter 18 concludes the book by summarizing the arguments presented throughout the book which suggest that 'money matters'. Money is described as performing a crucial role in determining the level and distribution of output and employment. Monetary theory is thus seen as central to economic theory. The chapter concludes with a discussion of future directions which monetary theory might take.

On a final, technical note, wherever we refer to 'billions' we are using the term in the American sense i.e. 1000 million.

1

What Are The Issues?

Money matters. To most of us this is not a controversial statement. But it is non-controversial in the sense that 'income or wealth matters', i.e. in the sense that it is important for most individuals, firms and governments to have command over real resources, the economist's proxy for welfare.

But would it 'matter' if we were paid income or held our wealth in something other than money? Is there something peculiar to money which gives it a different significance from other commodities, like oil; or assets, like houses? If so, what does this peculiarity signify?

These are the questions underlying the vast body of literature dealing with money and banking. Inevitably economists have differed not only over the degree to which money 'matters' but also in the manner in which money affects the economy. In the following chapters we attempt to provide answers to these questions from first principles. In so doing, the attempt is made to assess the different major contributions to money and banking theory with reference to these first principles.

Most theoretical contributions have arisen more in response to earlier theories than with reference to first principles. The attention paid to many of the issues which have dominated discussion can only be explained by this dialectic process among economists, which in many cases has not reached the synthesis stage. Most other dominant issues have been those prompted by particular policy problems, where a role has been sought for money in changing the values of important economic variables.

In this chapter we provide a very brief, simplified, overview of the more significant issues tackled by monetary economists, issues which will be explained in more depth in later chapters. These issues are expressed for the moment in terms of a common framework which is widely used: the IS–LM framework. Unfortunately, any methodology, like the use of IS–LM diagrams, implies a particular theoretical approach; but in order to compare different theories, *some* framework must be used. Indeed the theories of those who reject IS–LM analysis can be well represented by their reasons for this rejection. The framework is thus employed simply as a jumping-off point for the analysis in the chapters which follow.

The question of how, and how much, money matters must be expressed with more precision in order to be addressed within any particular framework. In fact, the form of the question is more or less common to all frameworks, as: 'how and by how much does the money supply affect important economic variables?' Thus:

(a) how and by how much does a change in the money supply alter the level of output?; and

(b) how and by how much does a change in the money supply alter the general price level?

To the extent that answers to these questions have suggested that money *does* matter, then the third part of the question assumes supreme importance:

(c) how and to what extent can the central monetary authorities effect changes in the money supply, in order to effect changes in the level of output or prices?

For many, particularly policy-makers, the answer is that the money supply *cannot* be controlled effectively, but that some financial rates of return (interest rates) can be controlled. In a sense this is the obverse of control of the money supply, since key interest rates are manipulated by changing some components of the money supply. But, if one must concentrate on interest rates for practical purposes, then questions (a) and (b) must refer to the effect of interest rates, rather than the money supply, on output and prices.

The matter is made more complex by the fact that the authorities may choose explicitly not to control the money supply, or even interest rates. Rather, these may be altered only as side-effects of other government policies, particularly fiscal policy. The effects of the resulting changes in monetary variables are thus enmeshed in the effects of the reason for their change, e.g. the particular form of fiscal policy. In this context the line between endogeneity and exogeneity of money supply changes becomes blurred: they are a direct result of government action, but not the instrument of control. In the simple IS–LM framework, policies are separable, i.e. it is possible to consider fiscal policy and its mode of financing as two additive components, so for the remainder of this chapter we concentrate simply on changes in the money supply.

We start by examining the *orthodox neoclassical approach,* often called the 'neoclassical synthesis', which is most closely associated with the IS–LM framework. Indeed the framework was first introduced by Hicks (1937) and developed by Modigliani (1944) in order to put different approaches to monetary theory on common ground. This orthodox neoclassical representation is shown in figure 1.1. (See Chick (1977), pp. 23–6 for a more detailed categorization of IS–LM systems.)

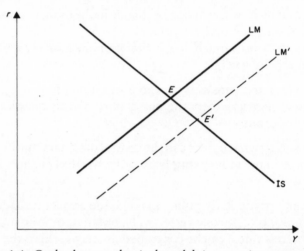

Figure 1.1 *Orthodox neoclassical model: increase in money supply*

The IS curve shows all possible combinations of income, Y, and a representative interest rate, r, which allow planned savings to equal planned investment. The LM curve shows all combinations of Y and r which allow demand for money to equal the particular money supply determined by the government. Thus we start off with the assumption that the money supply *can* be controlled. Wages and prices are also assumed for the moment to be fixed (in line with a common misinterpretation of Keynes (1936)). So the 'money matters' question is confined to question (a), the effect of a change in the money supply on output.

The positive slope of the LM curve reflects the combination of motives for holding money. Money held for transactions (and precautionary) purposes increases with income, while money held for speculative purposes falls as the interest rate rises. While Keynes' speculative motive (discussed in chapter 8) has been played down in the neoclassical model, a similar relationship between demand for money and the interest rate can be explained by the opportunity cost of holding transactions balances (see Baumol (1952)) and/or aversion to the capital risk for which high interest rates compensate (see Tobin (1958)). The LM curve is more steeply sloped the less interest-elastic is money demand.

The IS curve has a negative slope because a lower rate of interest is assumed to bring about a higher level of investment, which raises effective demand, income and savings. The slope is steeper the less interest-elastic is investment demand and the higher the marginal propensity to save.

It is then straightforward to show that an increase in money supply shifts the LM curve to the right, to LM', raising the equilibrium level of output. The higher money supply is met by increased demand both because income has risen and because the interest rate has fallen. The new equilibrium point, E', is on the original IS curve, showing that savings and investment are still equal.

As long as we accept that the system is stable, i.e. always approaches equilibrium, then the only room left for debate regards the slopes of the two curves. Monetary economists have been particularly concerned with the slope of the LM curve; the steeper it is, the more effect the money supply change has on income or output. The curve is steeper the less interest rates influence the demand for money. A vast amount of econometric effort has been expended in the task of estimating this slope (see Laidler (1977) and Fisher (1980) for a detailed coverage).

The usefulness of the resulting estimates of the money demand function is predicated on the acceptability of the assumption that authorities *do* fix the money supply (see Laidler (1977), pp. 114–17). If in fact in some cases authorities tend to respond to interest rate increases by raising the money supply, then the money supply is now endogenous and a positive function of r. (We say that government-induced changes are 'exogenous' if they are discretionary rather than automatic (see Chick (1977), pp. 83–90). If the money supply is endogenous a conventional LM curve, which assumes a given money supply, cannot be drawn. The slope of the curve would reflect a combination of demand and supply responses. This does not alter the answer to the underlying question about the effect of an *exogenous* money supply change on income levels, but it does alter the analysis of *how* that effect occurs.

The main source of endogeneity of the money supply considered by the neoclassical orthodoxy is international flows of funds arising from imbalance in international payments, when exchange rates are fixed. (This theory is central to 'global monetarism', which is discussed in chapter 16.) Money supply increases from this source too may be attracted by high interest rates. If interest rates rise relative to other countries' rates, and are not offset by a currency appreciation, then foreign investors will buy securities earning the higher return, in exchange for domestic currency which they have purchased with their own currency. This factor makes the LM curve flatter in the same way as when the domestic government increases the money supply when interest rates rise. But the endogeneity from foreign sources does seriously reduce the government's ability to control the money supply. (Having introduced the monetary effects of the foreign sector to the LM curve, we must also adjust the IS curve to reflect expenditure on imports and exports.)

An answer to question (b) on the effect of money on the price level can be tacked onto this type of analysis by means of identifying the full-employment level of output and allowing changes in the general price level. Then, if the equilibrium level of income is below the full-employment level, there is little pressure for prices rises. Above that level, however, any upward pressure on output will simply cause prices to rise. Thus an exogenous money supply increase which attempts to shift the LM curve to the right will raise the price level rather than output. The real purchasing power of the new, higher money stock falls, and keeps falling until all pressure on prices is removed, i.e. until aggregate demand equals the full-employment output level. The LM curve in terms of the *real* money supply remains in its initial position. Thus the effects of the money supply on output and prices are *alternatives* depending on whether or not the economy is initially at full employment. The mechanism of money's effect is, however, the same in both cases. (A wide range of overlap between output and price changes is the subject of Phillips curve analysis.)

The major modification to this type of analysis has come from the introduction of 'wealth effects' in a variety of forms. (Wealth effects are discussed in more depth in chapter 9.) In general it is postulated that the demand for money rises if wealth rises (in addition to the influence of income and interest rates). In strict monetarist models wealth alone determines the demand for money. Similarly, the demand for consumer goods rises as wealth rises.

Much argument has concentrated on what constitutes wealth, ranging from nothing but real goods, to real goods plus a variety of financial assets. If only real money balances (plus real goods) constitute wealth, then the LM curve shifts to the right as the money supply rises, but not by as much as without wealth effects because demand for money has at the same time risen; there is also a rightward shift of the IS curve as consumption demand rises. Whether the final increase in output is greater than or less than the outcome without wealth effects depends on the relative strength of the wealth effect on money demand and on consumer demand.

The most famous use of this form of the wealth effect was made by Pigou (1941) in response to Keynes (1936). If prices fall in a recession, then the rise in the real value of the money stock prompts an increase in consumer demand which pulls the economy out of the type of unemployment equilibrium situation depicted by Keynes.

If financial assets are added into the wealth measure, changes in asset values will have a greater effect on wealth. The traditional representation of an increased asset value is a fall in market interest rates (since that increases the *relative* return on existing assets). So demand for money and consumer demand now both increase for this reason when interest rates fall. This additional role of the interest rate flattens both the IS and LM curves, to ISw and LMw, as shown in figure 1.2. For a given fall in the interest rate there will be a greater increase in the demand for money than before, when the rise in wealth was not considered, and so a larger reduction in income is required to release

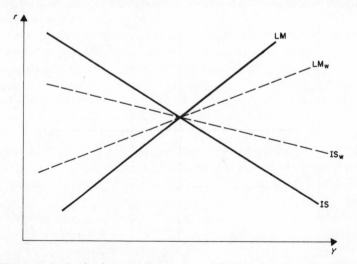

Figure 1.2 *Orthodox neoclassical model: introduction of wealth*

the necessary amount of money. Similarly in terms of the IS curve, a given interest rate fall now boosts consumer demand as well as investment demand, requiring a larger increase in income than before to maintain equilibrium in the goods market.

Again, whether a money supply increase raises output by more or less once these wealth effects are included depends on the relative strengths of the effects on demand for money and consumer demand.

The two major alternatives to the neoclassical orthodoxy can be described as the *extreme classical* approach and the *extreme Keynesian* approach. The extreme classical approach can be represented as shown in figure 1.3. It has many features in common with the modern monetarist model, which is covered in chapters 14 and 15. The LM curve is vertical, indicating that the demand for money is purely a function of income, as a proxy for wealth. Since money is a substitute for all assets, the interest rate on particular financial assets, like bonds, is not important in determining the demand for money. The IS curve is horizontal, indicating that investment and savings demand are purely a function of the interest rate. The interest rate is then a real variable, with no monetary significance. Its sole function is to equate the supply of savings and real investors' demand for them. Thus, while the IS–LM framework was designed to demonstrate the interdependence of the money market and the goods market, since demand in both markets is affected both by r and by Y, the extreme classical approach denies such interdependence. It is for this reason that the IS–LM framework does not focus on the central features of the extreme classical approach.

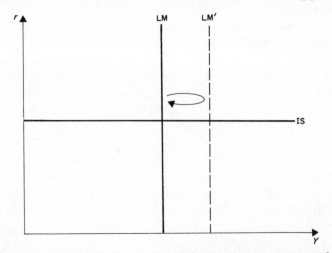

Figure 1.3 *Extreme classical model: increase in money supply*

All the monetary action occurs off-stage. A money supply increase (in this approach completely under government control) spills over into price rises since the economy is already, by assumption, at full employment. The *real* money supply is thereby restored to its original level. The tendency for the LM curve to shift to LM' is automatically reversed. According to extreme classicists, then, money only 'matters' in terms of its effect on the price level. But its supply is controllable so that monetary policy may be geared to determining the desired rate of inflation.

Modern monetarists qualify this approach in two major respects. Global monetarists view the money supply as being beyond the control of the authorities if exchange rates are fixed, or at least not *freely* floating. Any excess demand for money is met by supply through payments surpluses rather than price deflation. Any control over the nominal domestic money supply means relinquishing control of the exchange rate.

Second, continuing money supply changes cause continuing inflation. In the short run, incorrect inflationary expectations alter the IS and LM relationships, particularly with respect to expectations of the real interest rate. The money and goods markets thus become interdependent in the short run, but not in a way which can be analysed by IS–LM analysis. (The real interest rate concept originated in fact in Fisher's (1911) classical analysis.)

The '*extreme Keynesian*' approach appears to have some similarities with the extreme classical approach, when depicted in an IS–LM diagram, as in figure 1.4.

Now it is the money market which bears little relationship to the level of output and the goods market which is little affected by the rate of interest. Money is treated as a close substitute for only a few liquid assets so that its demand is closely related to the interest rate. When the LM curve is horizontal at rate of interest r_0, the economy is in a liquidity trap. Expectations are so strong that the rate of interest can fall no further (and so bond prices can rise no further), that the public cannot be induced to buy bonds at r_0. The risks are so great of capital loss when interest rates rise again, that there is an overwhelming preference for holding money. This speculative demand for money completely swamps transactions demand. But that rate of interest may be too high to induce a full-employment level of investment. Even if investment were not interest-inelastic (as shown in figure 1.4), then a change in the money supply has no effect on the interest rate, or on output, since the public are quite prepared to accept any increase in

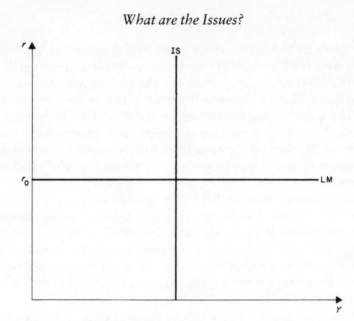

Figure 1.4 *Extreme Keynesian model*

money holdings in exchange for other financial assets, *without* any change in the rate of interest. In this sense, money does not 'matter' at all!

But the fundamental difference between the Keynesian approach and the classical approach lies in the reasons for rejecting this representation of the Keynesian approach. (Those Keynesians who do not accept an IS–LM representation of their ideas are often called 'Post Keynesians'.) If both demand for money and investment demand are not simply related to *actual* levels of r and Y, but are strongly related also to *expected* further levels of r and Y, then the IS–LM framework is missing an essential ingredient. Thus the standard IS and LM curves are indeed interdependent, in terms of these expectations, but in a manner which cannot be modelled in the normal deterministic manner because expectations differ among individuals, are often wrong, and are subject to periodic revision as events unfold. Thus changes in the money supply *do* alter expected asset values and rates of return, and thus impinge on investment demand and thereby output and prices. Money therefore does in fact 'matter' in a Keynesian system, in a way which will be explained in depth in later chapters.

This Keynesian analysis which differs from the IS–LM representation is also associated with the argument that the money supply cannot be controlled in the sense implied by the IS–LM analysis. The first major expression of this view was presented in the Report of the Radcliffe Committee (1959) in the UK. The money supply increases when interest rates rise, not only because governments choose to cause the increase to bring rates down again, or because they attract capital inflows, but also because the financial system itself expands to reduce the shortage of funds which had caused the interest rate to rise.

This process, described in detail in chapter 7, increases liquidity, i.e. the availability of assets whose value in terms of money is stable and which are easily convertible into money. Depending on how money is defined, the money supply may thereby have increased; if not, then money-holders will be induced to switch into alternative liquid assets (e.g. deposits with building societies), freeing up their money holdings for those who need money for real expenditure.

This type of approach raises fundamental questions about what we mean by 'money' in the first place. If it 'matters', what type of money are we referring to, and can it be changed exogenously by the government?

In practice, as we shall see in the next two chapters, modern banking systems in general generate money growth from a base which is not under direct control of the government. Governments can *choose* to influence the banking system's contribution to monetary growth, but institutional change may be required to allow them to do so.

In summary then, it seems that money does matter for both output and prices. How, and therefore how much, it matters is the question to be addressed in the ensuing chapters. But first, in the next six chapters, we address the question of how money is supplied, first in the long run and then in response to short-run developments. In the process, we form a view of what we mean by money in the first place.

2

Long-run Money Supply: The Development of Financial Structures

2.1 INTRODUCTION

Money itself is an institution; one institution within the institutional structure of the financial system. It is the vehicle for transactions which is *conventional* within a particular institutional structure. Institutional change is an inevitable feature of any society, so it is to be expected that the institution of money also changes, both in its nature and in the role that it plays in the economy.

Money is a particularly important institution because it is the vehicle for most economic transactions. And yet, because the acceptability of any asset in this role is determined by convention, it is vulnerable to changes in its acceptability as conventions change. An asset performs money-functions if it is generally acceptable as a means of payment. But other assets are very close substitutes for money-as-a-means-of-payment, and thus perform money functions because they can be readily exchanged for the means of payment. Assets are called more 'liquid' the more readily they can be exchanged for money without the risk of capital loss. (In this sense, savings accounts with credit unions, say, are much more liquid than company shares.)

Thus, when we are concerned with how much money supply is available, we must be concerned with the current set of conventions regarding means of payment, and the provision of liquid asset substitutes by the financial system. Once these are understood, it is possible then to consider how that system generates changes in the money supply in the short run. But any particular set of conventions, and financial structure, is the outcome of a series of institutional adjustments over the long run. In this chapter we attempt to identify some patterns in the historical development of money and financial institutions which are common to a variety of economies.

There are important reasons for studying the process by which this financial development comes about:

(1) there is a strong correlation between financial development and real economic development; money seems to 'matter' in the long run;
(2) long-run trends sometimes dominate short-run developments; it is important to understand those trends when setting short-run monetary policy;
(3) countries are currently at varying levels of financial, as well as economic, development; this fact colours the nature of international interdependencies, particularly in the form of international capital flows, which we saw earlier altering the levels of domestic money supplies.

We now examine each of these three factors in turn.

2.2 THE RELATIONSHIP BETWEEN FINANCIAL DEVELOPMENT AND ECONOMIC DEVELOPMENT

Financial development is commonly associated with economic development. Having said that, we must consider what we actually mean by 'financial development' and 'economic development', and form some view as to which causes which, if we are to make use of this observed phenomenon.

Economic development is like an elephant: hard to define, but you know it when you see it. For want of a better alternative, it is conventionally measured by the level of per capita income. This measure acts as a proxy for a variety of factors which imply a broadly based, high level of economic activity of a type which generates further activity in the future, and access to real resources.

Financial development is perhaps more easy to pinpoint, although, as we shall see, account must be taken of the *distribution* of access to financial markets, just as income distribution is a factor to be considered in measuring economic development. The best measure of financial development is Goldsmith's (1969) Financial Interrelations Ratio, or FIR. The FIR is the ratio of the sum of the value of all financial assets to the sum of the value of all real assets. The higher the FIR, the larger the financial superstructure, or under-pinning of real activity (depending on which you think 'causes' which). Goldsmith found that indeed the FIR does increase with per capita income, but at a decreasing rate as development proceeds. The relationship thus looks something like figure 2.1, where Y/N is per capita income.

This pattern seems to apply to individual countries over time: Gurley and Shaw (1967) estimate that the ratio of US financial assets to real wealth increased from about unity at the beginning of this century to 4.5 in the 1960s. A similar comparison can be made between countries at different levels of development in the 1960s: Gurley and Shaw estimated a ratio of around 0.1 for countries like Afghanistan compared with 2 for the UK and 1.5 for Japan. The Soviet Union has a low ratio relative to its per capita income, at around 0.4. Most countries seem to go through the stage of the ratio increasing faster than per capita income as the secondary (manufacturing) sector enjoys expansion. The growth of financial assets then slows down as the economy matures, activity shifting from the secondary to the tertiary (service) sector.

What factors explain this widespread pattern? If we consider an economy well to the left on the Y/N axis in figure 2.1, the economic structure would be one of subsistence, where goods may be exchanged by barter. This is an inconvenient and inefficient means of trading once trade expands, and once commodities are traded for which there are not well-known, uniform, values. Also, when it is difficult to find buyers who actually want to consume the goods they acquire (the 'double coincidence of wants'), it becomes necessary to value goods in terms of another good, i.e. in terms of money.

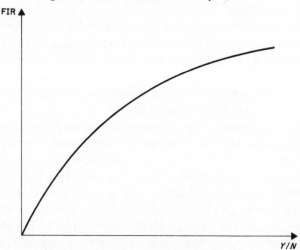

Figure 2.1 *The financial interrelations ratio at different levels of per capita income*

Throughout history different commodities have been used as the 'money' commodity, readily acceptable in exchange for goods. Gold still retains the peculiar qualities which have made it acceptable as money over centuries: durability, limited supply, portability, high use value in consumption and production. But other economies have used commodities more suited to their needs. A particular type of cowrie shell performed the function of money in West Africa, for example, until the turn of this century. Prolonged shortages were met by the introduction of alternative types of cowrie shells, which out of necessity became accepted as money. But it was the increase in transactions with European governments and traders, relative to domestic transactions which caused their replacement by conventional money, not the periodic appreciation and depreciation of their value as supply fluctuated (see Hogendorn and Gemery (1981) and Johnson (1970)). In the Canadian North-West in the eighteenth century, tokens called 'made-beavers' were used for transactions between trappers and traders, each token being worth an adult male beaver in prime condition (see Binhammer (1968), p. 29). The trappers had more confidence in the value of these pelts than in the value of cheques or coin issued by unknown financial institutions. This confidence proved unfounded once silk hats superseded beaver hats in fashionable circles; but to this day the Hudson's Bay Company often makes payment to native people in the form of credit at the local Hudson's Bay store, a modern 'groceries' version of commodity money (restricted to transactions between the Company and the employee/customer).

Commodity money is nevertheless inconvenient to carry round, and also presents a security problem. The medieval goldsmiths provided a security service which was an important precursor of modern banking. The receipts given to depositors began themselves to be used in transactions, i.e. as money. At the same time, since people found the receipts more convenient than gold, the goldsmiths could lend out some of their gold deposits knowing that a high proportion of holders of their depositors' receipts would not need to redeem them for gold during any given period.

Thus financial institutions began to develop, to provide pieces of paper as means of payment, and also to provide credit. The need for credit arises with the growth of economic opportunities. Just as money avoids the need for a double coincidence of wants in terms of goods, financial institutions avoid the need for a double coincidence of savings and investment. Direct finance, the direct lending from saver to investor, becomes inefficient once economies become large and complex. Financial institutions perform the function of indirect finance: pooling savings and providing loans.

This process is called financial intermediation. It is promoted by shortages of funds: the more costly borrowing becomes, the greater is the incentive for financial resources to be used more efficiently. Efficiency in the financial sense means the provision of assets and liabilities (financial instruments) to meet every requirement, so that as few funds as possible are left idle. Thus savers can, in a sophisticated financial market, choose between a wide variety of deposits, with different terms and conditions, and of securities such as bonds and equities. Borrowers similarly have a wide variety of types of bank loan, or public bond or debentures, to choose from.

A pattern indeed emerges for the path of *individual* financial assets over time (or as per capita income grows) similar to that for *all* financial assets in figure 2.1, forming an increasing proportion of total assets as per capita income increases, but increasing at a falling rate. A commodity money, or currency, becomes widespread as trade spreads it round the economy. As the division of labour proceeds and businesses specialize (and thus trade) more, the need for money increases more rapidly than output. After a time its use becomes costly or inconvenient, and constraints on its supply may threaten to hold back development. This induces the introduction of an alternative, more convenient, asset like bank chequing deposits. Again the same pattern emerges, with bank time or savings deposits superseding demand deposits as financing needs push up interest rates.

The ratios, then, of currency to real wealth (C/W), demand deposits to wealth (DD/W), and time deposits to wealth (TD/W) will conform to the patterns shown in figure 2.2. The patterns can be summarized as representing rapidly increasing use of a particular asset during periods of economic growth, followed by economizing on that asset as the economy matures, facilitated by induced financial innovation. In the process, each successive asset becomes more 'money-like'.

Financial development has been descibed so far as if it were the *result* of demand for a means of payment, demand for credit, demand for financial intermediation. In so far as these demands arose from the *real* economic development process, then it could be said that real economic development 'causes' financial development, at least in the long run. (Whether unsatisfied demand for financing will call forth its supply in the short run, i.e. whether the money supply is endogenous in the short run, is a matter to be discussed later, in chapter 7.)

It can also be argued, however, that financial development *facilitates* economic development. Thus, even if the impetus for financial de-velopment occurs on the real side (the supply of finance is endogen-ous), financial development can allow greater or lesser rates of income increase depending on the form it takes (money still 'matters'). This is a matter of considerable importance to developing countries where governments are trying, or are being encouraged, to promote financial development artificially in order to promote real development. They are in the business of 'supply-led' financial development, in contrast to the 'demand-led' development described above, which has more direct application to the already-developed countries.

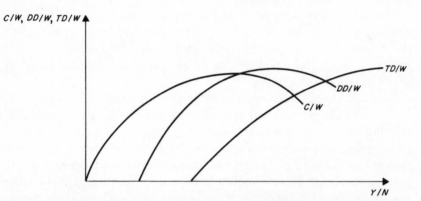

Figure 2.2 *Ratios of currency, demand deposits and time deposits to wealth at different levels of per capita income*

Drake (1980) suggests three ways in which the growth of financial intermediation promotes economic development:

(1) It augments real saving and investment, which generate growth. Financial intermediation provides instruments in which savings can be held which earn a higher return than alternative assets, thereby encouraging new saving. It also encourages those who save anyway to make their savings available to borrowers. Simi-larly, new sources of finance through financial institutions encour-age investment opportunities to be taken up.
(2) The productivity of investment is increased by improved alloca-tion mechanisms. If only direct finance is possible, savers are limited in their choice of borrowers. But indirect finance, through financial institutions, regularizes the lending process, pools infor-mation, and allows comparison between potential projects on a scale wider than that available to any individual lender. The selection of projects to be financed is thus improved.

(3) For any one country an increase in financial sophistication, represented by a broader range of available assets and liabilities, will attract the savings of residents of other countries, or at least reduce the outflow of savings. The scale of the financial structure, and thus credit, depends on the total amount of savings made available.

In summary, then, while economic growth and investment may generate sufficient savings to finance them, as a by-product of increasing income, these savings are only made *available* for investment if the financial structure so allows.

Financial development is not necessarily *sufficient* for economic development. Areas, for example, in London and New York closest to the financial districts (on the East side) do not display high per capita incomes. Financial development rather *facilitates* an underlying impetus to real development.

Nor is financial development necessary for economic development. It has already been noted that the FIR for the Soviet Union is low relative to its per capita income level. Indeed, in centrally planned economies, where the bulk of saving and investment is generated by the central authorities, the type of financial institution operating in the private sector of Western countries has no role. Alternatively, where saving and investment occur at the community level, on a community-wide basis, then investment is self-financed. Indeed, Baran, for example, argues that self-finance is more consistent with socialist development than indirect finance because of the surplus otherwise extracted by the merchant class (see Gurley and Shaw (1967)).

Indirect finance, and the concomitant growth of financial superstructures, is called into question more on practical than ideological grounds by Minsky (1975). He argues that financial institutions amplify cycles in expectations regarding real economic developments. These cycles are costly in themselves, but also present the periodic risk of financial collapse. (See chapter 11 for a full discussion of Minsky's theory.) To the extent that financial development does involve a risk of collapse, then there is also the potential for economic development to be retarded rather than promoted.

2.3 FINANCIAL STRUCTURE AND MONETARY POLICY

It has been suggested that, in general, financial development is often demand-induced. Thus, figures 2.1 and 2.2 can be treated as if they were long-run demand curves where the degree to which supply has accommodated that demand for financial assets determines per capita income, i.e. the position on the curve. Short-run demand changes, which must be anticipated if monetary policy is to have a predictable effect, take the form of fluctuations around this long-run trend. But most demand for money analysis is purely short-run, assuming a *given* financial structure; unpredicted shifts can occur in the short run simply because the underlying long-run trend is ignored.

Thus, for example, there was some consternation in the US when the *actual* demand for money, first in the early 1970s, then later in the same decade, turned out to be lower than predicted. Goldfeld (1976) made a thorough investigation of the problem which was referred to as 'The Case of the Missing Money'. After the fact, the problem has been diagnosed: a variety of changes in banking practice had been introduced to aid clients in conserving money balances which bore a high opportunity cost due to high interest rates.

Porter *et al.* (1979), for example, show that the introduction of various cash-management techniques reduced the level of demand deposits which businesses need hold. Savings accounts could be made available to cover overdrafts on chequing accounts when necessary, but otherwise earn interest. Balances on chequing accounts could be invested overnight by the bank, earning interest. Thus, not only was the opportunity cost of holding chequing accounts increased, but the liquidity of savings accounts was increased. This represents a relative fall in the demand for money defined as currency plus chequing accounts (M_1), but not for money defined as including these other instruments which earn interest but are now more readily available for transactions (more liquid). Indeed, the US money supply definitions have now been changed to take account of the changing nature of money assets.

Predicting these structural changes from year to year requires some theory of how banks operate. While recent work is beginning to fill the gap, there has been little in the way of a satisfactory theory of banks as firms. (See Baltensperger (1980) for a survey of the different approaches adopted so far.) Part of the difficulty arises from the tendency of the banking industry to adopt an oligopolistic structure, which is notoriously difficult to analyse.

Indeed, absence of competition in banking is often deliberately promoted by the state because the acceptability of bank-money depends on the confidence of the public that banking institutions will not go bankrupt (whereas perfect competition, in disequilibrium, necessarily involves the risk of bankruptcies). This point is illustrated in the next chapter where we look at the development of the Scottish banking system. Most national banking systems consist of a small number of major banks; e.g. there are only six clearing banks in England. The US is an exception in that banks may not open branches in states other than the one in which they are registered; in Illinois' case, banks may not have more than one office, anywhere. This system was designed to deal with the widespread fear (among non-New Yorkers) that New York would otherwise dominate the entire US financial system, with banks simply being branches of New York banks. (See West (1977) for a useful account of the development of the US banking system.) But even so, a single small bank in a small community can wield what is normally called 'local monopoly' power.

Nevertheless, trends in banking practice can be identified as profit-maximizing, and competitive within an oligopolistic structure. Successful cash-management techniques attract new clients, and also promote their continued profitability – by attracting their growing deposits, the banks thus also protect their own profitability. The latest major innovation on the horizon is an Electronic Funds Transfer System (EFTS). Curiously, this seems to be a supply-induced innovation in contrast to most earlier banking innovations.

High-level discussions have been going on for some time between government and banks in the US and Canada on the introduction of a standardized system of electronic transactions between households, business and the banking system, eventually wiping out all cash transactions. While the process would probably save on operating costs for the banks, and reduce the uncertainty over cash withdrawals, the main attraction presumably is that of the existing credit card systems – the ease with which bank customers would incur debt to their banks at relatively high rates of interest. Further, the entire population (unlike less than half, as in the UK) would have to open bank accounts. The implications for the money supply and how monetary policy would be conducted pose fascinating questions, which would be worthwhile bearing in mind as we discuss the role of currency in money supply (in chapter 4) and monetary policy (in chapter 17). (The effect of EFTS on monetary control is discussed by Flannery and Jaffee (1973) and briefly by Greene (1981).)

2.4 FINANCIAL STRUCTURE AT DIFFERENT STAGES OF DEVELOPMENT

Because economies are simultaneously at different stages of economic development and of financial development, it is important not to consider economies in isolation from each other. Financial development means the provision of saving and borrowing instruments which satisfy a variety of needs, thus making efficient use of financial resources (the money base). But if other countries provide the only type of savings instrument that domestic savers want to hold, then there will be inducements for savings to flow out of the country. Further, international transactions must be financed by foreign exchange, which is in effect part of the money base of the domestic economy.

Thus countries which have reached a relatively high level of financial development can, other things being equal, attract savings from outside to finance domestic investment. At the same time, countries at later stages of financial development are hampered in closing the gap if the fact of relative underdevelopment tends to reduce the availability of savings as well as foreign exchange holdings. In reverse, of course, borrowers in financially unsophisticated countries have access to a wider variety of sources of funds outside the domestic economy, because other countries have more highly developed financial structures. In this way, additional savings are made available to finance investment.

This implication of differential degrees of financial development is sufficiently important that we shall go into it in more detail in chapter 4. The issue is relevant not only to the North–South dialogue between developed and developing countries, but also to financial relationships within countries.

Before that, in the next chapter, we attempt to anchor the ideas presented in this chapter in the actual experience of a particular (and particularly interesting) banking system.

3

The Development of Banking Structure, with particular reference to Scotland

3.1 INTRODUCTION

I have heard it asserted, that the trade of the city of Glasgow doubled in about fifteen years after the first erection of the banks there; and that the trade of Scotland has more than quadrupled since the first erection of the two public banks at Edinburgh . . . that the banks have contributed a good deal to this increase, cannot de doubted. (Smith (1970), p. 394.)

Adam Smith clearly believed that the development of the banking system in Scotland was a major contributory factor to its economic development. In this chapter we look in some detail at the development of the Scottish banking system, and assess this view of its role.

The Scottish banking system is of particular interest for a variety of reasons:

(1) As Smith noted, even before the period of greatest economic and financial development, the development of the banking system was associated with spectacular economic growth.
(2) Many of the features of modern banking first saw the light of day as innovations in Scotland.
(3) Its development was free of much of the restrictive legislation and close relationship with government which featured in other banking systems. Thus it provides a good example of how a banking system develops under the primary influence of 'pure' market forces.
(4) The Scottish experience illustrates vividly the major principles of money and banking theory, to be drawn out further in later chapters (in particular the important part played by confidence in the banking system).

Rather than providing a detailed history, this chapter picks out major points of interest in the development of the Scottish banking system. A full account of the history of the Scottish banking system may be found in Checkland (1975).

Following the case study of Scottish banking in its formative years, comparisons will be drawn with other types of banking system. The chapter ends with a discussion of the related topic of the development of financial centres.

3.2 A SCOTTISH CASE STUDY

Scotland's first bank, the Bank of Scotland, was established by Act of the Scottish Parliament in 1695, 1 year after the Bank of England was established. At that time, Scotland was a relatively poor country, with per capita income at around one-quarter of the English level. Money consisted of a wide variety of coins, only one-half issued locally; the other half were the coin of major trading partners. Transactions were either conducted with coin, in kind, or, particularly in foreign trade, with bills of exchange. Thus traders arranging for delivery of imports in 3 months' time would pay with a bill to be exchanged for gold or another bill in 3 months' time. These bills in the meantime could be used as means of payment, at a discount from face value depending on the time until payment was due, i.e. the bills were negotiable. But because of London's dominance over trade, it was mostly there, rather than in Scotland, where bills were bought and sold and where the rate of discount was set, subject to a maximum set by the Usury Laws.

Because Scottish bills were settled in an unpredictable combination of other countries' coin, they tended to trade at a relatively high discount. This tendency was exaggerated during the periodic exchange crises in which any Scottish expansion culminated. Expansions had an immediate impact on the discount of Scottish bills because imports would rise more rapidly than exports, causing an increased net demand for credit, and then for gold, to make final payment. Since bills became too costly for importers when their redemption value was particularly doubtful, settlement would be made instead in coin, further fuelling the exchange crisis by causing gold and silver to go abroad.

This predicament is a familiar one for low-income developing countries today, whose monetary base is underpinned by foreign exchange holdings which must be run down in expansion in order to maintain the value of the domestic currency in terms of that of major trading partners. The particular problems posed by financial interdependence at the present time are discussed in the next chapter; but in the meantime it is a valuable exercise to consider the possible parallels between the historical Scottish situation and those of contemporary economies as we proceed.

The Bank of Scotland was set up to provide some solution to these currency crises which were seriously inhibiting commerce. Unlike the Bank of England, which was set up as a private bank by the governmeny to generate finance for war with France, the Bank of Scotland was purely commercial, the first joint stock private sector bank in Europe. It was, however, granted a monopoly in public banking for 21 years.

It conducted some deposit business, but its major activity, and source of revenue, was the note issue, put into circulation through interest-bearing loans. Such notes were redeemable on demand in coin. The convenience of this new form of money was so great, filling a clear need, that is was readily accepted as means of payment, which further increased confidence in its value. The notes were issued primarily in sterling, rather than the Scots pound, further enhancing their acceptability. Since each note was issued initially in the form of a loan, the Bank earned interest without having to relinquish any gold until a recipient of the note presented it for payment. The loans were, in the early days of Scottish banking, only short-term, to be repaid within 1 year. The borrower had to provide security in the form of land, personal possessions, or commodities, or pledges of credit-worthy associates. The borrower would generally use the note itself for whatever purpose the loan was made (often consumption, as well as investment), paying interest, and making repayment either in bank notes or specie.

The crux of note-issue banking is that holders of the bank's notes are content to use the notes as money, i.e. have confidence that their value will be maintained. As we shall see when discussing speculation (chapter 11) such a situation is potentially unstable: a loss of confidence expressed by a run on the bank will justify itself by causing bankruptcy, just as will the retention of confidence ensure solvency. In fact the shareholders were not provided with much information on which to base their views. But since it so happened that it was in the general interests of all concerned to display confidence, the Bank of Scotland could, with relative impunity, expand the note issue with a small capital base. The Invisible Hand was at work in the world of finance!

The Bank was not without its crises. One was caused by the emergence of a rival note issue put out, not by a bank, but by the Darien Company. This development caused instability because, should one issuer succeed in driving the other out of business, then that other's notes would become worthless. As a result, the public could become unwilling to hold the notes of either! The Darien Company had been set up in 1695 to establish a settlement in the Panama Isthmus, from where to provide a lucrative trading link between the Atlantic and the Pacific trading routes. Because of the large amount of Scottish capital sunk in the scheme, it had already posed problems of capital shortage for the Bank of Scotland. But it had been felt by the scheme's promoters that the prospects for profits were better abroad than within the Scottish economy. The project, however, proved to be a disaster, and all the paid-up capital was lost.

The threat posed to confidence in the Bank's note issue by competition appeared again in 1727 with the chartering of the Royal Bank of Scotland, whose capital was formed from the compensation paid to Scots for a variety of losses incurred on the union of parliaments in 1707 between Scotland and England. The constant threat that one bank might oust the other reduced confidence in both note issues. But each bank also used this fact in order to *try* to oust the other. Thus agents were charged to collect the other bank's notes and present them suddenly and in large quantities for payment. Each bank's customers were encouraged only to present the other's notes for payment in gold, keeping pressure on competitors. Notes were issued which would earn interest if not presented for payment within a certain time. If payment was insisted on, the bank would pay in inconvenient, small denominations. Customers were even pressurized not to present their own bank's notes for payment by the strong insinuation that it would ruin their chances of receiving loans in the future! (Not dissimilar tactics have been used in banking crises ever since, in efforts to retard runs on banks.) In any case, since many large bank customers were also its shareholders, they had a strong interest in supporting their bank's note issue. The Royal Bank won the first round of this battle, and the Bank of Scotland had to suspend payment on its notes for a period of 8 months in 1728.

This dangerously unstable situation was only finally curbed when a new wave of banks became a serious threat in the 1750s, and it was clearly in the interests of the two senior banks to combine forces in maintaining their dominance. One feature of this combination was the first instance of a regular clearing arrangement between banks so that their net payments position was known to them on a continuous basis. Other innovations emerging over this period included the introduction of overdraft facilities (in 1728) in the form of cash credits secured by bonding associates of the borrower, and the attempts to stabilize the exchanges between Edinburgh and London (during 1700–35). This latter involved the banks in buying and selling Scots bills of exchange to prevent excessive Scots borrowing which could cause uncertainty about the value of the coin to be used in final settlement. By reducing this uncertainty the banks tried to reduce the average discount on the Scots bills.

This concern over the balance of payments reflected the constant danger of withdrawals of coin, not only into people's purses as notes were redeemed, but also to London. The modern parallel is the persistence of phenomena like the us dollar area (in spite of the legal facility to float exchange rates). In effect, Scotland had a fixed exchange rate with England. The corollary was, however, that, as a small country, it was open to fluctuations in finance available from England, depending on the rate of discount on bills. Adam Smith (1970, pp. 426–8) describes how the American colonies periodically changed the value of their currencies with respect to sterling. But as similar small, open economies find today, allowing the domestic currency to depreciate does not correct a tendency to payments deficit if import demand is price-inelastic. (If imports continue at their previous level, but at a higher price, the problem of a deficit becomes worse, rather than better – unless, of course, exports increase dramatically.)

With the opening-up of new banks, and with the growth of capital in Scotland associated with the lucrative tobacco trade, the banking business expanded rapidly, coinciding with the emergence and expansion of Scottish industry. The wide extent of literacy among the population, the wide branching of banks throughout the country, and most particularly the practice of issuing small-denomination notes, all served to promote the banking habit.

The banks were, by modern standards, rather imprudent in their lending practices, not lending necessarily for productive projects and on less than watertight security. (The term of loans was, however, kept short, increasing their liquidity for the banks, a continuing uk banking tradition. These short-term credits were nevertheless often rolled-over so that the loan in effect became long-term.) Only very small reserves of coin were held against note issues – often as low as 1 per cent. The incidence of bank failure on these grounds is surprisingly low. The banking system in fact benefited from the prosperity of the economy;

when demand for local products is high and large investment projects at home (and abroad) are yielding high returns, loans tend to be repaid and the public recognize their own interests in supporting the banks' note issues.

There were nevertheless some spectacular collapses, in particular that of the City of Glasgow Bank in 1878. The problem arose because the bank's assets consisted of loans to US ventures which could not be recalled at all speedily, and loans to some foundering local firms who were debtors to other customers of the bank. The Bank's reaction to the situation was to continue lending to these firms so that they would not jeopardize their creditors' financial positions, and to buy up the Bank's shares in order to quieten rumours of bank failure. As a result the Bank's portfolio became progressively more unsound and eventually it had to close down. The directors were given jail sentences following a criminal trial for fraud. The collapse in turn caused large financial losses for the shareholders, which included some other banks; the Caledonian Banking Company failed as a direct result (although subsequently restructured and reopened).

The question of whether or not a banking system was stable generally revolved around the relationship between the note issue and other aggregates (such as gold reserves), just as now it revolves around the relationship between deposits and other aggregates, like income, or output. The implication was that there was some optimal ratio between the extent of note issue and the appropriate aggregate which would allow the most efficient use of financial resources without shaking confidence in the ability of the banks to meet 'normal' fluctuations in requests for coin in exchange for notes.

This is a question common to all financial systems, and depends to a considerable extent on what determines confidence. Thus, the 1971 collapse of the international financial system can be described as resulting from the amount of US dollars held by other countries, which was judged to be excessive relative to the US gold stock. The dollars had provided a very useful means of exchange until that point. How far it was in fact the relative gold backing and how much political considerations which caused the crisis of confidence is still a matter of debate. Nevertheless, the crucial factor is confidence, and how that is engendered.

There was much lively debate in the UK prior to the important 1844 and 1845 banking legislation over the appropriate aggregate to govern bank expansion. (A similar lively debate was conducted in the US when the Federal Reserve System was being designed during the period

1873–1913.) The two main schools of thought in Britain on the means of controlling the note issue were the Currency School and the Banking School, which in some respects have modern parallels in the monetarists and Keynesians respectively. The Currency School advocated gold backing for note issue above some initial amount, and centralized control governed by the major bank (the Bank of England), on the grounds that an 'excessive' note issue would be inflationary. Changes in gold stocks resulted from trade imbalance, i.e. changes in relative competitiveness. They were thus viewed as a good signal for changes in credit availability. Critics of the Currency School argued that economic development should not be impeded by tying the provision of finance to what they regarded as an arbitrary factor: the stock of gold.

The Banking School, pointing to the successful Scottish experience, argued that the basis should be real growth in the economy, which might not be reflected in gold holdings. Because of the banks' close connections with traders and industrialists, they should be allowed to continue to extend credit to finance real activity according to their own judgement, using liquid assets as backing in addition to gold. Indeed this is the principle on which the Scottish banking system had prospered – extending credit when there were real profitable opportunities to be financed, of which there were sufficient numbers of sufficient profitability to justify the policy. The development of the appropriate banking skills was a direct result of the extreme scarcity of gold and silver coin. The primary criticism of the Banking School, the 'real bills' doctrine, was that the same goods could be sold and resold over and over, with credit being extended in the form of bills for each transaction. The stock of bills would then grossly overstate the volume of economic activity.

An alternative, older, approach was the notion that land values could underwrite the banking system. A Scotsman, John Law, had earlier been unable to float the idea successfully in Scotland (although an experiment in land-banking was later tried and failed). His French land-banking scheme – the 'Mississippi scheme' – ended in disaster in 1720, but more because the issue was used to back the shaky Mississippi Company than problems of a land base as such. Throughout history since then, however, there have been instances of over-extension in land acquisition, where reversals in values have caused severe financial difficulties (see Kindleberger (1978), pp. 45–6). The Wall St Crash in 1929 was preceded by a spectacular speculative boom and then crash in the market for land in Florida (see Galbraith (1961), pp. 32–7). The problems of many financial institutions in the late 1970s can similarly be attributed partly to thwarted expectations of land or property price rises.

In the UK, after 1844–45, additions to note issue were to be backed by gold on a strict basis, both in Scotland and England. In fact eventually the gold backing was gradually eased out. The removal of the last trace of gold backing in 1970 was received without a murmur; clearly what generated confidence in one generation of bank customers was irrelevant to the next. Now too, the UK banking system, measured more by deposit growth than the note issue, is in effect backed by the Bank of England's stock of government securities, and those held by the banks themselves. Government behaviour, and particularly its borrowing requirements, thus have a direct effect on the growth of bank deposits, a theme picked up regularly throughout the remainder of the book.

For the Scottish banking system, the gold backing requirement enforced by the 1844 legislation was an impediment to expansion along the lines of its earlier history. The Scots banks were still allowed to issue notes, subject to the gold backing requirement. It can, however, be argued that this retention of note issue was a doubtful victory. The innovative power of the Scottish banks might have allowed extension of branching in England were it not that, in 1828, they were prohibited from circulating notes there, just after the field for joint-stock banking was opened up in England, in 1826.

The Scottish banking system seems to have lost its drive by the end of the nineteenth century. Competition was reduced by the fact that no new banks of issue could now be formed. Indeed in each bank there seems to have been the pattern of dynamism in its early years of life followed by a gradual accrual of caution; with no new banks on the scene, this pattern was reflected in the banking system as a whole. The proportion of deposits devoted to advances fell steadily throughout the nineteenth and the first half of the twentieth centuries, from a high of 104 per cent in 1877 to proportions under 40 per cent in the 1950s. With the fall in demand for Scottish products after the First World War went a relative fall in advances to Scottish industry. Only now, with the growth of North Sea Oil business, does the early spirit of innovative banking seem to have been given fresh impetus. The proportion of deposits employed for advances was over 70 per cent again by the 1970s (see Checkland (1975), table 45).

The general picture is thus of a banking system which emerged at just the right time to finance the development surge in Scotland. Indeed the banks overcame horrendous problems of specie shortage to achieve this. By the time the Scottish economy was going into relative decline, however, the banking system seemed if anything to exacerbate the situation by cautious lending practices. Caution may of course be perfectly consistent with profit-maximizing behaviour on the part of each bank, wishing to share in an expansion, but not be caught with depreciating assets in a decline. The net result, however, seems to have been that the financial system if anything amplified the trend in the real sector – or at least of expectations regarding the real sector. When real activity was expanding rapidly, the banks could extend finance freely with relatively low risk of business failure. When real activity stagnated, perceptions of low financial returns and high risk discouraged both the demand for bank credit and its supply, which may even have contributed to the low actual financial returns and high risk.

3.3 COMPARISON WITH OTHER BANKING SYSTEMS

The English banking system developed over the same period as the Scottish system, but in a quite different way because of its domination by the Bank of England; until 1826 there was a limitation of six partners for any other bank. This had two major consequences. First, because of the reliance of the government on Bank of England financing, its note issue was more geared to this concern than the provision of credit for business. Indeed the Bank had no branches until the 1920s. The country banks' note issue was used primarily for trade in local areas, but the limited range of these small banks prevented the emergence of widely used notes, and bank failures were frequent. Second, the country banks developed new practices, such as the use of cheques as a means of payment, in order to get round the restrictions placed on their scale and to meet local demands for finance. Indeed their strong local connections and willingness to take risks were useful attributes in promoting the development of local industry. A discussion of the inefficiencies caused by English banking legislation is provided by Cameron (1967), in a volume which compares the development of banking in a variety of countries.

The Japanese banking system (which developed in its modern form after 1872) was also strongly dominated by government involvement, with issues of government securities employed as an initial backing for the banks. Unlike the English government, however, the Japanese government deliberately promoted the growth of the present banking system in order to facilitate economic growth. To this end, the government provided a lender of last resort facility while encouraging the banks to make long-term loans; also competition and specialization were actively promoted, again with government safeguards against the normal consequences of competition (bank failures). Thus it was the government, rather than the banking system as such, which generated the public's confidence in bank money. To pledge the public credit in this way was totally alien to the British view that the state should separate itself from the supply of money and credit.

The US banking system is perhaps most noted for its development independent of central government, because of federal and state government legislation. First, the operations of the Treasury were initially (from 1833) quite deliberately separated from those of the banking system. Second, no bank could (according to state legislation) open branches outside the state in which it was registered; some states restrict branching also within state boundaries. As a result there are now over 14,000 banks in the US. Without this legislation, the banks in New York would no doubt have been able to use their established reputations to extend across the US by branching. But a profound mistrust of monopolies, particularly in banking, caused the other states to fight for state-based, unit, banking. Unfortunately, the cost of competition among a large number of small banks is bank failures, a hazard made more likely by the limitation of note issue to equal the value of paid-up capital, and the absence of co-operation between the banks. Galbraith (1975) is a fund of interesting accounts of the Wild West era of banking.

The debate between the Currency School and the Banking School in England and Scotland prior to the 1844 banking legislation was repeated in the US at a similar stage in the development of its banking system, between 1873 and 1913. The US banking system developed more according to the Banking School doctrine. Note issues were backed (except for a brief period, voluntarily) by both gold and commercial bills prior to the Federal Reserve Act in 1913. Thereafter, the Federal Reserve note issue was subject to mandatory reserves of gold and (primarily government) securities. The gold-backing requirement was finally removed in 1968. Bank deposits had been backed by reserves of specie or deposits with other banks, according to proportions mandatory under the National Banking Act of 1864. Under the Federal Reserve Act these deposits were to be held with the Federal Reserve Banks, which were in turn backed by assets consisting of corporate and government securities.

The Federal Reserve System was set up in 1913 in response to the problems caused by bank instability, while attempting to retain the balanced, decentralized features of the system. The institutional structure, based on twelve Federal Reserve Districts, and later backed by the Federal Deposit Insurance Corporation, provided a mechanism of support for banks in trouble, and supervision of bank practices to prevent 'trouble'. Further the switch from a capital base to a commercial bills base for bank expansion allowed for greater elasticity, and thus reduced the incidence of runs on account of reserves shortage. The increasing size of the stock of government and other nationwide securities provided a generally acceptable means of settlement between Districts which cushioned, at least in the short run, payments imbalances between regions.

Finally, returning to the Scottish banking experience, it is sometimes held up as an example of how much more successful a banking system is without a central bank. This case may have some merit when central banks, like commercial banks, are backed with gold. But now that a return to gold backing would put intolerable constraints on bank expansion, securities must be used instead. Since the securities which command the most confidence are those issued by the public sector, it is inconceivable that a banking system without government involvement could now survive.

3.4 THE DEVELOPMENT OF FINANCIAL CENTRES

In spite of efforts to the contrary to promote a balanced US banking system, New York is still clearly the financial centre of the US. Competitive forces thus have overcome legislative restriction. Through the correspondent system between banks, holding companies connecting banks in their portfolios and electronic access to market developments in New York, New York provides the same type of services for other parts of the US as London does for the UK where the banking system is already centralized.

In Scotland's case the first two banks happened to be established in Edinburgh, the capital. It was only later, when the West of Scotland became the locale of industrial growth, that efforts were made in the west to transfer the financial status to Glasgow. After some spectacular growth in banking, these efforts failed. Edinburgh is still the financial centre of Scotland, although long overshadowed by London. Only the oil business has been able to shake Edinburgh's status in Scotland, and even then only slightly, with foreign banks opening branches in Aberdeen. In the US and Canada, also, Texas and Alberta, the oil-producers, have performed the amazing feat of shifting some of the financial balance in their favour.

This is an 'amazing feat' because of the normally self-sustaining character of financial centres. They are widely regarded as benefiting from the 'Verdoorn effect', which postulates that productivity increases with growth itself: a virtuous circle is thus set in train once an advantage is gained. Economies of scale were very vivid in the case of note-issuing banks in Scotland: the larger and longer-established the institution the greater the public confidence in the soundness of its balance sheet, and therefore the more profitably it could allocate its assets. While modified by uniform reserve requirements and/or deposit insurance, the confidence factor is still important for modern banking. Added to this are economies of scale in terms of information-gathering, specializing in different types of transaction, and contacts with a variety of other financial institutions. (See Kindleberger (1974) for a detailed description of financial centre formation.)

The location of financial centres is a major factor in the financial interdependence of economies. In the next chapter we look more closely at the implications of financial interdependence for domestic money supply and demand.

4

Financial Interdependence

When studying individual cases of banking system development, it becomes clear that much depends on the international environment. The Scottish banking system, for example, was very much influenced by its trading position, particularly with England, and by the concentration of financial transactions in London. It was the tendency for specie to flow out of Scotland, a tendency exacerbated by dependence on London valuation of bills of exchange, which prompted the growth of Scottish banking in the first place.

Similarly, in this century, developing countries have sought to develop their own financial systems as a means of generating internal finance for economic development. The context is, however, rather different from that of the developed countries, whose banking systems emerged in a world with very little differentiation between the countries' financial sophistication. Further, these facilities arose in response to demand, while banking developments in developing countries now are primarily supply-led.

We shall discuss in some detail below the reasons for inducing financial development in developing countries and the particular problems the authorities are up against. In so doing we must investigate the current state of affairs in developing-country finance.

This topic is obviously of great significance for the developing countries themselves. It is also of significance for developed countries, since the economic and financial interdependence between the two groups of countries affects the monetary conditions in each. But, third, the contrasts drawn between developing-country and developed-country financial systems and the implications of their interdependence simply describe a polar case in all inter-economy relations. Thus, what we learn about the UK or the US *vis-à-vis* low-income developing countries is an exaggerated version of financial relationships between developed countries with different degrees of financial sophistication, or between regions within a country, or even between groups in a city.

Thus, while the bulk of this chapter deals with the developing countries themselves *vis-à-vis* the developed countries, we shall take some time at the end of the chapter to draw some conclusions for different manifestations of interdependence.

4.2 DUAL GAP ANALYSIS

For many years, the problem of financing development was viewed in terms of generating sufficient savings. The Industrialization Debate in the Soviet Union, for example, concerned the best way to generate savings to finance industrial development; the two possibilities under consideration were to force savings by paying low grain prices to farmers or by charging high prices for consumer goods. For a large centrally planned economy, fairly self-sufficient and also a gold-producer, the question of the *form* in which savings were generated was not important.

For a small, open developing country, however, the matter is not so simple. Certainly there is a savings constraint in the sense that, in the absence of a domestic capital market or overseas financing, savings are required *before* investment (even if investment generates the savings to finance it after the event). Only the anticipation among savers of high rates of return from an investment project, properly channelled into purchases of shares or bonds (by financial intermediation), will provide the savings at the correct time.

In addition, however, savings in the form of domestic currency are no help whatsoever if the investment project requires imported capital goods and materials, and if the expenditure generated by the income multiplier also involves a high import content. If foreign exchange holdings cannot meet the import requirements of new investments, even when savings are adequate, then the foreign exchange constraint is binding. It is because of the two potential gaps – between investment and savings, and between investment and foreign exchange – that the approach to the problem is termed 'dual gap' analysis.

Foreign exchange in these cases thus plays the same role as specie in the Scottish banking system and 'money' in modern developed-country banking systems. Keynes was not so worried about the savings gap for developed economies, since savings are generated by the income increase which follows investment and these savings are then made available to the investors. So what is required is 'finance' or liquidity to bridge the gap between the investment decision and the appearance of the savings following the investment. Keynes was thus concerned with the availability to investors of money, or finance, rather than savings:

> the public can save *ex ante* and *ex post* and ex anything else until they are blue in the face without alleviating the problem . . . the banks hold the key position in the transition from a lower to a higher scale of activity. . . . The investment market can become congested through shortage of cash. It can never become congested through shortage of saving. This is the most fundamental of my conclusions within this field (Keynes (1937b), pp. 668–9).

Thus it is the *form* in which savings are held and the portfolio behaviour of financial institutions which are important. When savings are lodged with financial institutions these institutions can, if they so choose, generate finance, or money, through the multiplier process (see chapter 5). If this money is not made available at a price to suit potential investors, then the investment cannot go ahead, no matter how high the flow of savings is.

Where most transactions involve the purchase of imports, they require foreign exchange. Foreign exchange is then money, the means of payment, and no other asset can perform that role. Thus most developing economies in effect back the banking system with foreign exchange in the same way that specie backed the Scottish banking system, and government 'promises to pay' now back most developed-country banking systems; in each case these are the assets in which ultimate confidence resides.

Developing countries in effect have two choices in the direction to take from here: either to promote exports, import-substitution and foreign borrowing in order to conserve foreign exchange, or to develop a domestic financial system to provide self-finance on a small foreign exchange base, conserving foreign exchange holdings for import expenditure. This latter choice could itself generate savings from abroad, attracted by higher financial rates of return, in addition to the new savings generated at home. The process of financial development itself thus discourages net outflows of foreign exchange by attracting capital inflows (or discouraging capital outflows), as well as expanding the amount of investment finance which can be supported by a given monetary base.

In contrast, in developed economies, the foreign exchange constraint is not so immediate, although it may be powerful beyond the short run. Where banking systems are highly developed, major foreign currencies are no longer necessary for use as money domestically, so that all holdings are reserved for international transactions. (The Eurocurrency market is a major exception to this; it will be discussed in some detail in chapter 6.) If there is a planned expansion involving high imports, then foreign exchange can be purchased with domestic currency. Unlike developing-country currencies, most developed-country currencies are widely traded and 'convertible' with each other. Beyond the immediate short run, continued purchases of foreign exchange drive down the price of domestic currency. But even this outcome may be averted if the planned expansion attracts foreign finance in the form of capital inflows. Thus, if national capital markets are sufficiently integrated that financial requirements are made known internationally, then not only does investment generate its own savings to finance it, but it generates savings in the form that it required, i.e. foreign exchange. Only if fears emerge of a currency depreciation possibly due to expansion-induced inflation, or if exports do not rise sufficiently to finance debt repayment, or foreign capital is available only at a rate of interest which chokes off planned investment (three eventualities which are highly interrelated) will the foreign exchange constraint become binding.

4.3 DEMAND FOR MONEY IN DEVELOPING COUNTRIES

Many econometric studies have been carried out to estimate the demand for money in developing countries, using the same techniques as for developed countries. Comparing the general picture presented by results for each type of economy is instructive in terms of the nature and role of money in developing economies.

As discussed in chapter 1, the major variables considered to determine the demand for money are income or wealth, and the rate of return on alternative assets. The proxy for wealth is conventionally permanent income, or the long-run accrual of additions to the stock of wealth; in turn, the conventional measure of permanent income is a weighted sum of past income levels (weights declining the earlier the time period). The rate of return on alternative assets is usually measured by the rate of interest on corporate bonds in developed countries, and government bonds in developing countries because of the relative absence of a domestic capital market. In addition, the expected rate of inflation often is taken into account, either because it determines the real rate of return represented by the rate of interest, or because it measures the opportunity cost of holding money rather than other assets which may retain their real value. The expected rate of inflation is measured in the same way as permanent income, i.e. using distributive lags. (See Laidler (1977) for a full discussion of these points.)

While we take up this whole question of the demand for money later on (in chapter 8), there are broad conclusions which emerge from comparisons between developed and developing countries which are very interesting. (See Drake (1980), chapter 4, for more details on particular studies, and in particular see the Adekunle (1968) study.)

(a) *Demand for money (in developing countries) is more closely related to actual income than the proxy for permanent income (unlike developed countries)*

The traditional explanation for this is that time horizons are shorter for decision-makers in developing economies; i.e. the future does not impinge so much on current decision-making. Alternatively, demand for money may not reflect past income experience, not because this experience is the proxy for permanent income, but because it represents past experience! What is interpreted as a weaker relationship between demand for money in developing countries and permanent income (compared with developed countries) could in fact be a weaker relationship with past income levels, pure and simple. Suppose indeed that money holdings are supply-constrained rather than an expression of demand, with supply highly correlated with foreign exchange earnings on exports, and thus with income; demand in turn is a function of planned expenditure, which involves imports and thus an outflow of foreign exchange. High income in one period is often the result of high export sales, and thus an increase in the money supply. The subsequent increase in planned expenditure increases the demand for money and reduces the money supply in the next period as foreign exchange earnings are spent on increased imports. Money supply, income and demand for money were all high in the first period but money holdings may be low in the next period, being determined only by export earnings minus import payments in that period, with no spillover from the previous period.

Thus the stronger link between money holdings and income in each period, than with income in previous periods, according to this interpretation, reflects the immediate constraining power of the supply of foreign exchange. Since this power is dampened in developed countries by the greater degree of financial intermediation, it is not surprising that the demand for money there should show the influence of past income experience as well as current income.

(b) *There is a higher income-elasticity of demand in developing countries than in developed countries*

This result confirms the analysis in chapter 2 of the changing role of money, by any one definition, as development proceeds. Income increases in developing countries, in the long run, are generally associated with increasing specialization in production, distribution and exchange. Transactions thus must increase relative to output, requiring higher money holdings in proportion to income. This factor generally outweighs (at early stages of economic development) the pressures to conserve an existing and prevailing form of money by using some alternative asset for some money functions. In mature developed economies the transactions needs for money are more static relative to income but financial innovations allow money conservation as income rises. In short, the income-elasticity of demand for money falls as income rises.

(c) *The rate of interest is a less significant determinant of the demand for money in developing countries than in developed countries*

Our initial discussion of the role of interest rates in the demand for money, in chapter 1, characterized the extreme classical theory as positing a high degree of substitutability between money and *all* assets, but more markedly between money and goods than between money and any one financial asset; hence the minor role given to the return on such an asset, its interest rate. The extreme Keynesian model, on the other hand, posits a high degree of substitutability between money and a few, liquid, financial assets which provide services similar to those of money; hence the importance of the rate of return on such assets. The evidence thus suggests that developing economies conform more to the classical model, and developed to the Keynesian model.

This is not surprising since the classical model was developed at a time when the financial sophistication of developed countries was more akin to that of developing countries now than that of developed countries today. If the inducement has not yet been sufficient for financial institutions to develop money substitutes and the state of wealth is not sufficient to support a full-scale domestic capital market, then interest-bearing alternatives to money are not available on a sufficiently large scale for them to be a major factor in determining the demand for money. In effect, the bulk of savings are held either in money or in real assets, so that the major choices are:

(1) how much to save, i.e. how much to spend on consumer goods and how much to hold in money or capital goods (real assets); and
(2) the composition of saving as between money and real assets.

In the classical world the two decisions are interdependent: savings are higher the higher the rate of interest, while investment in capital goods is lower the higher the rate of interest (determining the unique rate of interest at which savings equals investment). But if self-finance is predominant, as in many cases in developing countries, the two are positive functions of the expected real rate of return on capital, which may not bear a close relationship with the rate of interest. (See the discussion of interest rate policy below.)

In developed countries now, financial intermediation has filled in the gap between money and real assets with a wide variety of financial assets of differing degrees of liquidity, weakening the degree of substitutability between money and real assets. Thus alternative assets, like savings accounts with banks for example, perform some money functions and are easily convertible into a form of money which is acceptable as a means of payment, while earning a relatively low rate of interest. The high degree of substitutability between money by some definition, e.g. M_1 (currency held outside the banks plus demand deposits) and interest-bearing assets makes the rate of interest an important determinant of the demand for money in developed countries.

(d) *The expected rate of inflation is a more significant determinant of the demand for money in developing countries than developed countries*

The importance of the expected rate of inflation (measured by past rates of inflation) arises from its influence on real rates of return on alternative assets. In the case of consumer goods and real assets the dichotomy is clear: the real value of money falls with inflation but is more or less maintained on average for consumer goods and real assets. There is thus a strong incentive to switch out of money when inflationary expectations are strong.

In the case of comparisons between money and alternative financial assets the dichotomy is more muted. The nominal rate of return on financial assets does not generally fully reflect inflationary expectations; indeed in times of high inflation the real rate of return on financial assets, even in highly sophisticated financial markets, is often negative. This phenomenon is of great interest in itself. But the consequence for the demand for money is that there is a less strong incentive to switch out of money into alternative financial assets when inflation is high because the real value of these assets is not maintained either. It is this phenomenon which provides some justification for a return to the classical model. Since substitutability between money and real assets becomes more attractive again once inflation becomes persistent, relative to substitutability between money and the financial assets, the developed world may appear to be reverting to the classical mould. The similarity should not, however, be pushed too far: the important substitutability is between *all* financial assets (whose real return falls with inflation) not just money, and real assets (whose real value is maintained with inflation). In addition, it should be noted that other consequences of inflation may generate expectations of a weakening real rate of return on real assets, tending to diminish the degree of substitutability with money and other financial assets. These questions are pursued in depth in chapter 8.

4.4 SEGMENTED MARKETS

Before pursuing the implications of this evidence for the influence of money in developing countries, some closer attention must be given to the nature of markets in developing countries in order to assess the scope of the evidence discussed above. Most developing countries are characterized by segmented markets, i.e. by markets operating independently of each other. The most marked segmentation is between the rural sector and what is often called the 'export enclave'. (See McKinnon (1973) for a full description of this dualism, particularly in terms of financial markets.) The export enclave generally includes the bulk of industries and commercial activity in the economy, is urbanized, and has the closest ties with world markets. A high proportion of business, including the banking sector, is often foreign-owned.

Average incomes and wealth are relatively high in this sector, most transactions are monetized, and there is some financial intermediation through the banking sector, government agencies and international capital markets.

In contrast, the rural sector is primarily agricultural, average incomes and wealth are low, a large proportion of transactions is conducted in kind rather than with money and the primary form of financial intermediation is the activities of moneylenders whose interest charges are very high relative to the export enclave. Money-lenders' operations are often quite independent of the banking sector in the export enclave, being financed by an initial base augmented by interest charges.

There has been much debate about the reasons for these high rates, which can reach levels of 50, 60, or 70 per cent per annum. On the one hand, they reflect the poor security on loans (which is heavily dependent on the moneylender's valuation of collateral) and expected low rates of return on investment which increase the risk of default. On the other hand, because the financial market is segmented, with remoteness (physically and socially) from the export enclave precluding alternative access to bank lending, the local moneylender will exercise local monopoly powers. Moneylenders can thus maintain relatively high interest rates without fear of competition. Further, the high interest rates, combined with low income levels, mean that interest payments will have strong income effects. Indeed, rising interest rates may induce an upward shift in the demand for credit, since credit may be required to meet the interest payments themselves.

As a result, McKinnon (1973) postulates a strong incentive to self-finance investment in the rural sector, so that planned investment expenditure encourages an increase in savings held in the form of money. Thus an increase in the expected real rate of return on investment increases the demand for money. McKinnon describes this relationship as a positive relationship between the demand for money and interest rates (the converse of the conventional relationship).

There is cause for confusion about which 'interest rate' we are discussing here. If there are no deposit institutions, it cannot be the rate of return on money held with such institutions. If we mean the expected rate of return on capital expenditure, then certainly the demand for money to finance such expenditure will rise when the expected return rises. If we mean the loan rate charged for borrowing money, the relationship will not be so clear. Higher loan rates will encourage potential investors to amass their own money-holdings in order to avoid increased borrowing costs. Further, higher loan rates will increase the demand for money to meet higher interest payments. But the question of whether loan rates rise or fall when the expected real return on capital rises is still open. Other things being equal, an outward shift in the demand for money will push interest rates up (the local monopoly theory). But if the expected risk of default on loans is less when investment opportunities improve, then the supply of loans may shift out also, reducing the loan charge (the value-of-collateral theory). Actual money-holdings may then not appear to be strongly influenced by interest charges because of the two opposing (supply and demand) forces.

Because the rural sector and export enclave are so segmented, the published estimates of interest elasticity of demand for money probably in any case refer only to the export enclave, where financial institutions are more competitive. For those engaged in self-finance there, some interest-bearing alternative assets are available as a repository for savings: interest-bearing bank accounts in particular. Also, loan rates for those requiring external finance are arrived at in a more competitive environment. The banking sector expands when the real return on capital rises both because of increased demand for deposits among self-financers, and increased demand for loans among externally financed business. Particularly if rising real returns are associated with increased export earnings and thus foreign exchange reserves, this increased demand for liquidity need not push up financial interest rates. Again, the opposing forces of demand and supply may weaken the relationship between the demand for money and interest rates.

Money, in the form of currency, filters through to the rural sector in payment for agricultural products sold to traders in the export enclave, and it returns in payment for consumer goods and agricultural implements. If the demand for money rises in expectation of the need to finance an investment project (say, the purchase of a tractor) then that money in effect goes out of circulation until enough is collected to buy the tractor. If currency cannot be deposited with a financial institution, it cannot be used to generate additional finance.

Clearly the development of a banking system in rural areas (as is being promoted in India, for example) would be of benefit, concerning the currency supply for current transactions. Savings in the rural sector could then be amassed in the form of bank accounts (rather than stocks of goods, such as grain or gold), while the banks could use the resources to make loans, at rates lower than those charged by moneylenders. If in fact banks in that situation invested their assets in the export enclave instead, more financing would thereby be made available in the export enclave, and indeed savers in the rural sector would earn interest on their savings. On the other hand, continued dependence on moneylenders would reduce the overall capacity to save in the rural sector.

Since much of the financial development in developing countries is supply-led, choices are available as to the type of development to promote. The major issue has been the level of interest rates.

4.5 INTEREST RATE STRATEGY

The traditional strategy on interest rates was to keep them low (in the export enclave) as a means of subsidizing investment. The vicious circle of development was viewed as being so difficult to break out of that any assistance, e.g. in the form of low interest rates, would be beneficial. Thus loans from international agencies like the IMF and IBRD carry below-market interest rates. Governments in developing countries similarly provide financing at subsidized rates to businesses establishing plants or expanding within their countries. The low interest charges serve to offset perceptions of low real rates of return on investment, due to 'real' factors, political instability, etc. Finally, low real rates of interest have also been the consequence of expansionary government spending financed in effect by inflation (which erodes the value of the public sector debt burden, while expanding tax receipts).

This strategy has come under attack, primarily by McKinnon (1973) and Shaw (1973) who argue instead for a high interest rate strategy. Their argument in essence is based on the interest rate theory of the classical model. Higher interest rates encourage increased saving. At the same time, higher interest rates on loans, encouraged by increased rates of return, would encourage the institutional development of financial intermediation. The initial state of government-subsidized interest rates for business borrowers, together with inflationary government finance which reduces rates of return to lenders to the public sector, is called 'financial repression'. The growth of a private sector financial system is termed 'financial liberalization'.

The mechanism by which savings are generated differs as between McKinnon and Shaw. McKinnon concentrates on situations of self-finance, where money (in the form of currency and bank deposits) is the primary vehicle for savings, which in turn are generated by capital spending plans. Money and real capital are thus complements. Shaw on the other hand envisages a more sophisticated financial system where finance is direct, in the case of savers purchasing bonds issued by borrowers, or indirect in the case of banks lending out the deposits of savers. Then financial assets and real capital are substitutes as far as savers are concerned. The two approaches are quite consistent if McKinnon's applies to countries without a capital market and Shaw's applies to those at a higher stage of financial development. Indeed the evidence (see Fry (1978)) is consistent with such an interpretation. In both cases, higher interest rates generate more savings in the form of financial assets.

At the same time as reducing the savings gap, this strategy is also designed to reduce the foreign exchange gap. If there is less reliance on borrowing from abroad because of the additional finance generated domestically by financial liberalization and at the same time foreign exchange is conserved domestically by the greater use of other money assets, then the foreign exchange constraint becomes less binding.

The crux of the problem with this policy is that the interest rate does not *directly* determine the volume of savings, only the way they are held. An increased interest rate may induce savers to switch from holding real assets, or currency, to financial assets, and even to *attempt* to increase total savings. But income, and thus savings, can only increase if investment increases. So, the switch to financial assets may cause an increase in saving by allowing more investment to be financed (rather than vice-versa).

Increased savings could not be relied upon, anyway, to generate an equal amount of investment demand at higher interest rates. Certainly, if the financial development was extended to the rural sector, then even these higher interest rates would be lower than those charged by moneylenders. But, as Khatkhate (1980) argues forcibly, the essence of low-income developing countries may be relatively low real rates of return on capital. Shortage of financial capital pushes market rates of interest above this real rate of return, reducing investment demand, and thereby income and savings, further increasing the financial capital shortage. Neoclassical theory would suggest that the lower the rate of investment the higher the marginal return on capital, so that an equilibrium position *can* be reached. But it is reasonable to suggest that there is what is called a Verdoon effect operating at least in developing economies at early stages of development. According to this 'effect' more investment will generate more infrastructure expenditure, widespread acquiring of skills, more of an impetus to financial development, and so higher marginal rates of return on subsequent investment. In other words, growth itself increases marginal returns on capital. Khatkhate proposes, as a compromise, higher interest rates to promote financial development, but not higher than marginal real rates of return on capital (which are lower than marginal returns in developed countries).

Developing countries cannot, however, establish such a policy without attention to the implications for capital flows. A major feature of the export enclave is its close connections with international markets, including the international capital market. Suppose interest rates are established at a level below rates on international capital markets, in line with Khatkhate's proposal, by means of an increase in the money supply relative to demand. Asset-holders in the export enclave, particularly multinational businesses, are well aware of interest rates on the international money and capital markets; if a higher return can be earned there, then the act of placing funds on international markets involves an outflow of foreign exchange and thus a reduction in the money supply.

Again, we come back to the expected real return on capital. If it is sufficiently high, investment demand generates its own finance domestically and through capital inflows. If it is low, it causes outflows of what finance is generated domestically. Indeed, the Bank for International Settlements data on borrowing and lending on the Eurocurrency market shows that only the higher-income developing countries (with higher marginal rates of return on capital?) are net borrowers. The low-income developing countries generally hold more in deposits in the Eurocurrency market than they borrow from it.

It is this ready-made, accessible world financial market which makes it so difficult for developing countries to develop their own financial structures. Certainly there is a great deal of scope for extending banking into the rural areas, although it is an administratively costly exercise. But the major stumbling-block is the tendency for both savings and foreign exchange to disappear into international markets; at least, unlike the Darien scheme in Scotland, a good return may reasonably be expected! But, without controls on such flows, it takes an exogenous increase in expected returns on domestic investment to retain funds in the domestic economy and to generate growth in the domestic banking system sufficient to overcome the obstacle of foreign exchange shortage.

4.6 INTERDEPENDENCE AND THE MONEY SUPPLY

The lower the level of financial development, the narrower the range of assets acceptable as money, and thus the more vulnerable is that development to the supply of that narrow range of assets. In turn, the lower the level of financial development, the greater the tendency for narrow money (foreign exchange) to be attracted to other markets providing higher financial rates of return. Yet, it is unlikely that market forces (through 'financial liberalization') can alleviate the situation by promoting financial development unless there is strong investment demand. Once financial development has been achieved, however, the banking system is less dependent on underlying real rates of return; New York and London are no longer situated in the highest real growth areas, but still retain their supremacy in international finance. Finally, the foreign exchange constraint is more binding on less developed countries than on those with convertible currencies, access to international credit and a stock of international securities with which to purchase foreign exchange.

The way out adopted by many developing countries has been to acquire stocks of international securities and credit on international markets without going through the stage of development of the domestic financial system. That, and the greater involvement of international agencies in providing development assistance, is the main difference between the present North–South situation and that operating a century ago. Triffin's (1964) description of international relations at that time, under the gold standard, is, however, very instructive.

Capital markets at the end of the nineteenth century had reached a level of some sophistication in Europe, particularly in London. Developing countries relied on the London discount market for trade credit, just as they relied on London commodity markets for foreign exchange income. If expansion in Europe threatened to cause balance of payments deficits and thus gold outflows because of excessive imports, the situation could be alleviated by raising the London discount rate rather than waiting for price deflation. Demand for primary commodities dropped temporarily because of dearer credit in Europe, forcing the primary commodity exporters to finance unsold stocks with dear credit. The exporters would have to reduce the prices of their exports in order to move stocks, thus reducing credit costs and minimizing income losses. Payments balance could thus be restored for

Europe, with initial import levels restored, but their value reduced. In real terms, income has risen in Europe and fallen in the developing countries.

This depiction reflects in exaggerated form the consequences of differential financial development, with credit being supplied primarily from a financial centre, for real development in different countries. A more modern illustration is provided by the consequences of oil price increases. Without capital flows, the consequence would have been enormous balance of payments deficits for oil consumers and surpluses for producers. But, in fact, most of the increase in oil receipts found its way back to the oil-consuming nations, either in the form of payment for exports of consumer and capital goods (and financial assistance to developing countries), or as deposits in Western capital markets; financial returns on European and US capital markets provided sufficient inducements for oil producers to lend their surpluses.

It is this type of phenomenon which promotes the policy proposals for increased financial market integration; an important example is the European Monetary System (EMS) which was formed in the EEC in January 1979. Similarly, the observation that regions do not have balance of payments problems is attributed to the same cause. Banks within a country do not suffer 'specie' or resources shortage when they have a payments deficit with other banks, because settlement can be made with nationally acceptable securities, or they can borrow on national capital markets. Sooner or later, of course, any bank can run out of assets, just as ultimately even in developed countries the foreign exchange constraint can *eventually* bite. But the ability to borrow and lend because of the high degree of financial intermediation within a developed country allows a lot of leeway before that bite need be felt.

Between developed countries, as in the EEC, or between regions in a developed country, however, many of the same problems can arise as for developing countries. Differential degrees of financial development mean that pockets exist like the rural sectors of developing countries where financial operations are quite segmented from the rest of the economy. Half of the adult population of the UK, for example, have no bank account. Further, the interest rates charged by consumer finance companies, the main source of credit for low-income borrowers, bear the same relationship to bank interest charges as the loans of money-lenders in the rural sectors of developing countries.

More generally, where there is a low rate of return on capital, or where such a low rate is perceived by financial institutions in the financial centre, regions or countries cannot look to developed capital markets for credit. Thus regions or countries which are less developed financially as well as in real terms, and which are therefore more constrained by the effects of balance of payments deficits on the money supply, are more likely to experience net capital outflows than net capital inflows.

Of course, *if* the perceptions of real returns are correct and *if* marginal returns would fall with more investment in these less developed economies, then the capital markets are performing an 'equilibrating' role in allocating capital at the margin to its most productive uses. (Whether or not the consequences for the regions or countries concerned are acceptable is a political question.) But there may be misinformation about real return prospects in remote areas, which may be exacerbated by the divergence in financial centres between financial returns and real returns. (A full discussion of this phenomenon is provided in chapter 11.) Further, perceived real returns might increase at the margin if there were more investment, if only because increased activity itself reduces the creditor's risk of default.

With primary reliance on self-generated finance, only local perceptions of growth prospects are important. But world financial markets are becoming progressively more interdependent, emphasizing the importance of relative rates of financial return in different economies. This in itself serves to inhibit the development of local financial systems in areas where financial development has not so far taken place.

This was the kind of reasoning which promoted unit banking in the US, with self-finance at the community, state and Federal Reserve District levels, supplemented by a large active market in national securities. Indeed, it has been argued (by Naylor (1975), for example) that this unit banking system promoted an even spread of economic development in the regions of the US. In Canada, by contrast, the nationwide banking system employed the savings of the first-settled region (the Atlantic region) to finance development of Upper Canada to the detriment of the Atlantic region.

Market forces are, however, working against the unit banking system. The economies of scale enjoyed by New York as financial centre have attracted borrowers and lenders from across the US, further concentrating business there. At the same time, banks have been establishing links over wide areas, often connected by mutual ownership by holding companies. Financial concentration is clearly profitable.

In Europe, very deliberate steps have been taken by the EEC to promote the free movement of capital. The European Monetary System involves relative fixity of exchange rates, the creation of a common currency (the European Currency Unit) pooling of 20 per cent of members' reserves, and the establishment of a series of facilities to finance members in payments difficulties. In theory, then, with exchange speculation only relevant at times when the fixed parties clearly require adjustment, capital should flow purely in response to relative interest rates.

Since the consequence of capital flows is a change in the balance of payments and thus in national money supplies, the endogeneity of the money supply increases in the sense that it can no longer be controlled by the monetary authorities. This result is modified to the extent that intergovernmental capital flows (from the EMS financing facilities) offset the effects of private sector flows. The size of any one member's money stock is thus determined to a considerable extent by relative interest rates, which are in turn a function of perceptions of real rates of return, degrees of financial sophistication, and the demand for money for purposes other than investment in real capital.

This last paragraph has, as they say, opened a real can of worms. The way in which interest rates are determined – and what effect they have – is central to monetary theory. Taking things one step at a time, we go on now to examine more closely exactly *how* the money supply is determined in the short-run sense. *Given* a particular financial structure, *how* does an inflow of capital, say, generate an increase in the money supply? In the next chapter we adopt the traditional multiplier approach to answer this question, and then go on to consider other approaches.

5

The Money Multiplier Theory of Money Supply Determination

5.1 INTRODUCTION

The last two chapters have concentrated on the supply of money in the long run, as financial institutions develop and trading practices change. We saw how the supply of money, in some form, increased in response to demand for financing economic development. Now we turn to the supply of money in the short run, within a given institutional structure.

Even in the short run, of course, what is actually used as money, or regarded as performing money functions, may change in response to changing market conditions. This notion of 'moneyness' or liquidity, being applicable to most assets in some degree, is explored in chapter 8. Taking things one step at a time, however, we discuss in this and the next two chapters how the supply of the most 'money-like' assets is generated in the short run.

The first major approach to money supply determination is the money multiplier approach. This approach has a long pedigree, going back to the days when money consisted of note issue backed by gold. It was understood then that there was a stable relationship between the amount of gold and the size of the note issue, so that any change in gold holdings would bring about a multiple change in the note issue.

Now the approach is used primarily by monetarists, suggesting that demand deposits and savings deposits are stable multiples of bank reserves. If reserves can be controlled, then, so can the money supply. Further, it is regarded as not being of great significance which monetary aggregate determines expenditure, or for which monetary aggregate demand is most stable, if most of these aggregates are stable multiples of bank reserves.

In the next section we derive the multipliers which relate bank reserves to the different monetary aggregates, and then discuss the stability of the coefficients of those multipliers in section 5.3. The usefulness of the theory, assuming that the multipliers are stable, rests on the stability, or controllability, of bank reserves, also discussed in section 5.3.

5.2 DERIVATION OF MONEY MULTIPLIERS

Definitions of the various money aggregates differ from country to country. We shall see, however, that general principles can be derived as to the relationships between different multipliers. We derive here multipliers for aggregates called M_1, M_2 and M_3; definitional differences for particular cases can easily be incorporated in the formulae.

M_0 is defined as the monetary base, or 'high-powered money'. It is defined here as being made up of bank reserves, R, which we take to be deposits with the central monetary authority, and the non-bank public's holdings of currency, C:

$$M_0 = R + C \qquad (5.1)$$

Suppose the only liabilities of the banks are demand deposits, DD. Then we define the monetary aggregate M_1 as being made up of the non-bank public's holdings of demand deposits and currency:

$$M_1 = DD + C \qquad (5.2)$$

We now want to calculate the multiplier, m_1, which relates M_1 to M_0.

The banks are subject to reserve requirements imposed by the central monetary authority. They must hold a proportion, r, of deposits in reserves, so that they are always in a position to give currency for deposits, given the 'normal' fluctuations in cashing-in. (The ratio r could be maintained as a matter of prudent practice on the part of the banks, rather than as an official requirement; all that matters here is that the ratio be adhered to.) At the same time, the non-bank public habitually hold currency as a proportion, c, of deposits. Any high-powered money injected into the system, if fully utilized, must then be shared between bank reserves and currency holdings according to these two ratios.

From equations (5.1) and (5.2), we can derive the M_1 multiplier, m_1:

$$m_1 = \frac{M_1}{M_0} = \frac{DD + C}{R + C} \qquad (5.3)$$

Dividing the numerator and denominator by DD:

$$m_1 = \frac{1 + (C/DD)}{(R/DD) + (C/DD)} = \frac{1 + c}{r + c} \tag{5.4}$$

The multiplier is greater the smaller is the cash-deposit ratio, c, and the reserve ratio, r.

This tells us that if the monetary base is increased by an amount, x, then M_1 can increase by a maximum amount $[(1 + c)/(r + c)]x$. This is a matter of definition, summarizing the possible outcome of a process of bank expansion. The following numerical example shows how the increase in M_0 works through the system, eventually allowing an addition of m_1 times that amount to M_1. The example refers to the banking system as a whole, ignoring transfers of deposits between banks.

Suppose the reserve ratio and cash-deposit ratio are both 10 per cent. Then, according to equation (5.4), m_1 is 5.5. The public initially holds deposits of 100 units with the banking system, so reserve holdings and currency holdings are each 10 units. M_0 is thus 20 units and M_1 is 110 units. Since the banks only need to hold 10 units in reserves, but have deposits of 100 units, they can lend out the remaining 90 units and earn interest on them.

Now, the government gives out a tax rebate of 11 units, financed by borrowing from the central monetary authority. The public deposits 10 of the 11 units in the banks and holds onto 1 unit in currency. The banks now have 9 units of excess reserves (they must hold 11 units against the new deposit level of 110 units). They increase loans by 11 units, of which the public holds 1 unit in currency and 10 in new bank deposits (see table 5.1). The banks have thus lost 1 unit of reserves to currency holdings and must hold an extra unit as reserves against the new deposits, so excess reserves are down to 7 units. The banks keep increasing lending by 11 units for three more rounds, gradually reducing the amount of excess reserves they hold. In the final round, lending can only increase by 5.5 units, and all the excess reserves are used up. M_1 has increased by 60.5 units, or 5.5 times 11 units.

A broader definition of the money supply, M_2, would include time deposits (and savings deposits) as well as demand deposits. Although payment cannot actually be made directly with a savings deposit, it can be argued that withdrawals can be made so easily that these deposits affect expenditure decisions in the same way as demand deposits. M_2 is defined as M_1, plus time deposits TD:

$$M_2 = DD + TD + C \tag{5.5}$$

(Monetary aggregates are defined differently in different countries; for example, our M_2 is like the British M_3, while there is no 'M_2'.) If the reserve requirements and cash-deposit ratio are the same with respect to time deposits as to demand deposits, then the M_2 multiplier, m_2, is the same as m_1. But suppose the central monetary authority imposes a lower rate of reserve requirements, r', on time deposits on the grounds that their rate of withdrawal fluctuates less than for demand deposits. Suppose also that the cash–deposit ratio is still c against demand deposits, but zero against time deposits, and that time deposits are held as a stable proportion, t, of demand deposits. Then the M_2 multiplier can be derived as follows:

$$m_2 = \frac{M_2}{M_0} = \frac{DD + TD + C}{R + C} \tag{5.6}$$

Dividing both numerator and denominator through by DD:

$$m_2 = \frac{1 + (TD/DD) + (C/DD)}{\dfrac{rDD + r'TD}{DD} + (C/DD)} \tag{5.7}$$

$$= \frac{1 + t + c}{r + r't + c}$$

Table 5.1　*Bank multiplier process for entire banking system, given in arbitrary monetary units*

| (Excess reserves) | Banks | | | Non-bank public | |
| | Assets | | Liabilities | | |
	Reserves	Loans	Deposits	Currency	M_1
(0)	10	90	100	10	110
(9)	20	90	110	11	121
(7)	19	101	120	12	132
(5)	18	112	130	13	143
(3)	17	123	140	14	154
(1)	16	134	150	15	165
(0)	15.5	139.5	155	15.5	170.5

As expected, m_2 is larger than m_1, so that a given addition to M_0 increases the larger aggregate M_2 by more than M_1. Further, as with m_1, m_2 is higher the lower is the rate of cash leakage, c, and reserve requirements r and r'. Further, if the reserve requirement on time deposits, r', is equal to or less than that on demand deposits, r, then the multiplier is higher the greater the proportion of total deposits held in time deposits rather than demand deposits.

We can also derive a modified M_1 multiplier, m_1', which takes account of the need to hold reserves against time deposits (even though M_1 does not include time deposits). m_1' is thus calculated with a drain into reserves against time deposits as well as demand deposits.

$$m_1' = \frac{1 + c}{r + r't + c} \qquad (5.8)$$

Indeed, it should be clear by now that the technique can be applied to a wide variety of definitions of 'M' and of reserves and cash leakage rates. This multiplier also conforms to the pattern of being larger the lower the liquidity of the banks' and non-bank public's portfolios, i.e. the lower are r, r' and c and the higher is t.

This interesting pattern which is emerging confirms many of our observations of how banking systems have developed. The lower the proportion of wealth which the public hold in currency and the lower the proportion held in demand deposits rather than time deposits, the more the money aggregates M_1 and M_2 can expand. Similarly, the lower the reserves the banks hold against deposits the more can be lent out, returning eventually as increased deposits.

The Scottish banking system succeeded in expanding rapidly in spite of a small M_0 (specie holdings) because both the banks and the non-bank public were prepared to 'go illiquid'. In the case of individual bank failures, the desire among customers to hold currency, or other banks' deposits, increased; possibly because the bank's reserve holdings had fallen below a critical level. Thus the scope for such banks' expansion was seriously curtailed. Within 'reason', then, we have derived what seems to be a paradox, that the less liquid are desired asset-holdings, the more liquidity is made available by the banking system. Expansion of the entire system beyond some critical level can, however, carry the seeds of its own destruction. If the entire banking system becomes too illiquid, then the desire for liquidity on the part of the banks' customers will bring about a multiple contraction of the banking system.

Finally, before pursuing the subject of money multipliers in more breadth, we derive a further multiplier for the aggregate M_3. This aggregate is defined as including both M_2 and deposits with non-bank financial intermediaries (NBFIS). These latter are institutions like savings banks and finance companies, which were once small in relation to the banks, but which now provide a major source of liquidity. Thus, deposits with these institutions can be viewed as money; indeed some of these institutions issue cheques so that their deposits are as liquid as bank deposits to the extent that the cheques are widely accepted.

M_3 is defined as including M_2 together with the deposits of NBFIS, D'. To simplify the calculation, we assume that bank time deposits are subject to the same reserve requirements and currency drain as demand deposits, so they can be treated as if they were demand deposits. The public hold NBFI deposits as a stable proportion, d, of bank deposits. Suppose that the NBFIS are not subject to reserve requirements. Instead, as a matter of prudence, they hold a proportion, r'', of deposits with the banks. These deposits, $r''D'$, are then subject to the bank reserve requirement, r, just like the other deposits, D. The cash drain applies to NBFI deposits as to bank deposits, still at the rate, c. The M_3 multiplier, m_3, is derived as follows:

$$m_3 = \frac{M_3}{M_0} = \frac{D + r''D' + D' + C}{R + C}$$

$$= \frac{D + (1 + r'')D' + c(D + D')}{r(D + r''D') + c(D + D')} \qquad (5.9)$$

Dividing through the numerator and denominator by D:

$$m_3 = \frac{1 + (1 + r'')(D'/D) + c[1 + (D'/D)]}{r + rr''(D'/D) + c + c(D'/D)}$$

$$= \frac{1 + c + (1 + r'' + c)d}{r + c + (rr'' + c)d} \qquad (5.10)$$

Again, it transpires that the multiplier is higher the less liquid are portfolio preferences – the higher is d, the lower are r, r'' and c. The significance of the NBFIS is that they tend to hold their reserves with other financial institutions, particularly banks. So the reserves they must hold as they increase deposits are not a drain on the financial system as a whole. The more deposits get channelled into NBFIS, the faster the supply of M_3 can grow. Chapter 7 will be devoted to pursuing the implications of this phenomenon.

The multiplier equations have become rather complex even for these simple multipliers; but once the technique is learnt, it is possible to derive multipliers to apply to most institutional structures. All produce the same general result: the fewer the drains out of the financial system – into reserves and currency – the more the financial structure can expand on a given monetary base.

5.3 STABILITY OF THE MULTIPLIER BASE AND THE MULTIPLIER COEFFICIENTS

Chapters 2 and 3 on the development of banking systems demonstrated how the multiplier coefficients change in the long run. As banking systems develop, with more assets (bank liabilities) acquiring 'moneyness', the non-bank public have been prepared to hold progressively smaller proportions of their wealth in currency, then demand deposits, then time deposits and so on. Also, in general, improved banking practices have allowed banks to hold less 'cash' reserves (except when required to hold more for monetary policy purposes). Thus, as a broad generalization, c and r have tended to fall in the long run, and t and d to rise, allowing progressively greater expansion on a given monetary base.

Cagan (1965) has studied the cash–deposit ratio and the reserve ratio in the US from 1877 to 1960, as well as the high-powered money base, in order to identify their respective contributions to changes in the money supply. He concluded that the long-run changes in the two ratios only accounted for 10 per cent of the increase in the money supply; the increasing monetary base accounted for 90 per cent of the increase. He also observed short-run cyclical changes, concluding that the cash–deposit ratio was most important in bringing about increases in the money supply during expansions and decreases during contractions. The public's decision to conserve cash balances during expansions increased the money multiplier and thus the money supply; the stabilizing of C/D at a low level then stemmed further money supply increases, bringing about a peak in the cycle. Reserve ratio changes helped to curtail expansions and contractions in the money supply to some degree; changes in reserve requirements have been used relatively frequently in the US as a means of short-term monetary control.

In the UK, reserve requirements have been changed more by calling or releasing special deposits than by changing the reserve ratio itself. It is not surprising, then, that Sheppard (1971) should find that the cash–deposit ratio should have had more influence on the money supply than the reserve ratio. This was also the case before bank reserves became a tool of monetary policy, i.e. when they were held at conventionally prudent levels. Sheppard did, however, find that, like the US, changes in high-powered money were by far the most important factor over the period 1881–1960.

Black (1975) has conducted a similar study for the UK, quarterly, over the period 1960–70. His results show the cash–deposit ratio, and the monetary base, and, from 1967 to 1970, the ratio of bank deposits to NBFI deposits, as being the dominant influences on the money supply, relative to other multiplier coefficients. He uses the results to defend the use of the traditional simple multipliers of the type we have derived here.

But the more complex the multiplier, with the more coefficients, the less useful it becomes for predictive and control purposes. Even if all the leakage rates, and proportionate holdings of different forms of money (bank accounts, building society accounts, NBFI accounts, etc.) are more or less stable, the more there are in the multiplier equation, the more scope there is for overall instability of the multiplier due to random disturbances to the coefficients. The explanatory power of M_0 and c in Black's estimation was *relatively* strong, compared to the other coefficients, but still left a lot of changes in the money supply unexplained. Restricting attention to simple M_1 multipliers gets round this problem, but is only satisfactory if M_1 is the key variable with respect to expenditure and demand for money.

Further, the predictive power of the multiplier relationship, and its usefulness with respect to monetary control, is diminished if the monetary base cannot be controlled directly by the central monetary authority. This facility is available to the US authorities. Bank reserves consist, as in our examples, of deposits with the Federal Reserve Banks, and the Federal Reserve Board can limit the extent to which banks can top up their reserves by discounting bills. Indeed, since October 1979 much more attention has been paid to the rate of growth of the monetary base in order to control the broader monetary aggregates.

In the UK, however, from 1971 to 1981, required reserve assets included deposits with the Bank of England, but also Treasury bills, government stocks with a year to maturity or less, and call money (deposits redeemable 'at call') held with certain types of institution. Banks could thus top up their reserves by, say, selling government stocks with more than a year to maturity and buying those under a year. Further, unlike the Federal Reserve Board, the Bank of England did not place any limit on its lender-of-last-resort facility. Any shortage of reserves in the banking system could thus be supplemented by borrowing from the Bank of England. The Bank's control over the banking system depended both on the rate at which it bought and sold stocks and Treasury bills (and the interest rate required to sustain that rate of buying and selling) and the rate of discount charged for the lender-of-last-resort facility. The Bank could thus influence interest rates in an attempt to *induce* banks to hold the desired level of reserves.

Since 1980 there has been considerable debate about the merits of introducing a system of monetary base control into the UK (expressed in official form in a Green Paper, UK (1980)). The abolition of the reserve assets ratio in August 1981, leaving a ½ per cent cash ratio as the primary reserve requirement on the banking system, has moved the system closer to facilitating control of the monetary base. In addition, the 'discount window' (the lender-of-last-resort facility) is to be given less emphasis by the Bank of England, by a shift towards interest rate control through primary reliance on open market operations in bills.

But a change from controlling market interest rates to controlling the monetary base would require fundamental changes in the behaviour of all financial institutions involved. If the monetary base were fixed, there could be no lender-of-last-resort facility except in emergency situations. In order to ensure their liquidity and to retain the confidence of their customers, banks would have to be much more cautious in their portfolio management. The reserve ratio *chosen* by the banks would rise. Also overdraft facilities would have to be curtailed to prevent the banks from unforeseen reserves shortage; this would reduce the liquidity of borrowers. Further, since all the impact of exogenous shocks to the financial system would have to be taken by interest rates, monetary base control could cause violent interest rate fluctuations. Not only would these force the banks to be even more cautious, but they would also conflict with the Bank of England's role as money-raiser for the government. It would seem, then, that the introduction of a strict monetary base control system would actually reverse the process of financial development.

The important thing to note for the moment then, is that, unless the volume of reserves is controlled, the usefulness of the multiplier relates more to its role as an *ex post* identity (like the quantity theory equation, $MV=PT$) rather than a predictive tool. Given a particular reserves change, from whatever source, the multipliers tell us how each monetary aggregate can be expected to grow, only as long as the various coefficients are expected to remain stable.

But even then, the multipliers only indicate the *maximum* possible increase for given coefficients. In the numerical example of the M_1 multiplier, it was assumed that the banks would continue increasing lending until there were no excess reserves. If there was some uncertainty about whether potential borrowers would default, the banks might hold on to the extra liquidity until it seemed appropriate to increase lending. The banks might of course prefer to leave excess reserves in the short-term money market, to earn some return until better prospects turned up. By channelling excess reserves in a different direction from industrial or consumer borrowers, the new deposits created are subject to different leakage coefficients, affecting the size of the multiplier.

5.4   CONCLUSION

Multipliers show the relationship between the monetary base, which the monetary authorities *may* choose to control, and the various collections of money assets included in the definitions of M_1, M_2, M_3, etc. As financial systems have developed, attention has shifted progressively along the spectrum, from M_1 to wider ranges of assets as each has become more 'money-like'. The stock of what is regarded as money has thus become a progressively larger multiple of the monetary base.

In the short run, too, money multipliers may vary as the ratios vary between the money assets within the relevant range. A preference for more liquidity, expressed by a higher preferred ratio of currency to demand deposits, demand deposits to time deposits, etc. reduces the size of the multiplier and thus the supply of liquidity (for a given monetary base). Similarly, a preference for less liquidity raises the multiplier, and thus the supply of liquidity.

But the multiplier approach presumes that the money supply always rises to the maximum allowed by reserve ratios, without reference to demand. If liquidity preference does fall, raising the multiplier, will the additional deposits which the banks can then create actually be accepted? What influence do interest rates have, as a mechanism for reconciling contrary shifts in the supply of and demand for liquidity?

The alternative approach which attempts to answer these questions is the portfolio approach, which we discuss in the next chapter.

Before considering in more detail the alternative, portfolio theory, approach, it is worth while to complete this chapter by noting the uses to which multiplier theory is most suited. The two areas where the multipliers are most revealing are long-run analysis of money supply, and cross-section analysis, comparing financial systems at different stages of development.

When discussing the development of banking systems it was noted that increasing demand for finance was met by the emergence of new money substitutes, both in the sense of new assets acceptable in payment and of new assets providing a more acceptable medium for savings than money. From our analysis of the different types of money multiplier, working up from a simple demand deposits aggregate to one including liabilities of NBFIs, it is clear that money multipliers are higher for financial systems at higher stages of development.

This is of importance when designing monetary policy. A contractionary policy itself induces further innovation which allows the multiplier to increase, and stay higher even when the tight monetary policy is lifted. This must be taken into account if medium-term targets are to be reasonable. It is also of importance when considering financial flows between countries at different stages of financial development. Other things being equal, an inflow of foreign exchange in one country adds to the monetary base, raising the money supply by the appropriate domestic multiplier. The contraction in the monetary base in the country from which the inflow has come will cause a different change in the domestic money supply if the domestic multiplier is different. Further, differences in money multipliers are not only the effect of differences in financial development but also the cause in the sense that banks can make more efficient use of their resources in developed financial systems. These differences in financial competitiveness may induce capital flows towards the higher-return system, adding a contraction in monetary base to the lower multiplier of the less developed banking system.

6

The Portfolio Theory of Money Supply Determination

6.1 INTRODUCTION

The major alternative approach to money supply determination is the portfolio approach. This approach attempts to deal with the possibility that the multiplier coefficients themselves change whenever the supply of bank reserves changes. When bank deposits increase, for example, there must be other portfolio adjustments to accommodate them. Section 6.2 sets out the portfolio critique of the multiplier theory.

Section 6.3 discusses the Tobin, Goodhart and Radcliffe representations of the portfolio approach. Tobin's 'New View' established a framework for demonstrating how portfolios are chosen. Goodhart provides one of the many applications of Tobin's portfolio theory in a general equilibrium framework. Radcliffe also stressed the breadth of choice among assets, but without Goodhart's price adjustment mechanism.

Finally, in section 6.4 we use the case of the Eurocurrency market to consider the relative merits of the multiplier and portfolio approaches, and to introduce a more Radcliffe-like measure of the size of the market: the liquidity approach.

6.2 CRITIQUE OF THE MULTIPLIER APPROACH

It is the possibility that the coefficients of the multiplier will change with changing conditions in financial markets which is the spearhead of the portfolio critique of the multiplier approach. The money multipliers rely on a low degree of substitutability between money assets and other financial assets. Thus, when bank deposits rise as bank lending rises, the deposits are either held as additional balances, or used for expenditure on goods, thus turning up in the sellers' bank accounts, and so on. This is often called the 'hot potato' theory (after Tobin (1963)) whereby new deposits are passed round like a hot potato but are never 'dropped' (except in the sense that some are exchanged for currency as a proportion of additional deposits).

But suppose people are not willing to make deposits with banks indefinitely. Suppose the decision to hold demand deposits rather than time deposits, or time deposits rather than government bonds, etc., depends on the relative interest rates offered on different assets. In other words, suppose that all financial assets are reasonably close substitutes for each other, so that demand deposit-holders can be induced to hold time deposits instead, or cash-holders to hold interest-bearing demand deposits instead, by higher interest rates.

The propostion that this is so is the 'New View' put forward by Tobin (1963), to counter what was then the prevailing orthodoxy of multiplier theory. The article opens in resounding tones:

> Perhaps the greatest moment of triumph for the elementary economics teacher is his exposition of the multiple creation of bank credit and bank deposits. Before the admiring eyes of freshmen he puts to rout the practical banker who is so sure that he 'lends only the money depositors entrust to him'. The banker is shown to have a worm's eye-view, and his error stands as an introductory object lesson in the fallacy of composition. From the Olympian vantage of the teacher and the textbook it appears that the banker's dictum must be reversed: depositors entrust to bankers whatever amounts the bankers lend. (Tobin (1963), p. 408.)

It is a powerful (and political) notion, suggested by multiplier theory, that banks can continue to 'create' money as long their reserves increase. But Tobin's New View suggests rather that banks can only 'create' as much money as the public wants to hold, given the stocks of other assets. The size of the multiplier is determined by portfolio preferences with respect to the entire range of assets.

Consider the case of an increase in bank reserves resulting from deposited transfers from the government, as in our earlier numerical example. If financial markets start in equilibrium, then a fall in lending rates is necessary to induce increased demand for credit. At the same time, deposit rates must fall to maintain profit margins, so if demand deposits earn no interest, the ratio of time deposits to demand deposits, t, will fall. Since NBFI interest rates on deposits are more flexible than bank deposit rates, they will fall faster, reducing the ratio of NBFI deposits to bank deposits. In general, then, liquidity preference rises when interest rates fall, and the money multipliers fall. This outcome is intensified if the bank reserves increase was the result of monetary authority purchases of government securities, which could only be induced by sufficiently high prices, causing a fall in interest rates on other securities. The expansionary effect of the rise in reserves is modified by a fall in the multipliers. Correspondingly, the contractionary effect of a fall in reserves is modified by a rise in the multipliers.

In fact, as long as these offsetting changes in the multipliers occur in a reasonably predictable manner, as suggested by Cagan, then the multiplier approach retains much of its validity. Only if one adopts a view of financial markets as being continually potentially unstable does the multiplier approach become truly misleading. It was suggested earlier that banks may not employ their full lending potential if their perception of the viability of potential borrowers' projects is of possible failure and thus default. Such perceptions may or may not be accompanied by falling interest rates. Once portfolio choice is seen as being based on a variety of disparate expectations which are continually being modified, then the changes in the multiplier become less easy to predict – except in cases of very strong universal shifts in liquidity preference.

The other main form of critique of multiplier theory is based on the fact that monetary authorities have tended to concentrate more on control of interest rates than on monetary aggregates. Along with the view that all financial assets are potential substitutes goes the view that any one monetary aggregate does not constitute an effective constraint on expenditure. Rather interest rates, as well as determining the relative holdings of financial assets, also determine the acquisition of real assets (through investment).

The choice between controlling the money supply and interest rates is an exclusive one. If the supply of bank reserves is controlled, then interest rates must be allowed to settle at the level which keeps both the banks and their customers content with the volume of deposits generated. If supply is being held down, then interest rates will rise to curtail demand for bank credit on the one hand, and induce deposit-holders to exchange them for less liquid assets on the other. Conversely, attempts to increase the money supply require a fall in interest rates to increase the demand for credit and persuade bank customers to hold a higher proportion of their assets in deposits. We know from our multiplier theory that this very process reduces the ability of the authorities to curtail (increase) the money supply, because the interest rate fall increases (reduces) the value of the multiplier.

If the authorities choose to control interest rates, then they must supply enough bank reserves, and government securities, to maintain those rates. Because money market conditions are continually changing, it is not easy to predict from day to day what reserves are necessary to maintain a particular interest rate structure. The lender-of-last-resort facility allows banks to borrow as much as they need at the discount rate chosen by the authorities. Rather than allowing the multiplier coefficients to change in response to market conditions, this policy allows the monetary base to change instead. If, in addition, stable interest rates do not even keep the coefficients steady, because of other jolts to expectations about asset values, then the multiplier approach can be of little assistance.

6.3 THE PORTFOLIO APPROACH

The portfolio approach discusses how choices are made between different types of asset, and how monetary policy can affect that choice by changing the structure of interest rates. Tobin (1958) provided the basic tools for conventional portfolio analysis. He constructed his model in terms of the choice between money and bonds, taking account both of the expected return on each, and the risk of capital loss or gain. The analysis was presented as a formalization and extension of Keynes' theory of speculative demand for money, being a negative function of interest rates on bonds. We shall discuss later in this section how far this representation is faithful to Keynes.

Tobin postulates that individuals' utility in general is increased by a higher expected rate of return $E(r)$, but reduced by higher risk of capital loss or gain. This risk can be represented by the variance of an asset's return, σ_r. Money earns no interest but its money value is obviously constant: bonds do earn interest but their prices vary so that there is a risk of capital gain or loss when they are sold. Individuals will choose a particular combination of money and bonds which maximizes utility, given the interest rate on bonds and expectations as to the risk of capital gain or loss.

Figure 6.1 demonstrates the portfolio decision. The top quadrant of the diagram shows the possible combinations of return and risk associated with different combinations of money and bonds, with indifference curves U_0 and U_1. The shape of the indifference curves suggests that an expected positive return on the portfolio, $E(r)$, is a 'good' and risk of capital gain or loss, σ_r, a 'bad'. ('Gamblers', or 'risk-lovers', would regard both as 'goods', and would have conventional two-good indifference curves.) Each point on the indifference curves represents a particular combination of return and risk yielded by particular portfolios. The bottom half of the diagram shows the relationship between the proportion of assets held as bonds and as money and the expected variance associated with each proportion. The proportion of assets held as bonds is read down, from 0 to 1, on the left-hand axis, and the proportion held as money is read up, from 0 to 1, on the right-hand axis. For a given set of expectations, risk, measured by σ_r, is higher the higher the proportion held as bonds. OB_0 and OB_1 represent two sets of expectations, OB_1 suggesting a higher expected risk for any given proportion of bonds than OB_0.

The expected return from a particular portfolio combination is determined by the OC lines. They are like budget lines in that they each determine the maximum utility allowed by one going rate of interest. They are objectively determined, once expectations are set, by the expected return associated with each portfolio composition. For the

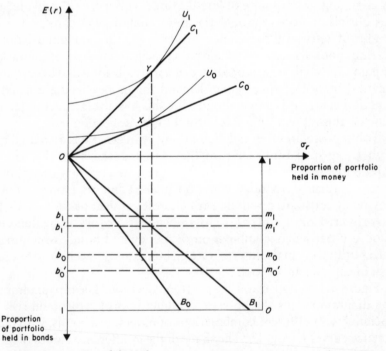

Figure 6.1 *Portfolio selection at various interest rates and states of expectation*

interest rate represented by OC_0, and expectations of risk represented by OB_0, utility is maximized at point X, implying a portfolio with a proportion b_0 of bonds and m_0 of money. If expectations of risk were represented by OB_1, then b_1 would be held in bonds and m_1 in money. If the interest on bonds rises, raising the 'budget line' from OC_0 to OC_1, then utility is maximized at a higher level, represented by point Y. The preferred proportion of bond-holdings increases to b_0' and of money falls to m_0' for risk expectations OB_0, and b_1' and m_1' for risk expectations OB_1.

This representation can be extended to the entire spectrum of assets, showing that, other things (like expectations) being equal, an increase in the interest earned on one asset will attract custom transferred from all other assets. Of course, reduced demand for all other assets will tend to raise the return on these assets also, modifying the final outcome, represented by a less marked switch into the asset whose return initially rose. The theory can be applied equally to the portfolio choices of financial institutions, firms and individuals.

This theory was welcomed as an improvement on Keynes, because it explained why most individuals hold both money and bonds, rather than one or the other as suggested in the *General Theory*. But in the process, much of Keynes' theory was lost. First, Keynes' concept of the portfolio decision was based on the notion that decision-makers hold a view as to the 'normal' rate of interest, or at least a view as to the direction of change from a particular level. The risk of capital gain or loss is thus a one-way phenomenon for each decision-maker (some of whom are usually wrong). Investors are attracted to bonds by the expectation of capital gain when bond prices are low and interest rates high; there is no symmetric concern in such a situation from capital loss as a result of falling bond prices.

Second, the decision to hold money rather than bonds is often made because investors *do not know what to expect* about returns on assets and the associated risks. This is one of the central functions of money; if in doubt, investors avoid a Tobin-style portfolio choice by holding money instead of bonds until better information is available. To quote from Keynes:

> ... our desire to hold money as a store of wealth is a barometer of the degree of our distrust in our own calculations and conventions concerning the future. ... The possession of actual money lulls our disquietude; and the premium which we require to make us part with money is the measure of the degree of our disquietude. (Keynes (1937a), p. 218.)

Third, as an extension of the first point, uncertainty about the expected return on an asset, and potential capital gains and losses, cannot neatly be captured as the mean and variance of a probability distribution. Tobin's use of this measure is perhaps helpful as a means of pinning down difficult concepts. But if people do not actually *behave* with such measures in mind, or if each individual arrives at these calculations differently, then they are of limited value. Again quoting from Keynes when amplifying on his use of the term 'uncertainty':

> Thus the fact that our knowledge of the future is fluctuating, vague and uncertain, renders wealth a peculiarly unsuitable subject for the methods of the classical economic theory.... The sense in which I am using the term ['uncertain'] is that in which the prospect of a European war is uncertain, or the price of copper and the rate of interest twenty years hence, or the obsolescence of a new invention, or the position of private wealth-owners in the social system in 1970. About these matters there is no scientific basis on which to form any capable probability whatever. We simply do not know. (Keynes (1937a), p. 217.)

Tobin's portfolio theory, however, has been widely adopted. It has the major attraction of being mathematically manageable, in a way which Keynesian uncertainty, by definition, cannot be. With its emphasis on the substitutability of all assets, on the basis of risk and return, the analysis is ideally suited to the general equilibrium framework. Households, firms, financial institutions and government, in such a framework, simultaneously make their decisions on the distribution of their portfolios among various assets, expenditure on goods and services, etc. with all the interdependencies between these decisions taken into account. The world portrayed is rather different from the Keynesian world, where decision-makers act on the basis of conflicting expectations, or do not act (i.e. hold money instead of any other asset or commodity) because they do not know *what* to expect.

Goodhart (1975) has set up a very elegant general equilibrium model, with portfolio choice represented for each sector. Each sector (government, banks, households, etc.) bases its choice on the expected return and risk of capital gain or loss from each asset (the latter is zero for many assets, like bank loans and deposits). The model makes clear the point made earlier about restrictions on the choices available to the government sector for instruments of monetary control. The government cannot fix the monetary base *and* the interest rate on government bonds, or the system cannot be solved. In the same way, the government cannot fix both the interest rate on bonds *and* the volume of bond-sales.

Suppose the government chooses to raise the interest rate on government bonds. This can only be achieved by selling bonds, which requires a fall in bond prices and a rise in interest rates to induce people to accept the bonds. In return the government acquires money, in the form of payments out of the banks' accounts with the central monetary authority. As the banks' deposits with the authority fall, so do their reserves. In the meantime bank deposits fall, because deposit-holders have switched into bonds; this switch is particularly strong if interest rates on deposits are fixed. The contraction in the banks' reserves requires the banks to reduce lending (some bank assets will already have been switched from loans to bonds). Investment is thus reduced because of the contraction in finance and the rise in lending rates which make that contraction effective. The marginal rate of return on capital is then hypothesized to rise (although in fact the contraction in aggregate demand as a result of reduced investment may reduce the *value* of the marginal product of capital).

Alternatively, suppose the monetary contraction were to take the form of a reduction of the monetary base, say, by the central monetary authority calling in special deposits. Banks would raise deposit rates (if they could) to attract more deposits (and thus reserves) and at the same time raise lending rates to reduce demand for loans to match availability. Bond-holders would be attracted to holding more bank deposits at the higher rates. The resulting attempts to sell bonds reduce bond prices and raise their yields in order to induce sufficient demand for the existing stock of bonds. Meanwhile, investment is discouraged by the increased lending rates, and the marginal real return on capital is hypothesized to rise.

The outcome in terms of the two means of monetary control is equivalent, in that a wave of increases in rates of return spreads right through the asset spectrum, the monetary base falls and economic activity falls.

An alternative portfolio approach, which also emphasized the interdependencies of financial systems, preceded the modern development of general equilibrium theory. It was set out in the Report of the Radcliffe Committee in the UK in 1959. The Report stressed the substitutability of financial assets, particularly at the liquid end of the spectrum. In particular, it was suggested that the demand for money is a demand for liquidity, an attribute in some degree of many assets, rather than a demand for a narrow range of 'money' assets. An asset is liquid if it may be easily traded for a means of payment ('money') without risk of capital loss. It is then an appropriate asset to hold until deciding what other asset to hold. In Tobin's terms, liquidity is greater the smaller is 'risk', the variance of the return on the asset. But the same assets vary in liquidity from time to time, even if only because trading activity (and thus the ease of selling) varies depending on market conditions. Further, institutional change affects the liquidity of assets. Deposit insurance, for example, increases the certainty that the value of deposits in small, new banks will be maintained. The expansion of NBFIS makes their liabilities more generally acceptable, particularly when they offer chequing facilities.

The Report concluded that 'liquidity' was what determined interest rates and real activity, but it is impossible to measure. Thus, the authorities should concentrate on steering interest rates in the desired direction, being the outcome of the demand for and supply of liquidity, whatever that is. While liquidity was viewed as governing real expenditure, not interest rates, the latter are the barometer of the former, and easier to identify.

Our discussion of portfolio theory started off with the critique of the multiplier approach, along the lines that the multiplier increases when interest rates increase. Further the monetary base may increase when interest rates increase, as banks sell securities to the central monetary authority or to individual purchasers who thereby release idle balances, to top up reserves. Thus, because asset-holders pay attention to relative returns on different assets, excess demand in the market for one asset, money, calls forth an increase in supply, attracted by rates of return which have temporarily got out of line.

This analysis also underpins the Radcliffe Report with an emphasis on the role of high interest rates in enticing money out of idle balances. If only the authorities could control the entire stock of those liquid assets which can step into the breach when money as such is in short supply, then they could hope to have some effect on expenditure. But, rather than emphasizing the role of substitutability of assets in transmitting interest rate changes throughout the asset spectrum, the Radcliffe Report emphasized the market imperfections which impede that transmission. In particular, the Report distinguishes between the mechanisms generating the supply and demand for credit.

Tight money markets, as we have seen, can induce an increase in supply of money through high interest rates. To that extent, financial markets work as suggested by general equilibrium theory. But banks do not in fact adjust their lending rates rapidly in line with rates they pay on, say, certificates of deposit, or with the prices at which they must sell bonds to acquire additional reserves. The shortage of funds available for lending must thus be manifested by rationing among potential borrowers. This reduced availability of finance has a more powerful effect on investment demand than a rise in lending rates, because loan demand is not highly interest-elastic. Figure 6.2 depicts the market for loans when the supply of funds has been reduced by, say, an open market sale of bonds which has increased bond yields and reduced bank reserves. (The notation is adopted from Chick (1977).)

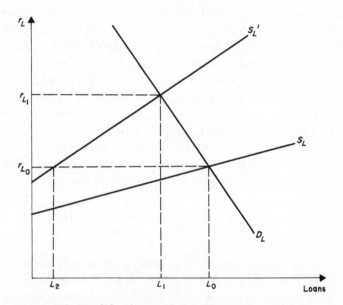

Figure 6.2 *Bank lending with fixed loan rates and rationing*

The supply of funds available for loans (or advances) is reduced from S_L to S_L', because of a relative rise in the rate of return on bonds, say, or in the penal lending rate of the monetary authority. The schedules are upward-sloping because a rise in the lending rate r_L relative to the return on other assets increases the relative attractiveness to the banks of loans. If r_L were free to rise to clear the market for loans, from r_{L0} to r_{L1} then lending would fall from L_0 to L_1. But if the lending rate stays at r_{L0} then lending falls by an additional amount, L_1L_2. Because of the bank practice of maintaining relatively stable loan rates, an interest rate policy is thus very powerful.

It is made more powerful also because of the segmentation of loan markets. Lenders, like borrowers, have their 'preferred market habitats'. If an entrepreneur's loan application is turned down by her own bank manager, then she may not be sufficiently familiar with alternative sources of finance to turn to them and attempt to establish a client relationship. Similarly, entrepreneurs may be reluctant to issue debentures rather than acquire bank loans. Continued rationing by banks in the face of strong investment demand will of course eventually break down these barriers. This segmentation contrasts with the high degree of substitutability between all assets and all liabilities postulated in the portfolio approach.

In summary, then, the Radcliffe Report sees the power of monetary policy lying in the *breaks* in the asset-substitutability chain. The high degree of substitutability between liquid assets from the saver's point of view makes attempts to control the supply of a particular monetary aggregate relatively impotent in terms of the effect on real expenditure; the control of that group of assets is offset by substitution with alternative liquid assets. But if interest rates themselves are increased, then this monetary tightness is amplified for 'real' investors because of the exaggerated reaction of the banks in rationing availability of credit. This has maximal effect on expenditure because reduced availability of credit is a greater constraint than high interest rates.

6.4   MONEY SUPPLY THEORIES AND THE
EUROCURRENCY MARKET

The whole question of how best to analyse the supply of money took rather a back seat to the theory of the demand for money for many years. Now the choice of approach has regained a sense of urgency in terms of analysing the growth of the Eurocurrency market and establishing policy guidelines for its operation (see McKenzie (1976)).

The Eurocurrency market is a market in short-term funds denominated in currencies other than that of the location of the deposit. It is said that the first incidence of such deposits was the dollar deposits of the Soviet Union held in Europe in the 1950s rather than the US for security reasons. But the market began its rapid growth with deposits of US funds in Europe (particularly in London) in the 1960s, which could be lent out to US firms as a means of evading US monetary controls. The market now covers deposits in many currencies held outside their country of denomination. But the major currency is still the US dollar, and most of the business is still conducted in London. By mid-1980 the 'gross' size of the market (the total value of deposits by the banks and the non-bank public) was over \$1200 billion, having doubled its size over the previous 3 years. Most deposits are made by banks with other banks; it is a lucrative market in which a bank can place assets for a short period. There is also a parallel Eurobond market which makes medium- and long-term loans in foreign currencies to commercial and government borrowers. These longer-term loans are often syndicated among groups of banks.

The immense growth of this market has been a source of concern for two main reasons. First, it allows evasion of domestic monetary controls, since these controls can only cover banks within the domestic economy. The US authorities attempted to introduce, in October 1980, penalties on dollar funds brought back from the Eurodollar market, in an attempt to separate the supply of Eurodollars from domestic dollars. The UK is experiencing more 'interference' from the Eurocurrency market now that exchange controls have been lifted, and banks can operate freely in the market.

Second, there is concern at the rapid rate of growth of a market which is not subject to the same prudential controls as bank operations in domestic currency. There is a fear that such a rapid expansion of a market can only lead to an equally rapid contraction. The banks in the market are highly interdependent because of the high proportion of interbank borrowing and lending; if one bank fails, for some reason, will the ripple effects on the other banks cause a crash? And yet the market has so far been extremely useful in efficiently recycling petrodollars and thus minimizing the dislocation effects on producer and consumer countries when oil prices rise. The authorities have therefore been hesitant to control the market and reduce its potency.

When the market first began to grow significantly, in the 1960s, the multiplier approach provided the main expression of concern. Most countries do not impose reserve requirements on foreign currency deposits with banks. If, further, there is no equivalent of the currency drain from banks reserves, then the simple multiplier of equation (5.4) becomes $1/0$, or infinity. If banks do not have to hold reserves against their Eurocurrency deposit liabilities, there is no limit to the amount of such deposits that they can amass.

Of course banks hold some dollar deposits with US banks as reserves for prudential reasons, although probably as a smaller proportion than required reserves on domestic currency deposits. There is also a leakage in the form of dollar deposits removed from a European bank and placed with a US bank. This leakage might conform to some preferred ratio of deposits held in the US to those held in Europe. The multiplier thus becomes finite, though possibly high. However, the base on which the multiplier operates, the reserves of the system, are deposits with US banks, held in the US. So increasing reserves against growing Eurodollar deposits do not cause a drain from the US banking system. The reserves stay in the US banking system as deposits, causing no drain on US banks, in the US. Rather an additional 'pyramid' of Eurodollar credit is built onto the same monetary base as the pyramid of domestic US credit, in the same way that non-bank financial intermediaries increase the money multiplier *within* the domestic financial system.

As with the domestic money supply, the portfolio approach points out that the demand for Eurodollars cannot be expected to increase indefinitely. Rather, portfolio choices between Eurodollar deposits and loans and US bank deposits and loans (and all other assets) are made on the basis of expected return and risk of capital loss/gain or foreign exchange loss/gain.

In particular, suppose that US interest rates rise as the authorities attempt to control credit. Deposits will return from the Eurodollar market attracted by the higher return, at the same time reducing the size of the Eurodollar market and increasing deposit rates there. Demand for credit is curtailed in the US market and diverted to the Eurodollar market, but supply there has decreased also. Similarly, the moderation in US rates diverts deposits to the Eurodollar market, lowering rates there but increasing the size of the market. Loan demand will, however, have been diverted back from the Eurodollar market to the home market.

In short, then, the Eurodollar market can only expand as fast as demand for deposits and loans; any attempt to expand at a faster rate will reduce Eurodollar interest rates, thus thwarting the attempt. Also, any tendency towards contraction of the market will be reversed partially by rising Eurodollar interest rates.

The third approach to analysing the size of the Eurocurrency market (see Niehans and Hewson (1976)) is more akin to Radcliffe's version of portfolio theory: the liquidity approach. Most banks perform the function of financial intermediation by borrowing short and lending long. Because of their dominance of domestic financial markets, banks can be reasonably confident that an adequate supply of short-term deposits will be forthcoming to finance long-term loans. The deposits total thus represents the liquidity 'created' by the banks on the basis of their reserves. This 'creation' is measured by the money multipliers.

But if banks make loans of short term to maturity financed by deposits of similar maturity, it cannot be said that they are creating liquidity – rather they are creating efficiency by bringing together borrowers and lenders. The shorter the term of a loan, the less liquid is the portfolio of the borrower; funds must be found within that term to pay back the loan. And in fact the maturities of deposits and loans within the Eurocurrency market are very closely matched; there is very little 'maturity transformation'.

If the growth of the market is only important in terms of its effect on expenditure, then the effect must be very small, since aggregate liquidity is scarcely increased in *net* terms. Further applying the concept of *net* growth of the market, by far the majority of transactions occur between banks. Banks borrow funds on the market and redeposit them at other banks, taking advantage of slight differences in rates. The Bank for International Settlements estimates that the net credit created by the market is much less than gross lending: $700 billion in mid-1980 compared with gross assets of $1200 billion. Further, as soon as Eurodollar credit is used for expenditure in the US, the Eurodollar market contracts again; the net payment must be made out of the reserves held with a US bank. Only if the recipient happens to place the funds with a European bank does the market not contract, until the loan is repaid.

So far, the market has survived without undue problems; the fears of the 'multiplier' theorists have not been realized. The market has nevertheless weakened domestic monetary control – as would any institutional change encouraging capital flows, whether subject to reserve requirements or not. It also continues to provoke fears of multiple contraction if some unforeseen eventuality caused the failure of major banks in the market. This concern with prudential control cannot be divorced entirely from control for macroeconomic policy purposes. The latter determines what growth can be called 'excessive'. Nevertheless, when financial markets take on a life of their own, independent of 'real' developments, prudential control over bank operations can at least prevent individual banks crashing, with ripple effects on other banks. This principle has been applied to a considerable extent to the domestic operations of banks. But the growing importance of their foreign exchange operations calls for an extension of that application.

6.5 CONCLUSION

The issues surrounding the Eurocurrency market have brought the whole question of short-run money supply determination right up to date. It highlights the importance of deciding what one actually wants to measure: a particular deposit total, the totals of a variety of liquid assets, or total net liquidity.

The total value of deposits, as measured by multipliers, indicates the size of the banking sector. A rapid rate of growth carries the danger of collapse of confidence in banking institutions, and a rapid rate of contraction of the same deposit total. Banking innovations allow more efficient use of the monetary base, allowing growth without confidence problems. Nevertheless, most banking systems have developed with prudential controls to limit the rate of growth of particular aggregates, albeit with periodic modifications to reflect new innovations in banking.

Particular deposit totals are, however, not appropriate for monetary control for short-term stabilization purposes. Control of the monetary base causes portfolio adjustments, with repercussions throughout the interest rate structure. These interest rate changes change the value of money multipliers, modifying the impact of the monetary base change.

General equilibrium portfolio analysis, however, represents the choice of assets to hold in a very deterministic manner, with the expected returns to an asset and capital risk derived from probability distributions. This approach is thus limited in its ability to predict portfolio reactions to monetary base changes, or indeed to changes in key interest rates if that is the chosen method of control. According to Keynes' original exposition of portfolio choice, expectations of returns are non-uniform (and thus, for most investors, wrong) and change erratically; capital risk similarly is perceived differently by different investors, with the risk generally perceived as being uni-directional (rather than symmetrical, as suggested by the variance measure).

In particular, the relationship between rates of return on financial assets and on real assets does not necessarily conform to traditional portfolio theory. A rise in financial rates of return may limit availability of funds for real investment, whose rate of return may fall through falling aggregate demand (rather than rise, according to the static model with increasing marginal return to capital). Interest rate control may not thus have the expected effect transmitted to real rates of return.

Nevertheless, the availability of credit to non-financial institutions for real investment at rates commensurate with real rates of return is the primary monetary instrument for influencing real expenditure. Thus the portfolio choice of financial institutions with respect to private sector lending is the crucial variable. The stock of liquid assets and liabilities in these institutions' portfolios is of significance for this choice, as are their relative prices or interest rates. But further, the influence of fluctuating expectations, and institutional rigidities which reduce the substitutability between assets, must be taken into account when assessing both the demand for and supply of liquidity.

The Eurocurrency market has posed a threat to monetary stability at the international level similar to the threat perceived in the growth of NBFIS. Indeed, the two sets of institutions have a similar relationship with domestic banking systems. In the next chapter we concentrate attention on the NBFIS and their role in influencing the short-run supply of money.

7

Non-Bank Financial Intermediaries

7.1 INTRODUCTION

It is becoming clear that financial institutions other than banks play an important role in financial markets. They represent an area of rapid growth in the financial sector, which poses particular problems for monetary control and the competitive position of the banks. For a long time, monetary theory concentrated completely on the banks as the fulcrum of the financial system. From the late 1950s, however, the role of NBFIS has been attracting progressively more attention as upsetting the traditional relationships between financial variables. In this chapter we consider how far NBFIS do differ from banks, how they should be analysed given these differences, and what implications may be drawn for monetary control.

The three criteria conventionally employed for distinguishing NBFIS from banks are the following:

(1) NBFIS have usually been subject to less stringent reserve requirements than banks, or none at all, giving them a competitive advantage both in terms of returns on assets and the capacity to expand their portfolios by higher multiples.
(2) NBFIS are relatively small, so that their multiplier potential is curtailed for each institution by leakages to other financial institutions. (Deposits arising from the expenditure of NBFI loans are more likely to be made in the banking system than in the lending NBFI.)
(3) NBFI liabilities are less liquid than bank liabilities (as are their assets); unlike banks, NBFIS are said not to 'create money'.

In section 7.2 the implications of these criteria are considered, in order to establish whether banks are in fact unique relative to other financial institutions, the NBFIS. Section 7.3 then considers the structural developments in financial markets which led to this segmentation into banks and NBFIS. Then section 7.4 considers the implications of this segmentation for monetary control, with reference to the major contributions to this area by Tobin and Brainard, and by Brunner and Meltzer, respectively.

7.2 ARE BANKS UNIQUE?

In order to decide whether NBFIS react differently to monetary policy and have a different effect on expenditure, compared with the banks, we must first consider how far they differ in function from the banks. Can banks any longer claim to be unique in financial markets?

The most clear distinction between banks and NBFIS relates to their treatment by the authorities. Traditionally, banks have been subject to reserve requirements, whereas NBFIS have not. To the extent that these requirements are a burden on the banks, – i.e., are in excess of reserves which would have been held voluntarily – the NBFIS enjoy a competitive advantage. This is particularly the case where bank reserves earn no rate of interest, far less a below-market rate. In addition, the banks do not have the flexibility to vary their reserve holdings cyclically. By reducing them in times of expansion, NBFIS gain maximum advantage from higher rates of return on alternative assets, and from excess demand for credit compatible with the higher money multiplier which results from lower reserve ratios. NBFIS do hold reserves voluntarily, for prudential reasons, usually in the form of bank deposits.

This regulatory distinction is no longer applicable, in the same way as a decade ago; or rather those institutions which we classify as NBFIS, by the criterion of reserves requirements, change over time. In the UK, for example, reserve requirements applied only to the large, 'clearing' banks until 1971, when the new form of requirements was extended to all other banks (the 'secondary' banks) and finance companies. In 1976 the Trustee Savings Banks were given full bank status, and thus became subject to reserve requirements. Building societies are also required to hold reserves, at a lower rate, under their own legislation. In 1981, after the reserve ratio was abolished, the main remaining requirement (a ½ per cent cash ratio) was extended to all deposit-takers under Bank of England supervision. This leaves insurance companies, pension funds, and investment and unit trusts as the only institutions completely free of reserve requirements. But at the same time, the foreign exchange liabilities of banks are also free of reserve requirements, so that this part of bank business can be analysed as if it were an NBFI subsidiary of the banks. This foreign exchange portion of the banks' portfolios represents transactions with the Eurocurrency market.

In the US also the classification of NBFIs has changed. In particular, the Depository Institutions Deregulation and Monetary Control Act of 1980 extended reserve requirements on 'transactions' deposits to all banks, whether they are members of the Federal Reserve System or not, and also to credit unions and mutual savings banks. The distinctions between financial intermediaries in the US are more a function of differences in reserve requirements than their presence or absence. Member banks in the Federal Reserve System, state-chartered banks, and other state-chartered intermediaries have all been subject to different requirements. Now the transaction account liabilities (demand deposits plus almost-demand, interest-bearing, deposits) are all subject to the same requirements and time deposits to lower requirements, eliminating competitive differences. Meanwhile, other liabilities are still subject to different state and federal requirements; whether that is significant for monetary control is a question to be addressed below.

The reasons for banks being subject to more stringent reserve requirements than NBFIs lie in the other features which distinguish NBFIs from banks: their size and their portfolio structure. These features in turn suggest that banks 'create' money while NBFIs do not. As producers of the note issue, governments earn 'seignorage', which is the difference between the value of the notes and their cost of production. Governments must control the extent of the note issue (or its equivalent in cheques drawn on the central monetary authority) in order not to erode the value of the notes, so much that they are not willingly held; an 'acceptable' rate of inflation enhances the seignorage gain. The note issue is a liability of the authorities. But when it is first issued, to pay for government expenditure, it buys more than after inflation has reduced its value. The value of the liability has thus been reduced.

Similarly, since bank cheques also serve as means of payment, banks earn profits from expanding their deposit base which is interest-free because of the attractiveness to deposit-holders of their 'moneyness'. Control of the expansion of the deposit base by means of reserve requirements limits bank profitability but also preserves it by preserving confidence in the banking system, and the acceptability of its deposit liabilities as a means of payment.

First, let us consider the role of size in denying NBFI liabilities the same 'moneyness' as bank liabilities. If non-bank institutions issue cheques, then they offer a means of payment. Such cheques are only acceptable to the recipient, however, if the institution is known and inspires confidence. In general, the larger an institution and the more widespread its presence, the more widely acceptable are its cheques in transactions. If the non-bank institutions do not issue cheques, then their liabilities are not means of payment. They are, rather, liquid assets. NBFIs in general 'create' liquidity rather than money as such.

The other function of size is in determining the redeposit ratio. In the numerical example of the banking system multiplier in chapter 5, the only possible leakages were into currency and reserves. Even when a leakage into NBFIs was incorporated, the banking system multipliers (m_1 and m_2) were unaffected, because the NBFI reserves were all held with the banks. The only possible difference would be if currency holdings were proportionate to liquid assets (including NBFI deposits) rather than bank deposits; then there would be an additional currency drain when NBFI deposits increased.

This has very important implications for the way we express the portfolio theory. Suppose the monetary authority makes an open market sale of bonds, pushing up their interest rate, and reducing banks' deposits with the authority (i.e. their reserves). Portfolio theory suggests that this reduction in the monetary base is offset in part by the rise in the multiplier brought about by higher interest rates. In particular, if bank deposit rates are fairly rigid compared with NBFI deposit rates, the latter will rise, attracting deposits away from the banks to the NBFIs.

As long as NBFIs hold bank deposits as reserves, the switch into NBFI deposits *increases* the multiplier, and does not add to the leakages from the banking system (except for NBFI till cash to meet any cash drain from their customers' deposits). In chapter 5 the money multiplier including NBFI deposits in the money definition is shown in equation (5.10). The switch into NBFI deposits attracted by higher interest rates can be represented by an increase in d in equation (5.10), the ratio of NBFI deposits to bank deposits. The multiplier *increases* when d increases, thwarting the government's attempt to curtail monetary growth by selling bonds.

This outcome makes sense if we consider an example. Suppose, following the increase in market interest rates (other than bank deposit rates) 100 units are taken out of a bank deposit and placed with an NBFI, say a building society (in the UK) or mortgage finance company (in the US). The transfer is made by a cheque drawn on the bank, payable to the NBFI. Suppose this bank happens to be the bank where the NBFI keeps its reserves. The 100 units is then simply credited to the

NBFI's account, adding to its reserves. The NBFI can then increase its lending, extending a loan of, say, 90 units, to a home-buyer. The loan takes the form of a cheque drawn on the bank. The home-seller deposits the money either in her bank, or her NBFI. If the latter, the amount is credited to the NBFI's bank account. If someone along the chain 'banks' with the NBFI, its reserves will be topped up again, and a further round of lending will take place. If not, the reserves of some other NBFIs or banks will have increased, so that they can expand their lending again.

But meanwhile, the bank has not lost any deposits until someone along the chain deposits the cheque drawn on the original bank with another bank. After the initial loss of bank reserves in exchange for bonds, resources have only been reshuffled *within* the banking system, but there has been no additional loss of bank reserves. Rather, the banks have to contract their lending because they have exchanged reserves for bonds, but by no more than if the NBFIs did not exist. But because some more of their deposits now belong to NBFIs, these NBFIs can extend additional loans. The total volume of credit may thus not in fact be reduced significantly as a result of the authorities' sale of bonds; it could even have increased.

For each NBFI, the extent to which new loans can be made on the basis of a new deposit depends on the likelihood of those along the chain started by the loans depositing their receipts with the NBFI, i.e. it depends on the redeposit ratio. For the banking system as a whole, the redeposit ratio is, as we have seen, very high. For individual banks, the redeposit ratio will vary considerably, depending on the type of banking structure. Each bank in the UK, for example, has such a large share of the national market that its own redeposit ratio will still be high. For unit banks in the US, the redeposit ratio will be small, with only a small proportion of its loans returning as deposits, just like most NBFIs. For small institutions, banks and NBFIs, then, the individual multiplier potential is quite small.

Suppose we use the numerical example in chapter 5 to represent one bank or NBFI in a financial system consisting of a large number of very small institutions. Suppose only 2 units of any new loan of 11 units are redeposited in the institution under consideration (compared with 10 in the earlier example). The multiplier process would then be as shown in table 7.1. The bank loses 9 units of reserves because only 2 units are redeposited, excess reserves are reduced to zero again immediately and the expansion ceases. The money supply has only increased by 13 units following an injection of 11 units of reserves.

Goodhart (1975) argues that redeposit ratios are unimportant in relation to the final equilibrium portfolio distribution. In the above example the redeposit ratio was 2/11. But the 9 units deposited elsewhere would induce interest-rate reductions, and repercussions involving new deposits in the first institution according to the re-deposit ratios of the other institutions. The final equilibrium is deter-mined by portfolio preferences.

Table 7.1 *Bank multiplier process for single financial institution, given in arbitrary monetary units*

(Excess reserves)	Small bank or NBFI			Non-bank public	
	Assets		Liabilities		
	Reserves	Loans	Deposits	Currency	M_1
(0)	10	90	100	10	110
(9)	20	90	110	11	121
(0)	11	101	112	11	123

But the portfolio behaviour of financial institutions is geared as much to the *process* of portfolio adjustment as to final equilibria. Consider the case of a small NBFI in a rural area which is subject to marked seasonal fluctuations in income. Loans are made at seeding time and repaid at harvest time. The NBFI is thus subject to a massive drain on reserves when loans are spent outside the local area on seed and farm machinery. The redeposit ratio rises after harvest time as the farmers build up some savings for the winter. Now, whatever the final equilibrium position, the NBFI has to have sufficient assets to cope with the spring drain. If not, it will collapse. Certainly the reserves loss was only part of the *process* to equilibrium. But the process itself has changed the final equilibrium by requiring the bank to hold more reserves. In terms of the example above, if *no* units were redeposited out of the loan, the bank would not have adequate reserves. (Excess reserves would be (-1)), and confidence in the bank may be reduced, perhaps encouraging further deposit withdrawals. The bank then has to raise its (reserves : loans) ratio, thus reducing the money multiplier, in order to avert a crisis.

In total, the size of the non-bank financial sector has grown immensely. By one definition of NBFI for the UK, the NBFI sector grew from a size slightly smaller than the banking sector in 1956 to 150 per cent of the banking sector in 1976 (see Carter and Partington (1979), p. 50). In the US the NBFIS were slightly larger in total than the banks in 1972, and were almost double their size in 1976 (see Nadler (1979)). Redeposit ratios for NBFIS as a whole have thus been increasing, and along with them the scope for expansion, i.e. for the 'creation' of liquidity.

How much liquidity is 'created' of course depends on both sides of the balance sheet. Deposits are more liquid for depositors the more readily they can be used in exchange, and more deposits mean more liquidity. But loans also vary in liquidity; a loan is more liquid for the borrower the longer she has to pay it back. Further, the more liquid a loan is for the borrower, the less liquid it must be for the bank. This brings us to the third difference between NBFIS and banks: the difference in portfolio structure. Bank liabilities (deposits) are very liquid. But because redeposit ratios are very high, most bank assets (reserves, loans, investments) can be much less liquid. A proportion of assets must nevertheless be held as liquid reserves to finance fluctuations in encashments (on the road to 'equilibrium'). Overall, however, bank liabilities are very liquid for depositors, while bank assets are overall-illiquid for the bank, i.e. the rate of 'maturity transformation' is high. Because bank loans and investments in general have a much longer term than deposits, banks 'create' liquidity among deposit-holders, but also for borrowers.

NBFIS also 'create' liquidity in the form of deposits. Because their deposits are generally not used as a means of payment, as are bank chequing deposits, the rate of encashments is much lower and so are fluctuations in encashments. NBFIS can thus hold less liquid assets than banks. NBFIS have therefore tended to lend longer-term to businesses, and for purchase of property, than the banks. It is not clear, then, how far the rate of maturity transformation, being the difference in term between assets and liabilities, actually differs, as between banks and NBFIS.

The overall extent of liquidity creation depends not only on maturity transformation but also on the scope for expansion of total assets and liabilities. The actual process of maturity transformation allows banks to expand deposits by a multiple of an initial deposit. An NBFI with a very small redeposit ratio can make an illiquid loan with a liquid deposit, but cannot then proceed to a second round of maturity transformation. As redeposit ratios grow, however, with NBFI expansion, NBFIs' behaviour more closely approximates that of the banks.

This increase in redeposit ratios can be attributed partly to attempts to control the growth of the banking sector. Since NBFI reserves do not constitute a leakage from the banking system, as long as they hold their reserves with the banking system, NBFIS can expand on the existing money base, as long as there is excess demand for deposits and credit.

Is there then, in fact, any fundamental difference between NBFIS and banks? The answer must almost resort to semantics. Banks and NBFIS appear to differ more in degree (of regulation, size and portfolio structure) than in kind. Once that degree becomes small, particularly in the second and third respects, institutions which were previously regarded as NBFIS become regarded as banks. Along with this development goes an extension of bank regulation to former NBFIS, thus removing remaining differences of the first kind. Any other financial institutions continue as NBFIS.

Further, as the net of control is cast wider, covering former NBFIS, excess demand for liquidity must reach further afield, so that the remaining NBFIS assume a new importance, and others may be expected to emerge. Alternatively, as in the case of the Eurocurrency market, NBFI-like activities arise *within* banking institutions. In the next section we consider how the particular division of labour between banks and NBFIS developed in the first place.

7.3 SEGMENTATION OF FINANCIAL INTERMEDIATION

The growth of NBFIS has largely been a response to portfolio preferences not satisfied by the banks. Why, then, did the banks themselves not meet these requirements? The simple answer is that banks have traditionally been controlled in terms of the structure of their portfolios. In particular, in some countries the banks have been discouraged from making long-term loans because of the need to preserve confidence in the ability of the banks to liquidate their assets if necessary.

In fact, much of the NBFI business has been conducted 'through the back door' of the banks, i.e. using bank capital, but under a separate institutional structure. Indeed the banks have been very conscious of their declining share of the financial sector and of total financial sector profits.

Nevertheless, it is also reasonable to suggest that, even without regulation of the banks, different types of institution would have emerged naturally, with different portfolio structures. The available evidence suggests that there are economies of scale in banking, but there is some suggestion that constant returns and even diseconomies of scale set in at a moderate bank size. The evidence is, however, not conclusive; bank size may be *inversely* related to monopoly power in that small banks in small communities exercise considerable local monopoly power. Profitability may be high for small banks because of this monopoly power rather than relative efficiency.

There are obvious benefits from specialization, both on the asset side and the liability side. Banks specialize in consumer and business lending with good collateral and a high probability of repayment within the short and medium term. Consumer finance companies, or hire purchase companies, specialize in readily accessible consumer lending at high interest rates to compensate for default risk. Mortgage finance companies or building societies specialize in lending for property purchase, with expertise in property values. For depositors, different types of insitution have different attractions. For the small saver NBFIS are often less intimidating than banks, and offer better terms. For the large saver a variety of savings instruments in different institutions allows portfolio diversification, to spread risk. Also, by maintaining good client status with a variety of institutions, the saver increases the chances of being granted credit when required. For many borrowers and depositors, then, small scale is often an attraction.

Gurley and Shaw (1955) suggest that the growth of an NBFI sector is a natural feature of financial development. Initially investment expenditure is self-financed, i.e. financed from the investor's savings. Then, as socieites develop, individual savers who do not choose to invest in real assets make their savings available to those with no savings who nevertheless do choose to acquire real assets. This is called direct finance, and involves a 'dual coincidence of wants' among surplus households and deficit households.

Financial institutions perform the function of indirect finance, which breaks the direct link between savers and investors. Banks thus collect savings in the form of deposits, and independently make loans to those wishing to invest. Whereas direct debt can only increase as wealth increases, indirect finance can increase faster than wealth. Financial institutions can economize on initial deposits of specie, or liabilities of the central monetary authority, by holding reserves only as a proportion of total assets. They can thus expand assets and liabilities as a multiple of wealth, to the extent that there is excess demand for such assets and liabilities.

As wealth increases, so does the demand for bank liabilities, 'money'. But there is a higher wealth elasticity of demand for alternative liquid assets. Gurley and Shaw thus suggest that the growth of NBFIS as alternative sources of indirect finance is a result of portfolio preference rather than controls on the banks. Of course, the 'moneyness' of bank liabilities depends on the confidence in bank liabilities which is generated by controls.

But while Gurley and Shaw correctly argue that NBFI liabilities are assets for savers which only differ from bank liabilities in their degree of liquidity, they did not anticipate the growing 'moneyness' of NBFI liabilities and hence their need for control also. The institutional distinction between bank and NBFI portfolios was destined to become even less than they had suggested.

They point out an interesting problem associated with NBFI growth which may help to explain the current trend towards *reduced* segmentation between banks and NBFIS. NBFIS have traditionally specialized in particular types of asset and liability, relying on expertise in their chosen area to attract borrowers and lenders. The resulting diversity of assets and liabilities satisfied the increasingly diversified portfolio preferences of borrowers and lenders. But, by the very nature of indirect finance, which separates borrowing decisions from lending decisions, there is the possibility that the wealth elasticity of demand for a particular NBFI's liabilities might not match the wealth elasticity of demand for its credit. Institutions which finance house purchase, for example, cannot always attract deposits at a rate sufficient to finance mortgage loans during a housing boom.

A shortage of lending outlets for an NBFI with an excess demand for its liabilities forces it to hold excess assets in, for example, government securities. This makes its subsequent lending decisions highly sensitive to variations in the capital value of these securities. Alternatively, an excess demand for NBFI's credit not matched by demand for its liabilities can only be satisfied by maintaining a close enough relationship with other institutions to have access to their excess funds.

Clearly, just as individual savers choose to diversify their portfolios to minimize risk, so it makes sense for financial institutions to do the same. Diversification of course is directed to the high-growth, high-profitability assets and liabilities. Thus NBFIS have striven to increase the 'moneyness' of their liabilities, by offering chequing services, or by setting up an extensive branch network, for example. The higher the degree of 'moneyness' of deposits the lower the interest rate which need be paid on them. Banks have greatly extended the range of deposit liabilities available, to meet the need for a diversified portfolio of liquid assets. On the lending side, banks in particular have extended their business into the traditionally specialized fields such as mortgage financing. It is harder for the smaller institutions to acquire expertise on a similar scale in new lending areas.

The trend, then, has been for financial diversification to occur 'in-house'. The difficulties for monetary control posed by the growth of NBFIS have now been diverted into the 'NBFI-like' segments of the portfolios of all financial institutions. Thus, liquidity is made available outside monetary contol *within* the banks' balance sheets. This development tends to increase the substitutability among financial institutions' assets, which should increase the effectiveness of interest rate control, easing its transmission through the rate structure. On the other hand, the ability of financial institutions to evade monetary controls is increased if the controls apply only to particular segments of their assets or liabilities. For example, if reserve requirements apply only to domestic currency deposits, then the banks and NBFIS are free to divert funds into their foreign exchange accounts.

Before continuing, in the next section, with the discussion of NBFIS and monetary control, it is worth while to use Gurley and Shaw's framework to suggest a new area of evasion of monetary control which may replace NBFIS as the concern of the 1980s. The growth of multinational corporations has brought with it a return on a large scale to self-finance. Orthodox portfolio theory does not take account of the importance to large corporations of secrecy in financial affairs, independence from lending institutions, certainty as to supply of finance, freedom to use transfer pricing in transactions between branches in different countries for purposes of tax avoidance, freedom from exchange controls, etc. All these considerations may reduce the effect of monetary restraint (or expansion) on investment expenditure since these corporations may use the surpluses of some branches to finance investment by others.

This insensitivity of expenditure to interest rate changes and availability of credit from foreign branches reduces the potency of monetary control. Of course, interest rate considerations will ensure that *surplus* funds at any point in time will be invested in the most profitable financial instruments, inducing capital inflows when the authorities are attempting to control credit. Because of the international character of these institutions, their investments will also take account of exchange rate fluctuations. By adding thus to 'hot money' flows, the multinationals may contribute to foreign exchange instability and may erode the effectiveness of monetary policy (see chapter 11 for an analysis of speculative activity).

7.4 NBFIs AND MONETARY CONTROL

While the case has been presented that NBFIs impede monetary control, an alternative argument suggests that they *amplify* the effect of monetary policy. Tobin and Brainard (1963) have put the former case by comparing a situation where NBFIs exist with one in which they do not. Suppose there are neither banks nor NBFIs, i.e. a very low level of financial development. Then savers may hold either currency or real assets. The preferred combination of currency and real assets depends upon, and determines, the marginal rate of return to real assets. Monetary policy has a direct effect on real expenditure since currency and real assets are the only two assets available. A reduced quantity of currency requires a higher marginal return on capital, to induce asset-holders to accept smaller currency holdings. This is only possible (if the marginal physical product of capital is downward-sloping) if real asset holdings fall, i.e. if real expenditure falls.

Once banks are introduced, their deposit liabilities provide an acceptable substitute for currency. Asset-holders can now choose between currency, deposits and real assets. The effect of a reduction in currency (the monetary base) on expenditure will thus be muted by the fact that some of the excess demand for currency can be met by increased deposits, reducing deposit rates. Because the remaining excess demand for currency is thus reduced, the required reduction in the rate of return on capital is much smaller than before.

However, if the banks must hold a set proportion of their assets in currency, then deposits can only increase to the limit set by available currency reserves; currency and deposits are in this sense complements, although still substitutes for bank *customers*. If deposits can be substituted for currency when the supply of currency is reduced, then there is less impact on expenditure than if banks didn't exist. If increased deposits require increased currency reserves, however, the overall degree of substitutability between currency and deposits is reduced, and so the impact on expenditure increased. However, if NBFIs emerge, and expand rapidly relative to the banks, and if they are not subject to reserve requirements, then their deposits are pure substitutes for bank deposits and currency, and the impact of monetary policy on expenditure is again reduced.

This is the key to Tobin and Brainard's argument that NBFIs dissipate the effectiveness of monetary control: they reduce the complementarity between the montary base (currency) and liquid assets such as NBFI deposits. As a rider, they conclude that, if there are no reserve requirements at all, so that currency and all types of deposit are regarded as substitutes, and if interest rates paid on deposits are fixed, then asset demand shifted from currency will spill over into real expenditure as well as deposits. The effect of monetary policy would thus be strengthened. (If the monetary base is reduced, then substitution into NBFI deposits would be curtailed if the deposit rate could not rise.) On the other hand, if there are reserve requirements, then monetary policy would be transmitted most effectively if deposit rates are flexible. A reduction in monetary base would limit scope for deposit expansion, so that deposit rates would be held down, and a larger impact would be felt on real expenditure.

In practice, banks have been subject to reserve requirements, and have tended to have relatively fixed deposit rates; these are the conditions which encouraged expansion of NBFIs because banks' capacity for attracting deposits and acquiring reserves to back them was thereby curtailed. The NBFIs on the other hand have, until recently, generally had no reserve requirements and have had deposit rate flexibility. According to Tobin and Brainard, this is the worst possible combination for the effectiveness of monetary control. Attempts to control the money supply in order to limit real expenditure have been thwarted by excess demand for credit being satisfied by the NBFIs, which were not constrained by reserve availability, and which could raise deposit rates relative to bank deposit rates to attract the deposits to finance the credit.

Brunner and Meltzer's (1963) defence of the role of NBFIs in transmitting monetary policy rests on the notion that demands for money and real assets are not closely related; a reduction in the supply of money need not have much effect on investment demand. Money and real assets are at either end of the liquidity spectrum. The more gaps along that spectrum are filled in, the more closely will each asset be substitutable for the others. A reduction in the money supply increases interest rates on deposits, interests rates on bonds, and interest rates on other liquid assets, which induces an increased bank lending rate and an increased yield on equities as their prices fall (as shares are sold for high-interest liquid assets), which discourages issues of new equities, and thus discourages investment.

Brunner and Meltzer see the most powerful variable as being the stock of wealth. If interest rates increase right along the liquidity spectrum, then the capital values of all assets fall, inducing a reduction in expenditure demand. Without NBFIs there would be a large gap in the liquidity spectrum which would impede transmission of interest rate changes along the chain from money to real assets, and the effect on wealth of changes in interest rates on liquid assets would be reduced.

Now, how far do controls on the banks impede this transmission mechanism? Silber (1969) argues that controls on financial inter-mediaries reduce the degree of substitutability between assets and thus the effectiveness of monetary control. But controls on only one type of intermediary (the banks, say) would only affect the substitutability between a small range of assets and would not signficantly affect the transmission mechanism. On the other hand, if controls are extended to cover NBFIS also, then the similarity, and thus the degree of sub-stitutability, between bank and NBFI liabilities is increased, although that between NBFI liabilities and, say, bonds, would be decreased.

Overall, Tobin and Brainard, and Brunner and Meltzer's con-clusions do not seem to be at odds with each other in terms of their policy conclusions. As long as interest rates are flexible, reserve requirements on bank and NBFI liabilities need not inhibit the trans-mission of interest rate changes right through the spectrum, allowing monetary policy to influence spending at the 'real' end of the spectrum. Of course, market conditions may impede attempts by the authorities to feed interest rate changes *into* the system. If there are widespread expectations of interest rate increases (as in a Keynesian liquidity trap), the authorities can buy up bonds without any rise in their price. There is no mechanism for feeding an interest rate reduction into the system. The financial intermediation which fosters this liquidity trap situation does indeed, as Tobin and Brainard suggest, reduce the effectiveness of monetary policy.

The main difference of opinion between the two approaches seems to relate to the degree of substitutability between money and real assets. Tobin and Brainard view them as potentially close substitutes, with the return on capital the 'price' of holding money. Financial intermediation drives a wedge through that relationship. Brunner and Meltzer rather view money and capital as being polar extremes; financial intermediation generates a chain of assets of intermediate degrees of liquidity linking the two extremes.

From our discussion of the development of financial systems it is clear that such a juxtaposition confuses economies at different stages of development. At early stages of development, currency and real assets are indeed the only assets available. Financial intermediation develops in response to demand for intermediate assets. As wealth and financial sophistication increase, demand becomes more specific.

Gradually the system increases the efficiency with which it uses the monetary base, providing assets and liabilities designed to meet those specific requirements at least cost, or at highest return.

The juxtaposition is certainly useful in analysing the relative effectiveness of controlling the monetary base in developing and developed countries. As we saw in chapter 2, a high degree of substitutability between money and capital does indeed allow monetary policy a powerful effect on expenditure (confirming Tobin and Brainard's theory for less developed financial systems). But for developed financial systems, it is not particularly helpful to imagine the outcome if financial development were to regress.

For developed economies, Tobin and Brainard's argument can be made somewhat stronger, but in a rather different way. Quite apart from the effectiveness of monetary policy, financial intermediation increases the availability of finance, but not always for real expenditure. Financial intermediation increases the scope for profitable investment in financial assets in markets whose short-term fluctuations may be quite divorced from real developments. Keynes, in chapter 12 of the *General Theory*, emphasized the different mentality and motivations of the financial investor (speculator) and the real investor (entrepreneur).

Unlike the former, the latter are not primarily concerned with interest rates, but rather with expected aggregate demand. The primary influence of financial markets is effected through *availability* of credit rather than its cost. As the major suppliers of credit, the banks and NBFIS are the main concern (taking account, of course, of their reactions to changing values of alternative assets).

Control of both banks and NBFIS by reserve requirements, or by interest rate controls, limits their total size by limiting the supply of, and demand for, deposits, respectively. According to Tobin and Brainard, money supply control would divert excess demand for credit to the bond market, say, raising bond yields, with the yield rise being transmitted to the equity market. Brunner and Meltzer would suggest that controls on bank and NBFI lending made them only weak substitutes for borrowing on the bond market, so that the spillover would be muted.

But banks and NBFIS hold government bonds in their portfolios. The fall in the bonds' capital value would dissuade them from selling bonds to finance increased lending. Thus, the greater the impact of monetary control on the markets for assets which banks and NBFIS hold as alternative to loans, the greater the impact on availability of credit.

Since in fact monetary control has traditionally been effected primarily through these very markets, its impact on availability of credit is very direct (as long as the size of the NBFI sector is controlled). But the range of assets currently of concern for monetary policy in the UK and the US is much more limited than that implied by Tobin and Brainard, and Brunner and Meltzer. A move to controlling bank reserves rather than total money, i.e. 'monetary base control', involves the loss of control of interest rates. But since the size of the money multiplier changes with interest rate changes, the size of total bank and NBFI portfolios is no longer controlled, so that the availability of credit is no longer predictable.

Further, control over financial institutions encourages the emergence of new institutions to satisfy excess demand for finance. Indeed the emergence of the NBFIS themselves was given an impetus to a large extent by control over bank portfolios (although they would have developed anyway to satisfy the varied financial needs of a maturing economy). Monetary controls have, over the years, taken account of rates of growth of a widening range of money assets, from M_0 to M_{11} and beyond. In this way the authorities have attempted to capture the diversion of finance from controlled intermediaries to uncontrolled (or less controlled) intermediaries. But experience shows that financial markets will always be one jump ahead of the authorities, innovating in ways to evade controls.

Suppose the monetary target is expressed in terms of M_3, which in most countries includes demand and savings deposits with banks. In order for this control to have the desired effect on availability of finance, and thus expenditure, the authorities must be able to predict the effect on M_4, M_5, etc. of achieving that particular M_3 target. Much depends on the relationships between NBFIS and the banks. If NBFIS now come under control of the monetary authorities in the sense that they are subject to reserve requirements, then control over reserve assets will also automatically curtail NBFI deposits at the same time as curtailing bank deposits. Indeed the competition for reserve assets from NBFIS could force banks to contract more than was intended. But if NBFI reserves consist of voluntary holdings of bank deposits, then the NBFIS can raise deposit rates, attract deposits and extend credit without actually causing a drain on the banking system. (Deposits transferred to NBFIS would return to the banks as NBFI reserves.)

Even if some NBFIS also must hold reserve assets other than bank deposits against deposits, some deposits may be exempted from reserve requirements, both for banks and NBFIS. Thus, from 1971 to

1981 in the UK, there was no reserve requirement on certificates of deposit ('CDs' – fixed-term deposits) if the banks themselves held CDs to the same amount with other institutions. The rapid expansion of CD business in the early 1970s, in spite of attempts at monetary restraint, demonstrates that this element of bank portfolios was performing an 'NBFI-like' function by allowing some avoidance of monetary controls.

Finally, along with concern over the weakening effects on monetary policy of NBFIS has gone a concern over their financial soundness. Chapter 12 discusses the secondary banking crisis of 1974 in the UK where poor banking practices brought about the collapse of secondary banks. The Bank of England stepped in to prevent the failures having ripple effects on other institutions, and then in 1975 proposed new methods of surpervising the secondary banks.

NBFIS are subject to particular dangers because of their specialization in particular markets. The collapse of property values can be disastrous for mortgage finance companies and building societies if there is default on mortgage payments and deposit growth is weak. Foreign exchange crises for banks heavily engaged in foreign exchange operations can cause similar difficulties. The more liquid their liabilities become, as NBFIS attempt to compete with banks, the more danger there is of large withdrawals once the NBFIS get into difficulties. A general deposit insurance scheme, as operating in the US and Canada, protects institutions from such withdrawals; attempts to introduce such a scheme in the UK have so far failed.

7.5 CONCLUSION

Non-bank financial intermediaries developed both as a response to demand for more diverse assets and liabilities, and as a means of satisfying demand for credit which the banks could not satisfy because of monetary controls. Because they have generally been subject to much less control of reserves and interest rates than the banks, they have reduced the effectiveness of monetary policy.

Because of the profitability of satisfying demand for new assets and liabilities, the banks have been extending their portfolios into the areas once reserved by the NBFIS. Similarly, the NBFIS have been attracted by the profitability of low-interest demand deposits to attempt to increase the 'moneyness' of their deposits. The portfolio distinctions between the two types of institution have thus been markedly reduced. Reserve requirements also have been extended, both in the US and the UK, to cover a large proportion of NBFI liabilities in the same way as bank liabilities, so that their scope for expansion has been curtailed to some extent. (The constraining power of reserve requirements depends on how tightly the supply of reserves is controlled.) The major scope for an NBFI-style erosion of monetary control lies in the segments of portfolios not subject to controls, particularly foreign exchange deposits.

NBFIS are important for monetary control because they are an alternative to the banks as a source of credit to finance real expenditure. Reserve requirements which limit their rate of growth thereby limit the total potential credit availability. But the return on alternative assets in their portfolios determines the actual availability of credit for real expenditure. Stringent control applied both to banks and NBFIS when credit demand is strong will, before the control of NBFIS, induce *some* institutional change whereby alternative sources and forms of credit emerge. The 'NBFI problem' is inherent in all financial systems once they have developed a degree of sophistication. Rather than applying to particular institutions which are defined as 'NBFIS', it applies to whatever area emerges as the means of avoiding monetary control.

8

Liquidity Preference and the Nature of a Monetary Economy

8.1 INTRODUCTION

This is the first of a series of chapters concerned with the reasons that determine how willing people and institutions will be to hold money instead of other assets, and with the consequences of their portfolio choices. Particular emphasis will be given to: first, the central importance in monetary economics of uncertainty about relative price movements; and second, the suggestion that monetary matters are the key to understanding the origins of involuntary unemployment. The latter contention has been challenged in an influential paper by Hahn (1977). We shall argue that Hahn's paper is merely an exercise in semantics which is flawed because it fails clearly to define what it means by a monetary economy. This chapter shows that a monetary economy can only be understood in institutional terms as an arrangement whereby agents can attempt to escape or benefit from the risks of relative price uncertainty. It is a distraction to attempt to see it as a concept bound up with the use of a particular physical commodity in the process of exchange.

The structure of the chapter is as follows. Section 8.2 examines the components of asset yields and concludes that all commodities which are not instantly perishable possess monetary characteristics in some degree. There is no such thing as a perfect monetary commodity. The implication derived is that there is a speculative element in the demand for all such assets. Section 8.3 analyses how speculative portfolio choices determine the level of employment in a monetary economy. Section 8.4 shows that a barter system would have no problem of involuntary unemployment, but that this benefit would be achieved at the cost of workers being forced to bear entrepreneurial risks of relative price fluctuations. Section 8.5 is a brief conclusion.

8.2 ASSET YIELDS

Portfolio choice is a complex, multi-dimensional decision problem. Assets that might be held can contain many different characteristics but it is often hard to decide which ones in advance of experience. For simplicity we shall follow Keynes' approach and suggest that an asset's yield is composed of the three components listed below:

(1) *Output*: the asset's yield as conventionally expressed, i.e. a flow of services or income, now or in the future, which may be of an uncertain magnitude.

minus (2) *Carrying cost*: any outgoing payable while the asset is being held. This may also be uncertain. The sizes of the other yield components may be dependent on the volume of resources used in the upkeep of the asset.

plus (3) *Liquidity premium*: 'The amount (measured in terms of itself) which [people] are willing to pay for the potential convenience or security given by [the] power of disposal [over an asset] . .. (exclusive of the yield or carrying cost attaching to the asset)' (Keynes (1936), p. 226). People are prepared to pay this amount, which may be positive or negative, and which has no obvious outward manifestation, in the light of their appraisals of the opportunity costs of holding an asset whose price may change against other assets while they are holding it, or if they are unexpectedly forced to sell it in a hurry. This is a particularly important consideration in markets where buyers and sellers arrive erratically and there is a high variance of possible prices or, if secondhand dealers are operating, the certainty of a high trade-in loss if a seller cannot wait to find someone who wants precisely what is being offered. It will also reflect any perceived tendency for the transactions costs of buying and selling the asset to vary according to time and place.

Some examples of asset yields may help to make matters clearer.

(a) Freezer food
  (1) Output: its expected value when consumed at some un-specified date.
  (2) Carrying costs: expenditure to run and maintain the freezer.

    (3) Liquidity premium: the price of fresh food may be expected to rise in the future; but if persistent electricity failures seemed likely freezer foods would command a negative liquidity premium and would not be purchased.

(b) A theatre ticket

    (1) Output: the expected value of the actual performance, given present information.

    (2) Carrying cost: negligible.

    (3) Liquidity premium: the value of person places on avoiding the risk of having to pay an inflated price to a ticket tout on the night of the performance, as set against the difficulty of selling it locally if it is bought beforehand and something happens to prevent attendance or critics give the show poor reviews, and the extra costs of using an agency to get it in advance instead of from the box office.

(c) A new factory

    (1) Output: an expected physical quantity, to be sold at an expected price.

    (2) Carrying costs: rates, maintenance, interest charges.

    (3) Liquidity premium: the negative value the firm contemplating its purchase assigns to it if there is the prospect of obtaining it more cheaply at a later date, or having to make a capital loss if it has to be sold off (or other assets have to be sold off because financial resources have been run down to purchase it) if expectations are falsified and there is a need for finance due to a business downturn.

(d) A time deposit in a bank

    (1) Output: expected interest payments.

    (2) Carrying costs: negligible.

    (3) Liquidity premium: the negative value the person assigns due to her unease about (a) the possibility that inflation might be faster than expected; (b) the chance of missing 'bargain' purchases if money cannot be obtained instantly; (c) the possible failure of the bank. This may be offset by the positive value conferred by the chance the ability to store generalized purchasing power gives the holder to wait and acquire further information before commitments are made to durable goods with low trade-in values relative to their initial costs.

It is evident that it is not possible to hold wealth in any form without it being necessary to speculate about future changes in its value against other assets. Even money is held on a speculative basis. Its real value in exchange is never entirely certain. Money is not a good store of value in times of inflation. It is not a good medium of exchange if it is deposited in a bank and cheques are not trusted, or if its owner is in a foreign land and can only make her domestic currency acceptable at a large discount. Not only is money as conventionally understood not even perfectly liquid in these senses, but the rate at which someone can exchange it for goods is not independent of the quantity she wishes to exchange, just as share prices vary according to the rate at which a large holder attempts to dispose of them on the stock exchange.

The possibility that the yields of all durable assets include positive or negative liquidity premia has, as Townshend (1937) observed, highly destructive implications for conventional value theory. Liquidity premia are dependent on expectations that can be prone to sudden shifts as consumer confidence changes. The demand for goods may be highly unstable even if long-run preferences with respect to the characteristics they offer are stable. Demand depends not merely on a consumer's ability to purchase but also, as Katona (1960) has emphasized, on her willingness to use up her liquidity. Shifts in consumer confidence have been shown by Smith (1975) to lead to highly unstable sales behaviour in the US car market. Since cars are usually scrapped in America long before they are unroadworthy it is easy for consumers to postpone replacement purchases if they are worried about, say, their future employment prospects. Extreme price shifts are avoided in so far as dealers are willing to hold stocks while waiting for demand to pick up, and if the manufacturers can cut production and lay off workers without further affecting confidence.

This view of the way that instability in expectations can affect the demand for durable assets leads to an unconventional view of the role of transactions costs. Instead of being a barrier to the orderly functioning of markets they appear to be necessary for markets to operate without extreme instability, particularly where the annual flow of production is small relative to the existing stock of assets. If transactions costs were trivial someone expecting a fall in house prices could sell her house and move into a smaller one, buying back a large house when she believed the price of such houses had bottomed. In this way she could probably increase her wealth sufficiently to offset the temporary loss of consumption of a large home and any fall in the value of small houses. In selling her large home for the small one she would be helping to set in motion precisely the kind of price shift that she expected. Without transactions costs to deter portfolio shifts, and the additional imperfection of quality uncertainty to cause lock-in effects (see Akerlof, 1970), many more markets for assets that can be used as stores of wealth would exhibit the sort of instability normally confined to commodity and stock exchanges.

To sum up: whenever someone accepts a durable asset as a store of wealth in preference to something which she is absolutely certain she will dispose of in the immediate future she is doing so because its current price in terms of other goods implies an acceptable real rate of return given her expectations concerning its output, carrying cost and future relative value. Whenever relative prices are not fixed, people who wish to avoid opportunity losses cannot avoid speculating about how prices may change, no matter how they chose to hold their wealth.

8.3　PORTFOLIO CHOICE AND EMPLOYMENT DETERMINATION

Given their knowledge of current prices, expectations of future prices, and fears about future financial flows and other contingencies, economic agents will choose portfolios such that no increase in their total yield could be obtained by increasing their holdings of some assets and reducing their holdings of others. In arranging their portfolios they face two constraints in addition to those concerned with information and their initial endowments. The first is that in some markets what they buy or sell will be rationed in quantity. For example, there may be waiting lists which prevent firms from obtaining rapid deliveries of investment goods, while workers may not be able to sell their labour at the current money wage rate and may be powerless to change it.

The second difficulty they may encounter is that only certain kinds of commodity may, at current prices or within legal constraints, form an acceptable means of payment. Clower (1967) suggests that in a monetary economy 'money buys goods and goods buy money, but goods do not buy goods'. This is not strictly true if 'money' is understood in a narrow sense. Previous chapters have shown that what is acceptable as 'money' varies considerably with the state of development of the economy and the market in question. In a modern industrial economy one can purchase a car part in barter by trading an existing vehicle in with a dealer and, often, partly with a cheque drawn in part against a time deposit in a bank. The barter component of the deal would not usually be possible, except at a massive discount, if anything other than a car were being offered in part payment. In many employment contracts workers are paid partly in kind, or enjoy an entitlement to purchase the output of their companies at attractive prices, which they can then resell. In such situations goods (i.e. labour services) are in effect buying other goods directly. However, although Clower's dictum is open to such qualifications, it will be most unusual for isolated transactions to be made in a manner vastly at variance with conventional institutional practices.

Through their choices of means of payment and portfolios agents can affect the velocity of circulation of particular monetary aggregates and, though not necessarily in any closely related way, the level of employment. Where flow supply prices of assets are not independent of the level of demand for them the general price level may also be affected. Agents are fortunate to have some historical knowledge of previously marked prices to guide them as they arrange their portfolios. Otherwise, as Townshend (1937) pointed out, they would have no idea of what relative or money price bids they should put in for assets, or ask for things they had to sell. Reasoned portfolio choice would be impossible.

To illustrate how shifts in portfolio choices can affect employment and prices we will consider what happens when consumers and firms decide, as a result of a change in confidence, to reduce their clearing bank deposits. A variety of outcomes is possible depending on which assets are initially purchased, and on what the sellers of the assets do with the proceeds:

(1) The purchase of new consumption or investment goods will encourage firms to hire more workers. These workers, in turn, may become less reluctant to run down their bank deposits in a similar way.

(2) The purchase of secondhand goods will tend to raise their prices and thus make the production of new, closely substitutable, products more attractive.

(3) If agents buy new shares or bonds, or make new loans (e.g. companies increase trade credit, parents lend to their children) the recipients of the money will be able to make expenditures that otherwise would not have been possible. Other firms may issue new shares or financial IOUs as a result of seeing how easily their rivals have been able to raise money.

(4) The purchase of existing shares causes their prices to be higher than otherwise and encourages firms to expand by buying new

plant instead of by buying up existing companies. Takeovers, unlike the building of new factories, do not directly create employment.

(5) If deposits are simply transferred from clearing banks to non-bank financial intermediaries the onus to spend passes to the managers of these institutions. To the extent that the NBFIS hold their reserves as clearing bank deposits this may not entail a reduction in the clearing banks' lending powers and total lending may rise in consequence, rather than there simply being a change in the composition of advances across financial institutions.

(6) The use of bank deposits in the purchase of non-reproducible assets, such as land, old masters and antiques obviously cannot be associated directly with employment, apart from that due to the increased need for auctioneers and other intermediaries. However, the rise in prices obtained for these assets will cause demand to spill over into substitutes in the long run: rising land prices cause tall buildings to be used instead of short ones, while people will be more willing to purchase so-called reproductions of furniture and paintings. There is also scope for the sellers of the assets to use the purchasing power they otherwise would not have had in a way which creates employment directly, or provides profit incentives by raising the demand for existing assets.

(7) If the reduction in bank deposits is accompanied by an increase in the volume of cash held outside the banking system there will be a multiple reduction in the volume of credit available, and hence in employment, unless the clearing banks are prepared to borrow from the Central Bank as a last resort or reduce their previously unused reserves of lending power. A similar effect on the volume of credit can occur if, instead of holding more cash, people increase their holdings of newly imported assets.

In all but the last of the seven cases above a reduction in the perceived return to holding clearing bank deposits relative to other assets leads to an increase in the velocity of circulation, along with rising prices or output. Whether or not a first-round rise in asset prices and output is subsequently maintained depends on what the first-round sellers do with the means of exchange they have obtained. If they are happy to hold on to their newly acquired assets because they can see no other commodities or securities which offer a higher return they are saying 'the bucks stop here'. To the extent that other people who would like to spend do not have acceptable means of payment these first-round sellers of assets are constraining them from doing so by their choices of portfolios.

If agents attempt to use the most commonly accepted media of exchange as stores of value, and there is a general consensus on which assets serve best in the latter role, the relative prices of other assets will fall. Firms will be encouraged to expand production of the former and contract production of the latter, thus causing shifts in employment. But the assets in demand may be commodities in whose production firms cannot invest, either very rapidly or at all. The most obviously strictly non-reproducible asset is currency. Private firms cannot employ workers to make this in times when people and institutions want to use it as a store of wealth instead of as a medium of exchange. If there is unemployment as a result of an excessive desire for liquidity it is up to the State to increase the supply of it or discourage people from holding it. Workers who would like jobs cannot make it possible for firms literally to make money simply by offering to work for lower money wages. The private sector can only create money that agents can use to buy assets if financial institutions and depositors reduce their desire to hoard cash reserves or borrowers are prepared to offer more (become less liquid and commit themselves to higher interest payments) to obtain loans.

The implication of the previous paragraph is that the key determinant of the level of aggregate demand and employment is the return people expect to obtain from holding on to assets that could function as means of paying for other assets, either at their present relative price or a lower one. If money, as conventionally understood, was the only means of payment we could say that the rate of return on money ruled the roost. But it is not strictly possible to accredit any single asset with this roost-ruling role when there are organized markets for many assets, and currency is not the only conventional means of payment. For example, the person who decides against buying a new car because the trade-in price of her existing one is unacceptable is allowing the yield on a potential means of payment to affect employment. Paradoxically, if people generally were more willing to trade-in their cars for new ones secondhand prices would rise as business activity and incomes rose, causing a multiple increase in spending. Individuals, however, merely observe a low current trade-in value and not the rise in income their purchase might initiate or, if they do perceive the latter, may not expect to share in it.

Too strong a desire for liquidity leads to a lack of demand for new goods. Too weak a desire for it causes excessive demand and inflation.

In a hyperinflation the roost-ruling rate of return tends towards zero as the money prices of assets rise towards infinity. Shifts in liquidity preference entail shifts in the velocity of circulation if the money supply (however defined) is given. Even in a situation where all money is credit money and no cash is held outside banks (what Gurley and Shaw (1960) have called an 'inside money' economy), employment will vary according to the desire people have to hoard money in their bank deposits instead of writing out cheques to spend it. Shifts in liquidity preference will usually affect the availability of credit, but not always: they may merely affect the rate at which money moves between bank accounts, with the total value of outstanding loans unchanged.

8.4 EFFECTIVE DEMAND IN A BARTER ECONOMY

We have argued that the perceived rate of return on assets that might be used as means of exchange, but whose owners prefer to use as stores of value, is the key factor in determining aggregate demand and employment. The implication is that monetary matters are at the root of what is to be learned from Keynes. Hahn (1977) has attracted much attention by producing a paper which challenges this conclusion by supposedly specifying a non-monetary economy in which there is scope for macroeconomic problems. Careful examination of his arguments, however, reveals that all he has done is to play around with various commodity definitions of money, ignoring institutional aspects which differentiate monetary and barter systems.

Hahn (1977, p. 31) suggests that conventional conclusions rest on an 'axiomatic restriction' of what constitutes money. In Clower's (1967) work, for example, a requirement that workers are paid in currency prevents them from selling their labour directly in return for a bundle of goods whose value does not exceed their marginal physical product. Hahn's paper replaces Clower's restriction with the assumption that the world consists of a computer-mediated economy where workers are paid in terms of units of land, and titles to land can serve as a means of payment and store of wealth. He demonstrates that with a given land wage an increased desire to use land as a store of wealth will cause unemployment to emerge because it entails a fall in demand for reproducible (i.e. non-land) commodities.

All this is quite correct in terms of our earlier analysis for, given the restriction that land is the only means of payment, the rate of return to holding land must rule the roost. If other assets offer a lower return agents will not hold them. Their demand prices may then fall below their supply prices and cause unemployment. Anyone who insists on holding land as a store of value is preventing other parties from trading non-land goods. But it is hard to view this economy as anything other than a monetary economy with a peculiarly narrow definition of money.

If one seriously wants to examine the origins of effective demand failures the appropriate focus of the analysis is on the institutional and class relationships involved in transaction-making in the economy, not on the consequences of using different physical commodities as *general* means of payment. From this perspective we can propose the following definitions of barter and monetary economies, definitions which overcome the difficulties of pinning down 'money' itself in a world of many durable goods:

A barter economy is any economy where workers are paid in terms of *current* output or titles to that output.

A monetary economy is any economy where workers avoid entrepreneurial risks by being paid in *other* than current output.

If agents are institutionally restricted to the barter system an arrangement will emerge which overcomes informational problems and general chaos which might arise from the lack of double coincidences of wants. The simple barter system of a primitive economy is not an appropriate reference point in this context. Trade would be arranged thus: a sulphuric acid worker, to take an example, would never see the acid constituting her pay and instead would be given a title to the acid which she would then take along to a commodity broker and exchange for a generally acceptable asset to use as a means of paying for the goods she wished to consume. This generally acceptable asset could even be normal currency or titles to land without violating the barter requirement. The acid dealer would then sell what is, strictly speaking, secondhand acid in return for the generally acceptable asset. The worker, likewise, would purchase 'secondhand' items for consumption.

In such an economy there could be no failure of effective demand and no involuntary unemployment so long as wages were flexible. In a barter system it is quite clear how the product of a firm will be divided up, given the level of productivity. This is not the case in a monetary economy, since a known wage is paid to produce a volume of output to be sold at an unknown price and firms can never know how much will be left over as profit. With the barter arrangement the firm has merely to decide whether what is left over would be worth enough when subsequently exchanged for something else. If providers of capital are not satisfied then a lower product wage may be agreed upon to provide them with more of the product so that if, say, its price falls against other commodities, their share still represents an adequate return. The institutional arrangement ensures that, as far as current output is concerned, the economy always has an *ex ante* and *ex post* marginal and average propensity to spend of one. So long as wages are flexible changes in portfolio choice behaviour will change relative prices and distributional shares but will not cause Keynesian unemployment.

Such arrangements for trade are, to say the least, not common as a general way of organizing production. Workers and capitalists usually prefer a monetary system. The reason for this quickly becomes apparent if we define workers as risk-averse agents who aim to avoid any losses of general purchasing power from their earnings when the relative price of what may make falls. Capitalists, by contrast, are risk-lovers. If workers are paid in terms of a non-reproducible commodity, and the general price level is an index of prices of currently produced goods expressed in terms of the wage commodity, they will be immune from entrepreneurial risks. The non-reproducible nature of the wage commodity means that the value of their wages cannot be eroded by an increase in its supply causing its price to fall. Moreover, in so far as wages are sticky in terms of the wage commodity and firms use some form of normal cost pricing, changes in the demand for the wage commodity which cause output to fluctuate will not affect the real wages of those who remain in employment.

In a barter system the acceptance of payment in product involves the acceptance, for the duration of the contract, of the risk that the relative price of one's output may change because of shifts in demand and supply conditions. As Shackle observes, in a barter economy a 'worker' is 'a merchant in Cantillon's meaning, a man who buys goods at a known price to sell them, later on, at a price which now he cannot know. . . . Suppliers of productive services who are willing to be paid in product are shareholders in the enterprise' (Shackle (1974), pp. 7–8). In an economy where wages are paid in, and are sticky in terms of, a non-reproducible good, workers almost entirely avoid entrepreneurial risks. But the cost of avoiding them is the risk that they may not be able to find employment.

8.5 CONCLUSION

If monetary matters are understood as being concerned with the choices of portfolios and institutional arrangements that agents make in order to avoid or profit from risks of capital losses due to swings in relative prices, then it can be said that monetary matters have a central role in the determination of employment in an economy. Any asset that is durable can serve as some kind of store of wealth; how well it performs in this function depending on what happens to its relative price. Whether it can also serve as a means of exchange will depend on its current price relative to its likely future price. An asset whose relative price against other goods is prone to high variance will be one that will only be held by people if they feel confident of which way prices are going to move and, if its price is expected to fall in future, if the cost of capital loss is offset by some other, physical or financial, component of the asset's yield. Speculation by present holders of most durable assets prevents them from acquiring a relative price per unit low enough to function as an acceptable means of payment for goods in general. Their prices would have to fall to make them acceptable to sellers because of the possibility that they might not be able to trade them for something else at a later date without a further capital loss. Changes in expectations will affect what constitutes an acceptable relative price and, if they alter the relative prices of newly producible and existing goods, will affect the level of employment. If there is a one-to-one correspondence between changes in wages and changes in the cost of making reproducible goods the obvious implication is that wage changes will only affect the level of employment if somehow they change the relative prices of new and existing assets. A cut in nominal wages which leads to a fall in the money prices of new goods without also causing a fall in the price of existing assets will cause demand to spill over from existing to new goods. Hence production and employment will increase. If, for a particular money wage, average cost curves for reproducible goods are not upward-sloping an increase in employment will not entail a cut in real wages so long as workers only consume reproducible goods.

9

Wealth Effects

9.1 INTRODUCTION

In the previous chapter we examined how portfolio choices are affected by expectations of relative price movements, particularly those associated with forced sales of assets, and how such choices affect the level of economic activity. In this chapter we consider how an economy's performance will be affected when shifts in relative prices actually occur, whether or not they conform with expectations. Changes in asset values can affect both the command a wealth-holder can have over resources and her willingness to exercise it. The two features combined are called wealth effects.

Our discussion of wealth effects is divided into three main parts, followed by a conclusion. Section 9.2 examines the origins of wealth effects and shows how they are possible even in economies where one person's assets are often another's liabilities. Section 9.3 discusses the incidence of wealth effects and assesses the role they play in determining the demand for new goods, and hence employment. Section 9.4 examines the importance of wealth effects in the context of the question that Keynes' *General Theory* caused pure theorists to ask; namely, was it logically possible for an economy with flexible prices to suffer an indefinite failure of at least one market to clear? Neoclassical economists used wealth effects, in particular Pigou's real-balance effect, to provide a negative answer. We offer an alternative, disequilibrium view of the problem.

Since we are only concerned with the consequences of changes in relative asset values we have no need to get entangled in tortuous discussions about the total value of 'wealth' in an economy. Readers interested in this puzzle will find a comprehensive analysis of it in Pesek and Saving's (1967) work.

9.2 THE ORIGINS OF WEALTH EFFECTS

It is instructive to begin by considering an example which, at first sight, seems somewhat perversely to suggest that net wealth effects may not exist. Suppose that some people do not have any money balances whatsoever, and own portfolios which consist entirely of durable goods. A second group keeps some of its wealth deposited in financial institutions, from which a third group has borrowed to finance the purchase of durable assets. Then assume there is a uniform rise in the money prices of durable goods currently being held as wealth.

The fall in the value of money has no effect on the first group's ability to use its wealth for consumption. Assets can now be sold for more money, but more money is needed to purchase other assets. The second group's command over consumable resources will have been reduced unless a rise in interest rates has occurred to make the value of deposits rise in line with money prices. This group will reduce its current expenditure to the extent that this is dependent on its current wealth-holdings. However, any such cuts in expenditure may be offset by greater spending from the third group, whose debts have fallen in value. This last group could sell off some of its assets, pay back its loans, and have resources left over which were not previously available. Unless the relationship between wealth and consumption differs between debtors and creditors it seems that the net wealth effect of the change in the relative price of money and goods is zero.

A rise in the general price level can only cause a net wealth effect if one of the groups in the economy holds currency as a store of wealth outside the banking system. When money prices rise holders of cash suffer a negative wealth effect. On the other side of the balance sheet the body to gain is the government, since, to the extent that cash is backed by government securities, the real value of its outstanding debt falls. But this positive wealth effect can be neglected for it is rather unrealistic to believe that it will cause an increase in government expenditure. Governments are not constrained in their spending by the current net value of their wealth if they can levy taxes or print money to cover their debts.

Currency or, as Gurley and Shaw (1960) term it, 'outside money' is, however, no more than a trivial part of most people's wealth. A massive change in the general price level would be required in a predominantly inside money economy before the kind of wealth effect we have been considering would have much impact on expenditure.

This point seems to have been forgotten by those who have attributed the rises in private sector savings ratios in OECD countries in the mid-1970s to attempts by people to restore their money balances as their wealth was eroded by the accelerating inflation that followed the oil crisis. Other things equal, any extra saving to this end should have been offset by the extra expenditure of debtors who were enjoying positive wealth effects: private sector savings are almost entirely 'inside money' deposits.

Although the trivial wealth effects associated with outside money balances have attracted most attention in this area other, more important, varieties do exist. As an alternative example consider what happens when a company issues shares to finance building a factory. While the new factory is an obvious addition to society's physical wealth the new issue that finances it may only be possible at the cost of a fall in the value of existing shares in the company. Against this, land prices in the locality and the share values of construction companies engaged to build the factory may rise. In this situation, in contrast to the earlier example, the positive and negative changes in real asset values are not 'back to back' on the same balance sheet, so there is no necessary reason for them to cancel out. These wealth effects may be augmented by changes in spending by purchasers of the new shares and construction workers if they see events as raising their lifetime incomes, either from dividends or from employment. But we cannot say *a priori* in which direction the net effect will operate.

The magnitude of any net wealth effect associated with a particular change in a country's capital stock will vary according to the state of expectations. If the purchasers of a new issue of securities hold a particularly rosy view of the consequences of the investment for the future of the company it may be possible to float the issue without causing a fall in the value of existing shares. In this case, in contrast to our earlier scenario, there will be no negative wealth effect.

Significant wealth effects can also occur when share prices change as a result of expectational shifts rather than attempts to float new issues. Consider first what happens on a rising market. When confidence increases, holders of wealth may revise their expectations of the yields from equities and/or how likely a fall in share prices might be. If they then decide to use idle bank deposits to buy shares they transfer their bank deposits to sellers of shares, with share prices rising in the process. Those who decide to off-load their shares once their prices have reached a particular level may then purchase gilt-edged securities in anticipation of an easier monetary policy. They pass on bank deposits to others while driving up the price of gilts; and so on. With an increase in confidence the economy thus experiences rising asset prices and falling interest rates.

The rise in asset prices means that agents who have not shifted their portfolios and still hold gilts or equities will find that their capital gains enable them to buy more currently produced goods or non-reproducibles. Gilt-owners suffer no reduction in income streams while equity-holders may be expecting higher dividends. In this situation individuals may expand their consumption, while companies may increase the scale of their operations. To the extent that they do this by selling off their assets or increasing their borrowing they will tend to moderate the rise in financial asset prices. But it is quite possible that they will use up idle balances instead; either their own, or those of other agents whose expectations are rising and who become more willing to take chances and add to the supply of loanable funds.

Now, while the rise in share prices confers a positive wealth effect on existing shareholders it also causes an opportunity loss to managers who were planning to take over existing companies as a cheaper way of breaking into a market than buying new factories. But this loss is, paradoxically, likely to lead to higher employment. If the money is used to buy a new factory instead, despite any lower return this might offer, investment takes place instead of a mere exchange of assets, even though its extra cost means that the agents will be somewhat out of pocket and may reduce their expenditure elsewhere. Their other expenditures fall but their total expenditure on new goods rises.

The only group to suffer when interest rates fall are people who keep their wealth in variable-interest bank deposits rather than variable-price securities. Their capital will then accumulate at a slower rate and they may reduce their expenditure in consequence (e.g. as with people trying to save up for a house deposit of a given amount). But such reductions will be offset by the increased spending of those who have borrowed at a variable rate of interest and are finding that their repayments are falling (as with people who have mortgages). This counterbalancing subgroup of wealth effects is a variant on our earlier 'inside money' example. It arises because of a change in the inter-temporal money price of money with no necessary change in money prices of reproducible goods, whereas in the earlier example the money rate of interest was constant and the money prices of goods changed.

In a pessimistic market falling asset prices cause a reduction in wealth and expenditure, which further aggravates the problem of falling prices. But to analyse wealth effects in such a situation by simply reversing all the signs in the previous four paragraphs would not be adequate. There is an additional problem to consider. Previously we have assumed that wealth effects cancel out if associated with an asset which is someone else's liability. It was reasonable to do this for a rising market, but in a situation where everything denominated in money terms is falling in value, except for money debts and fixed-money interest obligations, bankruptcies may occur.

Fixed-money debts represent an increasing real burden if the income or profits streams from which they are financed are falling with the general price level. Even if money interest rates are falling it may not be possible to refund the debt at a lower rate of interest that is more manageable, since the value of the asset against which the loan has been made has fallen and it may now represent inadequate collateral. If the debtor cannot meet her interest charges and goes bankrupt the creditor *may* be fortunate enough to receive a sum of money whose real value has not fallen despite the fall in the money value of the assets involved. But, while the creditor may just have lost an unrealized gain in her wealth, the debtor now possesses negative real wealth and will be highly constrained in her future expenditure.

The scope for refunding debts is likely to be very limited in an economy where the price level is falling and bankruptcies are occurring. Pessimism is likely to reflect itself in rising interest rates as agents become more cautious and share prices fall, with less real funding being made available to secondary banks or new share issues. The negative wealth effect of higher interest rates, where prices of existing assets collapse faster than those of new goods, compounds, and is compounded by, the negative net wealth effect of bankruptcies.

9.3 THE INCIDENCE OF WEALTH EFFECTS

We have argued that significant wealth effects are associated with changes in the prices of existing financial assets and previously produced goods against new goods rather than, the bankruptcy problem aside, changes in the money price level for currently producible goods. That is to say, we are emphasizing what Leijonhufvud (1968) calls 'Keynes' windfall effect' rather than the real balance effects upon which neoclassical economists focus their attention. The implication of this is that wealth effects of consumption are likely to be most significant in economies where security ownership is widespread, the

US being the obvious example. This is somewhat disturbing if the liquidity preference approach to the demand for consumer durables, which we discussed in the previous chapter, is also put into the picture.

The wealthier the community the more likely consumers will be to hold their wealth in a form whose value is prone to fluctuation. Similarly, in a wealthy community the proportion of expenditure which can be classed as discretionary, as dependent on confidence rather than goods actually having worn out, will be relatively high. Shifts in confidence such as seem to have occurred in 1957 (following the Russian demonstration of superiority over the US in the space race) and 1974 (due to the oil crisis) can lead to mutually reinforcing collapses in share prices and expenditure on consumer durables.

The extent of demand instability associated with fluctuations in security prices will depend on how far these are treated as permanent. If consumption is a function of permanent income (the long-run flow from human capital and interest-earning assets) and some conception of permanent wealth 'Keynes' windfall effects' will be unimportant: we are in the stable world of Friedman. If consumers take a short-run view and treat wealth effects as permanent, as well as having consumption partly as some function of expected income in the near future (including expected returns from securities) we are in the potentially highly unstable world of Keynes, Shackle, Katona and Smith. Both sides claim empirical findings inconsistent with each other's world views (e.g. Friedman (1957); Katona (1960, 1976); Smith (1975)).

In countries where security ownership is concentrated in the hands of firms, institutional bodies such as pension funds, and a tiny minority of exceedingly rich families, wealth effects will manifest themselves more in shifts in investment rather than in consumption expenditure. If share prices fall, the institutions will have to draw upon their reserves to meet pension and insurance payouts to their clients. Their ability to subscribe to new issues of bonds and equities will thus be reduced, even assuming they are not afraid to do so because of the prospect of further falls in asset prices. Corporations that hold their investment funds and general reserves as securities to earn a higher yield than would be possible on bank deposits will feel locked into their existing portfolios if taken by surprise by a discontinuous fall in asset prices. If asset prices are expected to recover fairly soon it will be foolish to sell out now, and prudent to postpone marginal investment schemes unless these have exceptionally high expected returns.

In principle, companies might be able to carry on investing in a 'lock-in' situation (assuming their confidence in the new schemes had not evaporated) by running down whatever reserves of cash they had or increasing their borrowing. In practice, however, this will be seen as a dangerous thing to do in a recession. Companies will be keen to hold on to their reserves in case their customers default on credit payments, or because loan financing involves a commitment to particular interest payments and thus a greater risk of bankruptcy. A further deterrent may be a rising cost of borrowing – indeed, a rise in interest rates may have been the original cause of the fall in asset values. Rights issues would avoid interest-rate problems but would cause management teams to incur the wrath of their shareholders by forcing them to suffer a further capital loss.

The significance of these wealth effects in practice depends once more on the willingness and ability of asset-owners to treat changed asset prices as temporary phenomena. To escape the kaleidoscopic situations about which Shackle (1974) has written we need unshakeably confident managers and a financial system that contains much buffering, in the form of unused borrowing power. The more willing managers are to risk upsetting their shareholders, chance a less liquid corporate asset structure, and take a long-run view of the business cycle (particularly if their investment projects have long gestation periods as in, say, the chemicals industry), the smaller 'lock-in' wealth effects will be. However, where firms finance investment from retentions, are reluctant to seek new equity and gearing issues (see Whittington and Meeks, 1976), and hold accumulations prior to large chunks of investment as securities, wealth effects will be powerful. They will also be compounded by shifts in profit levels and expectations if managerial outlooks are dominated by what happens in the short run.

Wealth effects appear to be inextricably linked with the speculative dimension of a monetary economy and, as such, may be difficult to model econometrically. This is particularly likely to be a problem in times of rapid inflation. Evans (1980) has shown that price changes become more uneven the faster the general rate of inflation. The 'noise' in the system that this cross-sectional variance represents will make it hard for people to decide what their wealth positions are, or will be in the future. This of itself may seem sufficient reason for hesitancy in expenditure while information about trends is being acquired. The inclusion of wealth effects enhances our understanding of the possible texture of economic systems but makes accurate predictions likely only when an economy is stable and such effects are not occurring.

9.4 WEALTH EFFECTS AND SELF-RIGHTING PROPERTIES
OF ECONOMIES

Wealth effects achieved prominence in economics as a result of being used in attempts to challenge Keynes' (1936) conclusion that even an economy with flexible prices had no inherent tendency towards full employment equilibrium. In order to understand, and then evaluate critically, the way in which neoclassical economists used, particularly, the real balance effect to make their challenge we must first examine how Keynes reached his conclusion.

Keynes argued that lower money wages offer no direct remedy if there is a tendency towards unemployment when firms find they cannot sell the full employment volume of output at a price that offers an acceptable return. When wages are cut they reduce purchasing power, not just industrial costs. Sooner or later, *even with falling wages*, firms will cut their volumes of output and employment if events keep falsifying their expectations that wage cuts will restore profitability. The multiplier process will then take hold, just as it will do anyway if there is resistance to wage cuts. Hence money wage cuts, which may be difficult to implement, do not directly assist in solving the problem. What is needed is more real expenditure.

If money wage cuts cause the price level to fall the amount of loan finance or cash reserves necessary to finance a given real volume of activity will fall in money terms. This appears to offer an indirect mechanism whereby wage cuts may restore real demand. If the volume of finance available does not fall due to bankruptcies or people becoming less willing to deposit their cash in financial institutions and buy new debt issues – a rather big assumption – the falling price level causes the real supply of loanable funds to rise. This may spill over into demand for new goods, either directly (e.g. clearing banks reduce their loan charges to attract more customers), or indirectly via the 'Keynes effect' type of wealth effect (e.g. clearing banks buy gilts for their portfolios, driving up their prices and causing sellers to spend more by giving them capital gains).

But there is no guarantee that this process will actually lead to a sufficient fall in interest rates and rise in asset prices. If holders of cash have inelastic expectations speculation will delay the fall in interest rates. Any delay lengthens the period during which losses are being made and the multiplier is being given a chance to work. Losses and falling sales will cause investment to be cut. Thus what might have been a rate of interest low enough to generate a full employment level of expenditure, had it been achieved immediately, will fail to do this when, eventually, it is reached. An even lower rate of interest will be needed. But the greater the delay and the more prices and wages have to fall, the more likely it is that bankruptcies will occur and agents will become less willing or able to lend money, causing an offsetting upward pressure on interest rates. The attempts of companies to avoid redundancies or irreversible factory closures as they make losses may also add to the real demand for finance faster than the falling price level causes its real supply to rise. Seats in the financial 'lifeboat' thus get more expensive unless the Central Bank raises the credit base of the economy.

Neoclassical economists completely fail to spot that Keynes' vision of financial systems implies the possibility that falling wages and prices might lead to rising interest rates rather than the more convenient reverse result. Consequently they assign great significance to a feature Keynes includes as a special case; namely, the liquidity trap. Wage cuts are prevented from restoring full employment even indirectly if a 'floor' is hit in money markets before an adequately low rate of interest is achieved. Hence, further wage cuts cannot further stimulate expenditure through their effects on interest rates and asset prices: the Keynes effect ceases to work.

Conventional explanations of the liquidity trap proceed, without any reference to institutional details, along the following lines. A falling price level associated with falling wages and insufficient aggregate demand causes agents to find their transactions balances in excess of their daily needs. They then have to decide what to do with their excess balances. If they are afraid to buy bonds because the rate of interest is below their normal expectation and they think it will shortly rise, they will merely hoard their cash. There is then no upward pressure on bond prices and the interest rate fails to fall. Alternatively, if they are prepared to buy bonds they find they can purchase them without driving up their prices because existing holders sell out at the slightest tendency of interest rates to fall. (This second way only works if there is consistently present a group of bond-holders indifferent between bonds and cash, whose bonds are worth at least as much as the value of new excess transactions balances which are not being hoarded.) These processes are repeated every time the price level falls and reduces the transactions demand for money.

In a modern economy with banks and portfolio diversification the mechanics of the liquidity trap are somehat different. If the private sector demand for loans falls as the price level comes down banks can buy up existing securities from this sector. If there is no effect on security prices we appear to have a liquidity trap situation. But such a policy will cause bank portfolios to become top-heavy with marketable securities rather than personal and corporate loans. The dangers of a capital loss on these securities thus become greater. To avoid them banks can do either of two things. They can attempt to expand the real value of new loans by lowering their interest charges or removing any credit rationing. In this case the liquidity trap ceases to operate unless people are afraid to borrow any more because the recession raises doubts about their ability to repay the money. Alternatively, banks can obviate the difficulties that might arise if security prices fall, or marginal borrowers default, simply by leaving interest rates where they are and avoiding becoming fully loaned up. Until the economy recovers its confidence and the prospect of capital losses fades away it may thus be gripped firmly in the liquidity trap.

Neoclassical economists argue that Keynes' conclusion must be dependent either upon an assumption of wage rigidity or on the dominance of the liquidity trap. Following Pigou (1941) they suggest that it is a conclusion which can be overturned, so long as money wages are flexible, by the real balance effect, even if the liquidity trap binds. Although further cuts in money wages cannot lead, indirectly, to further falls in interest rates in this situation, the value of money balances will be rising. Eventually this extra wealth will spill over into increased real expenditure which will put a brake on further falls in wages and prices by restoring the demand for labour. Hence, on the neoclassical argument, the real balance form of wealth effect, ignored by Keynes, guarantees that an economy will not languish in an equilibrium of involuntary unemployment so long as wages are flexible. In terms of static, institution-free, textbook expositions, the neoclassical use of the combination of flexible money wages and the real balance effect can appear a powerful critique of Keynes' work. But it needs to be asked first, whether this combination of factors is necessary to discredit his pessimistic conclusions, and second, whether it is sufficient. It is particularly important to raise these questions since, as Trevithick (1978) has shown, these factors are also responsible for the conclusions of the celebrated works by Barro and Grossman (1976) and Malinvaud (1977) on the theory of employment.

Even if fixed money wages prevent the real balance and Keynes effects from occurring, there is no reason to assume that an economy in which there has been a failure of aggregate demand will languish for ever at an *equilibrium* position of unemployment should be no expansionary government policy be forthcoming. Normal IS–LM analysis neglects the fact that unemployed workers have to live, somehow, and that durable consumption and investment goods, the postponement of whose purchases may have caused the recession, do not last for ever. Recognition of this forces us to take a dynamic perspective.

The need for unemployed workers effectively to be subsidized by their families in the absence of deficit-financed dole payments or their own liquid reserves means that the average propensity to consume rises as a recession takes hold. To the extent that supportive relations have sacrificed their own consumption they will maintain a very high propensity to consume if anything happens to restore demand and removes the burden of financing the unemployed. This, and the wearing-out of the unemployed group's durables, will mean that any increases in income will be more than usually likely to be spent. Such injections of spending may come either from firms replacing worn-out machinery or from other consumers still wealthy enough to afford to replace durables that have finally worn out and whose replacement can no longer be postponed. That is to say, even without wage flexibility and Pigou effects, trade cycle forces will stop an economy from settling down into a particular unemployment equilibrium once a recession has occurred. The Keynesian view of the potential for speculation and the instability of expectations in markets for all durable assets implies a multiplier process that is uneven and an inherent tendency for the level of economic activity to oscillate. However, Keynesian business cycles, dependent as they are on expectational movements, will have no reason to be regular or always to hit the full employment ceiling before turning downwards. The speculative forces that can set in to stop upturns from continuing indefinitely are there regardless of the source of an upturn – real balance effects, capital replacement mechanisms, straightforward shifts in confidence, or whatever.

The sufficiency of the combination of flexible wages and real balance effects as a device for ensuring economic recovery in a recession is even more open to question than its necessity. We have already emphasized how negative wealth effects associated with bankruptcies can tend to push interest rates up and real expenditure down as the price level falls, and how, even if interest rates do fall in a recession, their sluggish adjustment increases the scale of the fall in price level required to bring the Keynes effect to bear. The greater the fall in the price level, however, the greater the danger of bankruptcies. If the liquidity trap does set in and prevent the Keynes effect from operating, the bankruptcies that occur while the price level is falling to a level low enough to bring the real balance effect to bear may vastly outweigh any gains to be obtained from the latter. This is particularly so in a modern 'inside money' economy, where a dramatic shift in prices is necessary to generate a significant real balance effect. The result of an attempt to cure unemployment by imposing wage cuts is therefore likely to be a further reduction in output, an increase in real interest rates and the destruction both of confidence and of business institutions. Furthermore, there is no guarantee that the least efficient firms will be the ones to suffer most. These will occupy the seats in the financial lifeboat first of all, leaving relatively efficient companies, who would be surviving but for a falling price level raising the real value of their debts, unable to scramble aboard.

9.5 CONCLUSION

Relative price changes in certain circumstances can change net wealth and may thus affect expenditure. But economists do not agree on the relative importance of various kinds of wealth effects which can occur. Monetarists and neoclassical 'Keynesians' believe that economic systems are well-buffered and people act with regard to their long-run wealth and income positions. Although they see changes in relative yields as playing an important role in determining portfolio choices they play down the consequences for asset values that yield changes involve. Furthermore, since they neglect the complexities due to contractual commitments in modern financial systems, they see the real balance effect of changes in the overall money price level as an important stabilizing force. Keynesian economists, with their emphasis on short-run speculation and the consequences of fixed money wage and debt obligations, see shifts in relative *money* prices of assets as destabilizing and real balance effects as normally ineffectual but approached by a pathway too dangerous to traverse.

10

Crowding Out

10.1 INTRODUCTION

In this chapter we are concerned with an occurrence which makes economic management difficult even if there is not also the problem, discussed in chapters 8 and 9, of speculation causing investment and consumption functions to be unstable and the multiplier to have a variable value. The feature is called crowding out and it may be said to be occurring when a fiscal expansion fails to have the multiple effect on GNP implied by the economy's marginal propensities to consume, import and pay taxes. The increased net government expenditure displaces private expenditure and, depending on the size of the displacement, the value of the multiplier is reduced, in the limit to zero.

Monetarists tend to argue that the limit case, complete crowding out, is the usual long-run result, so that attempts at reflation increase not the size of GNP but the proportion of it consisting of government expenditure. In this chapter we present a Keynesian perspective on the problem and argue that the result depends very much upon the composition of injections of expenditure and the state of expectations. On this view there is thus no unique and stable percentage value for the magnitude of crowding out, though total displacement seems most unlikely unless an expansion is very foolishly engineered.

In section 10.2 we consider the nature of two kinds of crowding out, physical and financial, and the senses in which they 'matter'. The mechanisms and inevitability or otherwise of financial crowding out are the subject of section 10.3. The method of analysis in this section is completely at odds with conventional IS–LM investigations of the problem and in section 10.4, which is followed by a brief conclusion, we explore some of the difficulties of using IS–LM diagrams in this context.

10.2 THE NATURE AND IMPORTANCE OF CROWDING OUT

Crowding out, as we observed in the introduction, is occurring when the effect of a reflation is less than the value implied by coefficients usually used to derive the multiplier, because some private expenditure which would have otherwise occurred is displaced by the extra state expenditure. Both private sector investment and consumption expenditures may be displaced, for either physical or financial reasons. But so long as the displacement is not as much as the increase in government expenditure some addition to GNP is generated, although the value of the multiplier may be rather small. If crowding out is not total, expansionary policies work, albeit with limited leverage for a given stimulus. So any criticism of such policies must logically concentrate on any harmful effects on the long-run well-being of the economy resulting from an increase in the share of government in GNP and the loss of particular private sector expenditure schemes.

Financial crowding out may occur when a government atempts to increase its expenditure and finances it by floating new bonds on the money market rather than by credit creation. The government successfully sells its bonds but, as a result, the private sector is unable to obtain finance on as favourable terms as otherwise would have been available and so decides against implementing some spending schemes. Total financial crowding out occurs when the value of extra bond-financed government expenditure is equal to the value of displaced private sector spending. If financial crowding out is total the implication seems to be that only monetary measures can stimulate aggregate demand, a fiscal expansion *per se* has no effect.

It is important not to make the same mistake as proponents of the 1930s Treasury View, who argued that a fiscal expansion could not work because there was a fixed pool of 'saving' from which investment, public or private, could be financed. Finance and saving are different things. Saving is that part of current income which is not spent. It can be lent out to finance expenditure by others but, equally, it can be hoarded. Money held in bank deposits as a result of current saving only represents an addition to the supply of finance in so far as it is a new deposit rather than merely a transfer from another account. If an increase in expenditure can be financed initially, by borrowing money that otherwise would have been hoarded or by borrowing from the central bank ('printing money'), there will automatically be created an equal amount of saving, which people *may* choose to make available to finance the *subsequent* injections of expenditure by the government or private sector to keep demand up to its new level. But such saving can only occur from the extra income generated by the injection of expenditure: finance for this must come first.

Physical crowding occurs when the government's addition to the demand for factors and intermediate inputs in inelastic supply drives up their prices and causes private investment schemes no longer to be viable. For example increased defence expenditure may result in higher wages being paid to lure specialist scientists away from private sector electronics factories. In the longer run high wages may act as an incentive for people to train as such specialists; if this happens the physical crowding out is just a temporary problem. As Keynes recognized in letters to *The Times* early in 1937 (reprinted in Hutchison, 1977), at a time when one person in 7 was out of work, bottlenecks may occur even when there are substantial volumes of unemployment. This means that *ad hoc* measures should be used to increase demand in sectors where shortages do not exist. Selective industrial subsidies are, if chosen wisely, less likely to cause physical crowding out than blanket reflationary measures if there are barriers to the short-run sectoral substitutability of labour and machinery, and an uneven distribution of unemployment.

If short run crowding out is only partial a refusal to stimulate demand by selective fiscal means in an economy can only be justified with reference to short run government crowding out if such a policy produces damage to the economy in the long run. There are four main kinds of long run damage that warrant serious attention but each can be overcome or shown to be misconceived. They are as follows:

(1) In so far as financial crowding out arises through a rise in interest rates it may cause asset prices to fall and thus be associated with destabilizing wealth effects. Furthermore, rising mortgage charges will raise the retail price index and may lead to higher wage demands. The obvious solution is to accompany the fiscal expansion with an accommodating monetary policy.

(2) Even if the total value of investment expenditure increases in a situation where direct government investment partially crowds out private sector investment it may well be the case that in the long run this greater value of investment has a lower level of productivity, due to, say, X-inefficiency. The flaw in this argument is that, because crowding out is incomplete, short-run demand is higher than it otherwise would have been. This may have a 'pump-

priming' effect by stimulating private investment so that continued government injections are not necessary. The total of private investment then rapidly becomes greater than it otherwise would have been. From this standpoint 'unproductive' public investment schemes are then only undesirable if they are propped up when the economy is later thriving and, through their demands for skilled personnel, physically crowd out superior private investments.

(3) Extra public current expenditure can crowd out private sector current consumption which may be viewed as being undesirable for freedom of choice reasons. However, while higher interest rates can cause reduced first-round consumer credit expenditure this may be desirable for reasons of equity if the public expenditure is directed at lower income groups, and, to the extent that crowding out is less that 100 per cent and there is a pump-priming effect, a rising national income will *increase* the volume of private consumption expenditure.

(4) Extra public current expenditure may crowd out private sector investment and thus reduce the long-run output potential of the economy. This may be true but it is, point (2) aside, an argument about the *composition* of the fiscal stimulus rather than an argument against any kind of stimulus to demand. Again there is the possibility that the increase in demand will cause a shift in investment expectations and thus have a pump-priming effect. It should also be said that an autonomous increase in private credit-financed consumption expenditure as a result of Katona-style shift in confidence could have a similar crowding out effect on private investment, but again, this argument would apply only to the first-round effect.

Although the above arguments about crowding out have each been shown to be misplaced, they at least have the merit of focusing attention on the long-run economic implications of deficit-financed government expenditure and not merely on its short-run consequences for the orderly management of financial markets. The latter are considered in the next section, but before moving on to this we offer an example to impress on readers how important it is to consider the composition of crowding out effects before pronouncing they are inevitably harmful, should they occur. Increased direct public sector enterprise investment may crowd out current private consumption expenditure. To the extent that the former has a lower import content than the latter the tendency of an expansion to worsen the balance of payments is partially offset. Better still, in the long run the capacity created by the public investments may help to reduce any tendency towards a cumulatively increasing propensity to import.

10.3 HOW DOES FINANCIAL CROWDING OUT OCCUR?

There appear to be four main mechanisms by which financial crowding out may occur, but it will become evident that all could be offset by a careful choice of expansionary expenditure, or by favourable shifts in confidence. Let us consider them in turn.

(1) Banks are attracted to buy gilt-edged securities and reduce their issues of new loans to the private sector. The attraction of the gilts is the higher return that the government offers in order to sell them. In the first round crowding out can be total by this mechanism and will only have beneficial multiplier effects if the recipients of the additional government expenditure have a greater propensity to purchase domestic goods than would the recipients of the revenue from the private expenditure that the banks would otherwise have financed. If the higher government deficit reflects not increased direct expenditure but tax cuts to the wealthy, there may be an actual first-round fall in expenditure if some of the tax cuts are simply saved: i.e. the multiplier would be negative. However, even though a bank purchase of government debt reduces bank loans to the private sector by an equal amount, it is still possible that there may be a net increase in expenditure. For example, the government could make grants available to the public to cover part of the cost of insulating their homes. To the extent that grant recipients make up the difference by reducing their bank deposits below what they otherwise would have been in that period there is an addition to expenditure even if there is a tendency to substitute insulation expenditure for other private expenditure. Government subsidies to companies for investment may have a similar effect if the companies would otherwise simply have hoarded their contributions to the expenditure in bank deposits. The implication is that this kind of crowding out may be avoided by an appropriate choice of increased government expenditure. Subsidies to industry that encourage increased expenditure on domestically produced goods are 'appropriate'; income tax cuts are not.

(2) Private expenditure may also be crowded out if the non-bank sector is attracted to purchase government stock by high interest rates instead of purchasing goods for current consumption or as new investments (either directly, where companies buy gilts, or indirectly, if the higher interest offered by the government deters companies from making new debenture or equity issues to finance expenditure schemes). The power of this form of crowding out to work against an increase in expenditure clearly depends on the extent to which the private sector purchasers of extra government debt finance their purchases by running down idle balances, instead of by cutting their expenditure on new private sector financial assets and output.

Precisely which idle balances are used to purchase government debt matters too. If time deposits in clearing banks are used to purchase debt the only reduction in demand in the first round, if these balances would not otherwise have been spent, is as a result of bank lending falling slightly due to the government expenditure coming back initially as current demand deposits, requiring the banks to have somewhat more liquid asset portfolios. If wealthy building society depositors buy government debt and reduce their balances with building societies home loans may initially be reduced. This will reduce the rate of increase in house prices and deter new house starts as well as reducing expenditure that would otherwise have taken place as a result of house-moving – carpets and so on, whose purchase will be postponed. However, this is very much a short-term effect so long as crowding out is not complete since, if the pump-priming effect comes into operation, higher savings from higher incomes may be deposited in building societies on a larger scale than before.

Again it should be emphasized that such forms of crowding out can be offset by an appropriate choice of government expenditure.

(3) If the extra government debt can only be sold with a higher rate of interest, existing holders of debt and of closely substitutable securities whose prices fall may reduce their expenditure – i.e. we have another example of an adverse wealth effect of the 'Keynes' windfall effect' variety. New purchasers of government debt may feel wealthier than before since they may expect to have more resources available for their lifetime consumption than previously because such high interest yields were not then available. However, this group are in a minority when the increment to the stock of outstanding national debt is small. This effect could only be

avoided if all debt were financed by short-term bonds and there were no closely substitutable assets of a longer date (e.g. equities) whose prices might fall when the short-term rate of interest increased.

Artis (1978) has mentioned a further complication in this area, which he calls the 'coupon effect'. When dated debts mature they will have to be refunded at the new higher rate of interest and, to the extent that interest on the National Debt is deficit-financed, this would imply a still higher Public Sector Borrowing Requirement in the future – i.e. the goverment would have got itself into a vicious circle. It should be noticed, however, that so long as crowding out is not complete and the initial increase in the deficit has a pump-priming effect on private expenditure (because the higher aggregate demand affects confidence favourably) the deficit will not need to be so large in later periods and this will offset the 'coupon effect' in some degree.

Where interest payments are usually financed by increases in tax revenue the monetarists suggest that higher interest rates associated with a larger government borrowing requirement will cause people to anticipate higher future tax payments so they will reduce their consumption now in order to be able to meet them without a discontinuous drop in their consumption in the future. We regard this effect to be absolute nonsense as a device for explaining why fiscal expansions do not work. We, as Keynesian consumers, expect that crowding out will not be complete so that our future incomes will rise as a result of an increased government deficit at present and do not anticipate that it will lead to higher taxes in the future. We also believe that as economists we can be somewhat arrogant and assert that we know more than laymen about how the economic system works. However, we would also be quite prepared to confess that we do not know what precisely is the relationship between increases in the Public Sector Borrowing Requirement and taxes. As a result we do not believe that even we as economists can form rational expectations of what *will* happen on average, and we do not believe laymen can, or do, either. Laymen could equally hold a Keynesian view of the functioning of the economy instead of the monetarist one usually assumed by monetarists and rational expectations enthusiasts who offer such conclusions on the failings of fiscal expansions.

(4) A fourth kind of financial crowding out was suggested by Keynes (1936, p. 120): 'With the confused psychology which often pre-

vails, the Government programme may, through its effect on "confidence", increase liquidity preference or diminish the marginal efficiency of capital, which, again, may retard other investment unless measures are taken to offset it.' The confidence effects may be of a macro or micro nature. A micro example would be where a government subsidy increase to a private firm caused a close rival, which had been anticipating benefiting from the demise of the firm, to put off investment planned to take advantage of the extra market which it was otherwise expecting. On the macro level expenditure may be reduced if firms believe that in the long run government expenditure is a bad thing for the reasons discussed above, without being aware of the objections to them, or, even if they do not themselves believe that such expenditure is *per se* undesirable, they may believe that other firms will react as though it is.

If the government has not announced that it is deliberately pursuing an expansionary fiscal policy, and attempts to float the extra debt in a series of tranches, the rise in interest rates that the first sale of debt causes may lead to expectations of a further rise when the next instalment is announced, even though, to the extent that the first instalment has increased national income, there will be an additional volume of savings which may find their way into a demand for new securities. This seems to have been the problem that Mr Denis Healey, the then UK Chancellor of the Exchequer, was facing in 1975–7. Since would-be purchasers of gilts did not know what new heights interest rates might reach when the new instalments were floated there was a tendency for gilt rates to rise steeply until Minimum Lending Rate was raised to provide some indication of the effective rate of interest which the *government expected* to have to pay. This then led to a fall in gilt rates and rapid over-subscription of new issues when they were made.

The kind of money market behaviour just described leads us to an important point about financial crowding out. It does not necessarily arise because of any actual shortage of cash which the private sector *could* use to purchase government debt. Such financial resources may exist in principle but their owners choose to hold on to them for what they believe to be sound liquidity premium reasons. If a government deficit expansion occurred at the same time as, or actually promoted, a reduction in liquidity preference it could be financed with no rise in interest rates at all. But when a large debt issue is announced speculators do not know what is going to happen to interest rates. All they can look at are past experiences and signals from monetary authorities. If the latter indicate that they will act, if necessary, as residual purchasers of long-dated debt in order to prevent a rise in interest rates, the new securities may find a ready market at existing interest rates. But if no such indication is provided the kind of experience of the UK in the later 1970s may be repeated: a late government signal of a somewhat higher rate may moderate an even higher rate which had emerged on the announcement of the forthcoming gilt issue. It will thus provide speculators with a history to look back on in which public sector deficit expansions that are not accompanied by an expansion in the money supply lead to a net rise in interest rates. If the monetary authorities had provided appropriate cues an entirely different picture could have been observed and used as a basis for expectation formation.

This section has attempted to show that the extent to which an increased budget deficit will serve merely to displace private expenditure is not independent of the composition of the extra net government spending or the state of confidence in money markets. Conventional discussions of crowding out, based on the stable functions of IS–LM diagrams and extreme aggregation, ignore both of these points. To the extent that participants in money markets are affected in their behaviour by the arguments derived from such discussions evidence will tend to be generated which supports the conventional view which is in fact merely a special case of the more general analysis we have proposed. Sometimes even the conventional IS–LM analysis is misused and we cannot end the discussion of crowding out without some comments on some of the IS–LM treatments of the subject.

10.4 CROWDING OUT IN IS–LM MODELS

In many orthodox texts the differences between monetarists and Keynesians over fiscal policy, monetary policy, and crowding out, are often said to amount to a debate over whether or not the LM curve is vertical, for a vertical LM curve quite obviously implies complete crowding out. This seems to be a mistaken way of looking at things. To put it bluntly, the Keynesian view proposed in this and other chapters is completely at odds with the neoclassical 'Keynesian' IS–LM approach to macroeconomics, while IS–LM analysis should also be rejected by monetarists as being irrelevant to an exposition of monetarism.

The IS–LM methodology deals with a world of stable behaviour functions in order meaningfully to separate real and financial markets. Our analysis of the nature of a monetary economy in chapter 8 indicates that such attempts at separation can be misleading. We have shown that confidence shifts are all-important in determining the volume of crowding out associated with a given fiscal expansion. We have emphasized, too, that the magnitude of displacement effects depends on the compositions of aggregates affected by a change in the public sector deficit. IS–LM analysis cannot allow anything but an aggregate treatment of crowding out and misses such subtleties.

In monetarist models long-run real magnitudes are independent of both monetary and fiscal matters. Eventually, in the absence of disturbances, real income is thought to settle down at that output level associated with the so-called natural rate of unemployment (see chapters 14 and 15). Although the monetarist assumption of a negligible interest elasticity in the demand for money implies a vertical LM curve, in the long run the point where this meets the horizontal axis is determined by underlying real forces. Given the rate of monetary growth, adjustments in the price level are assumed to bring about the real rate of interest necessary for equilibrium at the natural rate of output. This makes the notion of the IS curve seem rather irrelevant in equilibrium. In the long run there is no curve as such, merely a point of intersection with the vertical LM curve, a point which shifts as the price level adjusts and generates an appropriate real rate of interest. As in our Keynesian view, the two 'curves' are interdependent, but for entirely different reasons and with different results.

Neoclassical 'Keynesians' sometimes use their chosen framework to derive bizarre anti-Keynesian conclusions on crowding out, owing to a failure to appreciate how wealth effects work and how they should be incorporated within IS–LM diagrams. Blinder and Solow (1974, p. 53), for example, reach the conclusion that under certain conditions 'the net impact of an additional government bond is contractionary'. If these conditions prevail the fall in income will provide a signal for a further reflation. The additional sale of government debt that this will involve causes the process to repeat, reducing national income still further; and so on. This example of a negative multiplier is argued with the aid of an IS–LM diagram similar to figure 10.1.

Initially the economy is in the equilibrium position implied by E_0, the intersection of IS_0 and LM_0. The expansion of the government deficit shifts the IS curve out to the right to IS_1, with the interest rate rising as the necessary bonds are sold and activity increases. Blinder

and Solow suggest that these bonds represent an increase in wealth and
'as long as the wealth effect on the demand for money is positive the
LM curve shifts upwards to LM_2' (p. 52). They then suggest that the
shift in the LM curve

> mitigates the increase in income caused by the original government
> spending. Of course the new bond issue also has positive wealth
> effects on consumption, raising the IS curve further, to IS_2. In princi-
> ple, then, when deficits are financed by bonds, E_2 may lie either to the
> right or to the left of E_1. If it lies to the left the bond financed increase
> in spending is ultimately perversely deflationary, though it may take
> a long time to become apparent (1974, pp. 52–3).

Their analysis incorporates two important flaws, in addition to the
obvious one that they should use E_0 as the reference point, not E_1,
when discussing whether or not the end result is deflationary. First,
even if one accepts that wealth effects cause the curves to move
around, they have neglected the negative wealth effects due to the
capital losses sustained by existing bond-holders when the rate of
interest rises. These, as we have observed before, are likely to dominate
where the existing stock of debt is large relative to the increment: what

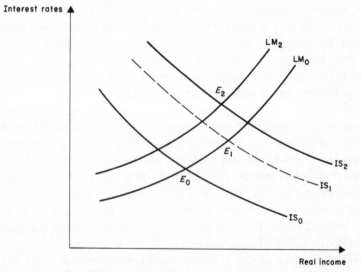

Figure 10.1 *The effects of increases in real government expenditures
financed by bonds on short-run equilibrium positions of IS–LM curves (after
Blinder and Solow (1974) p. 53)*

matters is not the number of bonds but the value of their total stock. Second, they do not realize that whatever wealth effects occur are already incorporated into the curves IS_1 and LM_0. Buyers of debt are only more wealthy to the extent that they expect to earn a return which formerly was not available. In this way they are just like purchasers of consumer goods or investment goods when they shift their spending propensities as a result of a change in confidence. Since, with given expectations about interest rates, demand can *only* be increased when some agents or the government decide to spend more, it is not possible to *move along* a given curve without such wealth effects occurring. Hence the curves must already incorporate any wealth effects. Blinder and Solow are double-counting wealth effects and, worse still, their wealth effects may have the wrong sign.

10.5 CONCLUSION

This chapter has been concerned with whether a fiscal expansion which is not accompanied by an expansionary monetary policy will succeed in raising aggregate demand or whether it will merely displace an equal amount of private expenditure. It has been shown that the answer depends very much on the nature of the additional government net expenditure – industrial subsidies and income tax reductions, for example, having completely different effects – and on the expectational environment in which the government attempts to finance its deficit. Physical crowding out may occur independently of any financial effects even at less that full employment if the extra expenditure makes demands on sectors where there are bottlenecks, so again we find the composition is all-important.

So long as crowding out is incomplete a bond-financed fiscal expansion will serve to raise demand and, if it affects confidence favourably, may be discontinued having served a pump-priming role because private expenditure will have been stimulated. It should be added that any autonomous increase in private expenditure could crowd out other private expenditure in both, or either of, the senses of the term. Consumption expenditure could crowd out private sector investment through its demands for credit or for inputs, but so long as it is incomplete, and does not harm the long-run productive position of the economy because pump-priming effects on future investment outweigh current capacity losses, this does not seem to matter. If it is believed that there is no involuntary unemployment then complete physical crowding out will always occur when expenditure is increased by the public or private sectors .

Tom Wilson (1979) has recently objected that many of the discussions of crowding out are rather futile since if financial crowding out is a problem then monetary expansion can be used to finance an increased budget deficit. This may be so with some governments but those of a monetarist inclination may refuse to expand the monetary base through fear of inflation, despite mounting unemployment. If financiers familiar with conventional discussions then conclude that a higher government deficit will mean an increase in interest rates then crowding out on a large scale may occur due to a speculative withholding of funds. It is to be hoped that the less conventional analysis of this chapter may suggest ways in which governments who feel constrained by monetary targets can, nonetheless, quietly pursue an expansionary fiscal policy and reduce unemployment. Financial crowding out effects are due largely to the direction of budgetary expansion being unwisely chosen or to adverse expectational effects rather than any objective shortage of finance.

11

Speculation and Financial Instability

11.1 INTRODUCTION

Changes in the relative yields of durable assets, both physical and financial, are of central importance in monetary theory. Changes in yields, both actual and expected, lead to changes in capital values as wealth-holders trade until marginal returns to holding assets are equalized. Where relative prices and yields of assets are uncertain maximizing agents have to speculate. The need consciously to speculate and the scope for mistakes due to speculation to have dramatic implications are particularly great where the gains and losses from valuation changes may vastly out-weigh income streams over a long period. In this chapter the aim is to look at the processes and possible consequences of speculation, with particular attention being devoted to the extensions of Keynes' work made by Minsky (1975).

Speculative activity and equilibrium analysis are fundamentally incompatible. As Shackle has repeatedly pointed out, asset prices are held where they are at any moment because many decision-takers expect them to be somewhere else in the near future. The person who holds her wealth as a time deposit in a bank and gets a lower rate of interest than a government security may be making an expensive mistake if bond prices rise in the near future. However, by holding her wealth in a bank deposit she may avoid the expensive mistake of buying bonds and then finding that their price falls with a rise in the rate of interest. If the rate of return on bonds fails to rise the expectations of cash-holders will tend to be revised and they will purchase bonds, whereupon bond prices rise and they enjoy a capital gain, confirming their opinions that they were right to abandon the belief that it would be best to hold cash as bond prices were about to fall. Having impressed this inherent tendency towards change upon our readers we can now proceed to a more detailed analysis.

The discussion is divided into four main sections, followed by a brief conclusion which serves as a bridge to chapter 12 where there is a case study investigation of some of the bank failures of the 1970s in the light of the theories we are about to examine. Section 11.2 considers the theory of speculation contrasting the Keynesian view that it is destabilizing with the conventional assumption that it reduces price fluctuations. Section 11.3 attempts a clarificatory exposition of Minsky's theory of investment, which shows how shifts in confidence affect the volume of investment and degree of indebtedness of a firm. The analyses of sections 11.2 and 11.3 are then brought together in section 11.4 to illustrate Minsky's theory of systemic fragility. Section 11.5 points out a number of features of modern financial systems that may help to explain why the disasters predicted by Minsky's theory are often avoided.

11.2 CLASSICAL AND KEYNESIAN APPROACHES TO SPECULATION

Keynes' (1936, pp. 155–6) conclusion that prices in speculative markets are determined by participants attempting to guess what the average opinion expects average opinion to be, concerning short-run pricing rather than long-run yields, is in sharp contrast to the classical theory of speculation. In classical approaches traders are assumed to be specialists who attempt to predict the price level warranted by the underlying supply and demand conditions in a single market. Supply and/or demand conditions are implicitly assumed to be variable in the short run, but variable in a regular way: i.e. there are no discontinuities other than those which accord with some known probability distribution. A commonly given example is the grain speculator who buys at harvest time in the hope of selling at a higher price later on in the year when other people's stocks have run down. She thus helps to keep up demand relative to supply when the latter has increased dramatically owing to the harvest, stopping the price from collapsing, while she prevents the price from rising later in the year as she runs down her stocks on the expectation of prices falling somewhat at the next harvest. Such traders reduce price fluctuations to a minimum if their predictions tend to be correct, as indeed they will be if they are the only holders of buffer stocks and if their experience has endowed them with a knowledge of particular kinds of irregularities occurring on either side of the market. In the classical model no-one holds the product who is not a professional trader in the market or about to *use* it in production or consumption.

When discontinuities occur due to wars or substantial harvest failures (such as that of Russia in 1973) existing buffer stocks may be wholly inadequate to match supply flows and demands without a rise in price outside the usual narrow range of fluctuations. The professional speculators are in a new situation in which they lack experience upon which to base their stockholding policies. As a result there is no guarantee that they will all interpret the situation in the same way. They will watch what happens in the market to see how others have gauged the situation. When they do this they are all taking their cues from each other and initial price adjustments will be provoked by a minority of adventurous speculators adjusting the rate at which they unload/purchase stocks in the market.

Once prices have begun to move beyond their usual ranges of fluctuation any attempts of professional traders to continue to try to assess the price warranted by the new real conditions will be frustrated by the activities of a new breed of non-specialist holders of stocks, identified by Irwin (1937), in a much neglected paper, as 'movement traders'. This group are essentially hedging speculators attempting at all times to increase the value of their portfolios by switching them into whichever markets happen to be rising most rapidly. They only enter markets where prices are already on the move. As non-specialists they are not concerned with the price level warranted by existing conditions. Instead of attempting to predict it they simply sell out when the market stops rising or begins to rise less rapidly than another market.

Participation in markets by movement traders may make prices prone to rapid fluctuation once professional traders have started prices moving and prevent the attainment of whatever equilibrium value would have been warranted by underlying genuine supply and demand conditions. Irwin provided a neat analogy to illustrate the problem: in 1919 a crowded troopship returning to New York was almost capsized after the lookout boy shouted that he could see the Statue of Liberty, for nearly all the troops rushed to what had been indicated by the boy to be the landward side of the ship.

Once a professional trader becomes aware that the exceptional demand for her asset stock arises not only from the conventional users of the product whose flow supply has suffered a relative reduction but also from movement traders, she is forced to speculate in the manner described by Keynes unless she wants to sacrifice income possibilities. Since movement traders have no use for the asset the moment its price ceases to rise, and because they cannot all take their profits simultaneously without bringing about a fall in price, the professional speculator will maximize her return if she attempts to predict *turning points* instead of warranted prices. In a world of discontinuities it will not be safe to presume that turning points will fall within a regular range (which converges to the warranted price in the case of perfect classical speculation); rather, as Keynes observed, success will indeed depend on guessing correctly what the average opinion expects the average opinion to be. All the while movement traders, who have no opinions on price levels, will be tending to confuse matters. When markets are subjected to disturbances of unusual magnitudes prices are likely, then, to fluctuate substantially and if some traders are making profits from price movements others will be making money losses. When losses are made they may be so severe as to entail bankruptcies, which represent further discontinuities, as was shown in chapter 9. It seems safe to assume that the wider the band of price fluctuations, the greater the likelihood of bankruptcies.

11.3   MINSKY'S THEORY OF INVESTMENT

It is perfectly possible to follow the analysis of a Minskian financial instability cycle in the next section on the basis of the arguments of the previous section and chapters 8 and 9, without examining Minsky's attempt to show graphically how much investment a company will undertake and the ratio of internal to external finance. However, it seems important to present a concise outline of his theory at this juncture in order to make life easier for those of our readers who trouble to investigate primary sources to which we refer. Minsky's exposition of his own theory is none too clear in his (1975) book, being marred by misprints and unhelpful graph-labelling. This section attempts to remedy these deficiencies and also to show how the theory can be adapted to cover banks in a way which helps make clear the layered nature of modern financial structures. Minsky's main diagram is shown in our revised form in figure 11.1.

Notes

(1) QQ is a rectangular hyperbola showing how much investment can be financed internally at different prices.

(2) DPK_1 and DPK_2 show the firm's demand price for capital func-

tions under, respectively, relatively pessimistic and relatively optimistic expectations, given the current cost of new assets (PI) and
the capitalized value of expected earnings per unit of investment in
the proposed schemes *(PK)*. If *PI* > *PK* no new assets will be
purchased. These curves slope down to the right as a result of
diminishing returns to expansion and increasing perceived risk
due to expansion in a particular market. Minsky labels them
borrower's risk curves when he really means that their shapes are
dependent on borrower's risk – in this case the risk to managers of
losing their jobs and value of any stocks they hold in the company
should their investments be unsuccessful.

(3) *SPK₁* and *SPK₂* show the supply price of finance functions facing
the firm under, respectively, relatively pessimistic and relatively
optimistic expectations about *PK* by would-be lenders of money.
MSPK₁ and *MSPK₂* show the respective marginal cost of finance
curves under alternative expectational states. The slope of these
curves is *dependent* on perceived lender's risk – of the lender losing
her own money. Minsky suggests that they will only tend to slope
upwards to the right of the intersection of *QQ* and *PIPI* because
the company will not be worried about losing its internally generated funds.

(4) *I₀* is the maximum volume of investment which can be financed,
given *PI*, without resort to external finance. In the light of the
Cambridge Controversies in the Theory of Capital, discussed by

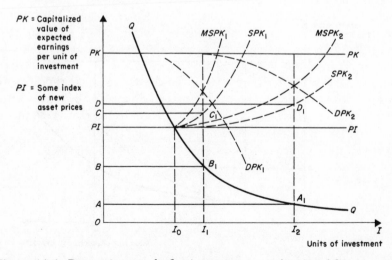

Figure 11.1 *Determinants of a firm's investment and external finance ratio*

Harcourt (1972), we are rather wary of speaking about quantities of 'investment' in a world of heterogeneous capital goods. The lack of an obvious index for quantifying investment also poses problems for PK and PI unless we assume we are dealing with firms that only use one particular production method regardless of their scale of output. The revision of Minsky's model shown in figure 11.2 is immune from such difficulties and enables much simpler labelling of axes.

(5) I_1 is the maximum volume of investment the firm will wish to undertake in a relatively pessimistic expectational state. Borrowed funds amount to $BPI.OI_1$ and interest charges on these are $CPI.OI_1$. If the investment turns out to be successful and not to suffer from diminishing returns PK will not fall and profits will be equal to $CPK.OI_1$.

(6) I_2 is the maximum volume of investment the firm will wish to undertake to maximize profits in a relatively optimistic expectational state. Borrowed funds will be $API.OI_2$ and interest payments will be $DPI.OI_2$. If PK does not fall profits will be equal to $DPK.OI_2$.

It is evident from this that, in the example shown, in the relatively pessimistic state external financing accounts for only a small fraction of a relatively small volume of investment, whereas in the optimistic state it accounts for well over half of a much greater expenditure. Although, with an increase in confidence, a substantial increase in

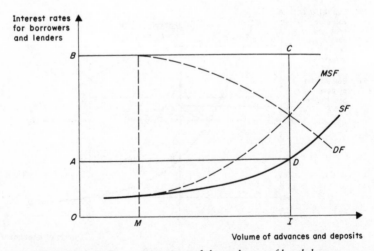

Figure 11.2 *Determination of the volume of bank loans*

investment can be achieved with little or no increase in the interest *rate* on loans (in fact it falls in the example shown) the *total* of interest charges rises dramatically. This will not be a problem if expectations do not turn out to have been over-optimistic but, if they have been, a failure to meet fixed interest loan commitments will entail bankruptcy. The problem is that during a boom 'the popular estimation of both of these risks, both borrower's and lender's risk, is apt to become unusually and imprudently low' (Keynes, 1936, p. 145).

Minsky's theory can be adapted to cover banks by recognizing that a bank's demand for finance will depend on its perceptions of the risks entailed in lending the money to someone else, perceptions which manifest themselves in the shapes of the *supply* prices of capital curves in figure 11.1. The bank's supply of finance function depends on the willingness of other agents to lend it money. In the case of secondary banks and other financial intermediaries these 'other agents' may be other banks – i.e. we have a layering of interdependent supply and demand for finance functions which may be prone to instability as expectation of possible yields shift. An adaptation of Minsky's theory to cover banks is shown in figure 11.2.

Notes

(1) *DF* is the bank's demand for funds curve, whose shape is dependent on the risks it perceives of defaults by borrowers and withdrawals by deposit-holders. When perceived risk falls this curve swings out towards the right. The perceived risk of the bank has this dual nature as a result of it borrowing short to lend long.

(2) *SF* and *MSF* are the bank's supply of finance and marginal cost of supplies of finance curves, the shapes of which are dependent on the perceived risks of lenders of funds to the bank. These curves will shift to the right if perceived risks fall.

(3) *QA* is the rate of interest promised to suppliers of funds, the amount of interest which must be paid being equal to *OADI*.

(4) *OB* is the rate of interest that has been negotiated on average, for the volume of lending *OI* that the bank makes in attempting to maximize profits. The volume of interest charges which borrowers must pay is equal to *OBCI*. If the borrowers do not default then the bank's profit will amount to *ABCD*.

(5) The ratio *OM/OI* is the ratio of the bank's capital base *OM* (the equivalent to *QQ* in figure 11.1) to its deposits. As the perceived risks fall *OI* will increase, implying that should withdrawals,

losses or defaults occur the bank will be less able to meet them. Thus, just as in the case of the company which increases its gearing ratio when confidence increases, the bank's position will become increasingly *fragile*, its survival depending on its expectations not turning out to be unduly optimistic.

11.4 MINSKY'S THEORY OF SYSTEMIC FRAGILITY

Shifts in confidence and expectations of price movements cause shifts in portfolios since they affect the willingness of industrial and financial firms to borrow or lend funds. Portfolio shifts then affect asset prices, causing futher adjustments of expectations. Minsky's central theme is that the combination of his theory of investment and Keynes' theory of speculation leads to a theory of irregular, speculatively generated, trade cycles, in which financial developments amplify or cause swings in the level of production and employment.

Consider the case of an economy in which there is substantial unemployment and where expectations are suddenly given a boost by some shock, such as the discovery of offshore oil deposits. Increases in investment, both actual and expected, to exploit the oil cause other firms to reduce their estimates of the likelihood of failure in given projects and their demand for finance schedules (cf. figure 11.1) to shift out to the right. To expand their investment they increase their borrowing. Gearing finance is cheaper than equity finance but entails fixed interest payment obligations as a cost. They expect that higher profits on their existing and prospective ventures will cover this. Finance can be raised without driving up the rate of interest if there is increasing confidence amongst those who possess idle balances. The latter either purchase debentures directly or purchase other financial assets whose sellers then purchase the debentures. Interest rates may even fall if, initially, the supply of finance schedule shifts to the right faster than that for the demand for finance.

Rises in income cause more people to have bank accounts, and cheque payments become more acceptable. This means that both the credit base of the clearing banks and the velocity of circulation may rise. With the increase in activity new market niches for specialist kinds of finance will be exploited by secondary banks. These will obtain their funds by borrowing from other banks – i.e. acting as intermediaries – and from depositors who are prepared to lend them their money in return for higher rates of interest, despite their less well established reputations.

However, as the boom gains hold prices may begin to rise due to bottlenecks in the supplies of factors, raw materials and stocks of foreign exchange (causing the currency to depreciate and import prices to rise). If profit margins are maintained this will encourage further gearing issues as the real value of corporate debt falls, including some issues on the expectation of further rises in money, if not real, profits from which interest payments can be met. There will be a feeling amongst companies that nothing can go wrong, of excessive confidence, of *euphoria*. Rising prices will also encourage others to seek inflation-proof ways of holding wealth. Commodity and property speculation, along with speculation in exchange markets, may then increase, bringing about expected price increases in these assets and encouraging market entry by movement traders. Where purchases have been financed by borrowing, rising asset prices will increase collateral values and make yet more borrowing attractive, with companies using higher-interest sources of finance, if necessary, on the assumption that even though yields from assets may be poor (or negative if they involve storage costs) they will be resaleable at a higher value at the time when loan repayments fall due. 'Lumpy' investment projects, such as the purchases of supertankers, which are usually paid for in instalments to spread risks, may be ordered without their buyers having troubled to arrange supplies of finance for later payments.

This boom situation can be brought to a sudden halt by a number of means. First, some of the investment schemes may be exposed as unsound even when money returns are still rising and bankruptcies may spread doubts about other, related, firms. Second, speculation in property and commodities such as gold which are not easily reproducible may begin to direct demand away from produced-goods sectors or may raise the cost of paying by instalments, or refunding loans, faster than had been expected. Third, there may be a slow-down in the rise of certain asset prices as some holders judge that such rises cannot go on much further because yields (e.g. land rent) have failed to rise in line with prices. The slow-down in price increases will encourage movement traders to sell out but they cannot all do this simultaneously without causing a fall in asset prices. Fourth, as a general point it should be emphasized that where non-specialists are entering markets and there is an urgency in the need to trade before asset prices rise, mistakes will be made on a larger scale than usual and doubtful assets may appear on sale. In a state of rapid change it will be difficult to keep track of whether less reliable customers of banks are not engaged in some form of deception. Fifth, companies may simply run out of investment ideas and wish to consolidate their existing positions while trying to spot new trends.

Once a reversal in price changes and investment demand has started it will be difficult to stop, owing to the layered nature of debt in the economy. A fall in property prices may leave property companies unable to refund debt with secondary banks as they had been expecting to, causing secondary banks to fail. This will cause clearing banks, who have lent them money on the interbank market, to suffer capital losses, while secondary bank depositors may have to default on their obligations elsewhere. This could cause a general scramble for liquidity: failing property companies will have their assets sold off, causing a further decline in prices; secondary bank depositors may be unwilling to trust even clearing banks as safe places to hold their wealth when they withdraw it from the secondary banks in case these fail. In short, the supply of finance dries up just as the decline in real expenditure due to a collapse of business confidence increases the deficit of the corporate sector and its need for finance.

If increases in unemployment are accompanied by falling money wages this, by causing a fall in purchasing power, will only tend to bring about a fall in prices in the produced-goods sector. If falling goods prices cause consumers to act as movement traders and hold on to their money so long as its value is rising, matters will only be made worse. The more prices fall the greater the real burden of fixed money debt payments and the greater the possibility of bankruptcy even for companies who have maintained their gross real profit streams (because their gross *money* profits are falling). As we noted in chapter 9, in a complex inside money economy the real balance effect (now just nullified by movement trading against produced goods!) may be a poor and inefficient stabilizing force. However, we will not be surprised should neoclassical economists attempt to point out that if the supply of inside money can easily be destroyed in a Minskian crash then, from somewhere, in amongst the debris, flexible wages would provide a full employment equilibrium solution by bringing about a real balance effect on the remaining supply of outside money.

11.5 MODERATING FACTORS IN MODERN FINANCIAL STRUCTURES

The picture suggested by the previous section – that in a multi-layered debt structure the effects of the financial multiplier may amplify any initial shifts in demand caused by the normal income multiplier when investment changes – seems somewhat less alarming once certain other features of highly developed systems are noted. In considering these we should emphasize that while they *may* be sufficient to prevent frequent disasters they cannot necessarily be relied upon to perform such a function.

First, the downward inflexibility of money wages prevents a downward flexibility in the prices of current outputs of an economy. This is of vital importance if debt interest commitments are fixed in money terms, since a proportionate fall in money wages and prices may bring about bankruptcies even if firms' gross incomes are constant in real terms.

Second, modern corporations tend increasingly to be conglomerates in structure, so losses due to speculation in one division may be borne by other divisions that have surpluses owing to more cautious behaviour and/or profits generated by the expansion of demand in the real economy which have simply been added to reserves. Minsky's approach tends to assume that additions to corporate funds automatically get spent on new investment schemes with very little time lag. He is thus ignoring work on the theory of the growth of the firm by Penrose (1959, 1971) and Richardson (1964) which suggests that often firm growth is constrained by a shortage of managerial expertise, rather than by finance, once market opportunities have been perceived. Of course, if euphoria manifests itself in a failure to recognize such managerial limitations then we can expect precisely the kind of ill-considered behaviour which Minsky puts at the centre of his theory.

Third, if the financial system is decomposable (see Simon, 1969) into sub-units that are, nearly enough, separate from each other, it is entirely conceivable that dramatic crashes in one area may fail to feed through to the economy in general. For example, if secondary bank funds consist largely of deposits which otherwise would have rested in clearing banks (as opposed to interbank loans), and if secondary banks lend not to the real sector but against the speculative purchasing of existing assets as inflation hedges, then a secondary bank crash need not harm the flow of finance to productive activities. The failure of the secondary banks may be caused by a transfer of their deposits to the clearing banks, so the latter only suffer if the value of their investments falls. Those who are hardest hit are the secondary bank depositors and property company creditors who are slow to see what is happening. If their demands on current output are trivial in relation to their wealth any wealth effects on demand will be small and may be partly offset by those of successful speculators who bought at the bottom and sold out in time. Such decomposability is possible in theory, but there is always the danger that falling property and bank share prices will filter through more generally and that there will be a run on clearing banks that is not warranted, given the latter's more balanced asset portfolios.

Fourth, some cushioning may be provided by clearing banks not being fully loaned up just in case companies choose to make use of hitherto unused overdraft facilities – though if the banks have not left sufficient slack to cope with many companies wishing to do this simultaneously expectations may be disappointed.

Fifth, a crisis may be averted due to prompt action by the Central Bank as lender of last resort. In the US, for example, the Federal Reserve Board keeps a watchful eye out for problem banks and is prepared to step in at an early stage to buy the good assets of weak institutions. If this rediscounting activity is insufficient the Federal Deposit Insurance Corporation steps in and pays sound banks to take over weak institutions, including the bad assets of those institutions. Effectively this means that all deposits in banks are insured instead of merely the first $40,000 of each account that the law decrees banks must insure for their customers.

Sixth, it is important to recognize that clearing banks may support other financial intermediaries to avoid enforcing their liquidation, being supported in this by the Central Bank if they are fully loaned up. A good example of this concerns the real estate investment trusts (REITs) in the early 1970s. Following the collapse of the Penn Central Railroad in 1970 the REITs could not borrow in the commercial paper market without arranging for bank loan backup commitments in case of any refunding problems. When the commercial paper market dried up in 1974 due to the failure of the Franklin Bank the banks honoured their commitments, restructuring their portfolios at a loss on their income accounts to avoid losing even more on their capital accounts. Thus whereas at the end of 1972 REITs had $7.0 billion bank debts and $4.0 billion open market paper debts, at the end of 1974 they had $11.5 billion bank debts and a mere $0.7 billion open market paper debts.

These fifth and sixth factors combined meant that despite the collapse of a number of banks and of the US property market in 1974 no bank depositors or significant creditors of failed property companies were forced to take a loss.

Seventh, fiscal intervention helps to stabilize both the financial and real sectors of the economy, as well as automatic stabilization as increasing transfer payments cause the public sector deficit to rise. In any period the net acquisitions of financial assets by the Government, Personal, Corporate and Overseas sectors must sum to zero. Hence an increase in government debt sales to finance a higher deficit may find a ready market from funds that people have decided to withdraw from the corporate sector. The government deficit can thus prop up weak firms without crowding out strong investment, either directly by subsidies or indirectly by measures to prevent expenditure from falling. To the extent that banks are prepared to lend more to avoid having their customers go bankrupt they too can help stabilize a collapsing system by shifting their loans between sectors – a reduction in borrowing by one group simultaneously increases the need of another group to borrow to maintain activity and, should the latter group wish to do this, provides the necessary funds. It is important to note, however, to avoid any Say's Law-style confusions, that a reduction in expenditure may not release any funds and the losing sector may simply run down its holdings of cash and reduce activity, with no necessary change in sector acquisitions of financial assets.

11.6 CONCLUSION

This chapter has been concerned with the ways in which speculation may tend to destabilize a monetary system instead of acting to moderate fluctuations. Against Minsky's theory of systemic fragility we have proposed a number of moderating features which may come into play to prevent extreme instability. But there is no guarantee that they will necessarily work to prevent Minskian crises from breaking out on occasions as the result of misguided attempts to make money by speculation. It should be emphasized, further, that a number of the moderating factors are aspects of government and central bank *intervention* and such stability as is observed is not necessarily the result of the free working of a market economy. We may not often go over the brink but speculative activity may bring us very near to doing so at uncomfortably close intervals. The next chapter looks in detail at some recent examples of financial failures to see how closely they fit into Minsky's speculation-centred theory. However, before turning to this task it may be appropriate to close this chapter by considering an example of how speculative activity by bank managers may also prevent a failure by a cunning appeal to mass psychology.

In the Great Depression a small Chicago bank had to find some means of stalling queues of customers, who were attempting to withdraw their deposits, while it attempted to find support. Cashiers were instructed to pay out money as slowly as possible, in small denomination notes, checking every transaction very carefully. Thus the first day of the run was survived till closing time.

Before opening the bank the next day the manager instructed his staff to pay out money as *quickly as possible* but also had them put up signs outside, requesting customers to queue in the streets. As a result the early morning queue was rapidly paid off and the length of the queue reduced to a barely noticeable minimum. There was no signs of chaos inside the bank, and customers passing by assumed the run was over and left their desposits in the bank instead of going inside to withdraw them. Thus the bank survived and expectations were self-fulfilling. If speculation *always* worked like this, Minsky would hardly have felt it necessary to write his book and, hardly surprisingly, this example is one that we owe to Milton Friedman's television series *Free to Choose*, in which the unimpeded working of markets is shown to lead inexorably to coherence rather than chaos.

12

A Case Study Investigation of Minsky's Financial Instability Hypothesis

12.1 INTRODUCTION

Perceptive readers may be suspicious that the title of this chapter contains a methodological contradiction: it seems to imply that an atomistic approach will be taken in the evaluation of what is a systemic theory. In Minsky's theory the economy as a whole is subject to waves of optimism and pessimism. These alternations of prevailing mass psychology are reflected in the asset and liability structures of an *intensely financial* economic system in which money is much more than just a veil over real variables. We thus get a succession of financial states alternating from robust to fragile: in the euphoria of a boom the financial sphere is characterized by very rapid credit expansion and the layering of financial transactions, with the increasing importance of fringe banks and risky liability structures. There will be a rising ratio of bonds to equities involving fixed interest obligations in future, and the financing of long investments by short loans which generate cash flow and refunding obligations for the future. Any interruption to the growth of the system will give a sudden turn to the financial state, bringing about a 'debt deflation'.

In looking at cases of bank failure in this chapter we attempt to set them in the context of the system as a whole, so as to capture the spirit of the Minskian approach while providing details of how particular financial institutions came to fail. In section 12.2 we provide an overview of the bank failures and financial climate of the mid-1970s showing that it was very much a world-wide problem. Section 12.3 contains more detailed examinations of five failures. The first four are examples of isolated banks where prompt intervention by the authorities or other (rival or parent) banks prevented the shock waves from spreading out too far and reduced the scope for adverse wealth effects. The fifth case, while occurring at much the same time, is almost perfectly in accordance with Minsky's systemic view but, again, *intervention* prevented the crash from spreading to engulf the whole system. Given that, despite the many financial failures of the mid-1970s, the 'sky did not fall' (to use one of Minsky's phrases), section 12.4 considers what policy lessons are to be learnt from the events. It is followed by a brief but far-reaching conclusion.

12.2   AN OVERVIEW OF DEVELOPMENTS IN THE POSTWAR FINANCIAL SYSTEM.

Since it is not easy to quantify shifts in mass psychology or structural complexity, probably the best way of getting a systemic perspective on the cases we examine is to view episodes of financial instability together rather than separately, and in their historical context. The US has perhaps the longest postwar history of monetarist policies and most episodes of financial instability. (As we shall suggest in the conclusion, attempts to control the money supply with sharp shifts in interest rates are likely to go hand in hand with financial instability.) The first major crisis was that of the Savings and Loan Associations in 1966, caused by the effects of rising bank interest rates on their deposits and property prices. There followed in 1970 the Penn Central Railroad Crisis. Here long-run investments had been financed by short-run borrowing which proved impossible to roll over, and this collapse was a severe shock for the commercial paper market. The largest crisis came in the 1973–5 period. This crisis was, for the first time since the Great Crash of 1929, a world-wide affair, as is clearly shown in the League of Bank Losses reproduced as Table 12.1.

To understand the world-wide nature of the mid-1970s crash it is important to recognize how interlinked the world financial markets had become, and, perhaps more significantly, how in 1973, for the first time since the war, all of the major OECD countries had been experiencing boom conditions simultaneously. Greater coupling together of finance markets and the rise in importance of multinational corporations meant that more companies were of a viable size to speculate against movements in currency parities by switching their funds around the world. Divergences in growth rates, and in inflation and balance of payments positions, caused the break-up of the Bretton Woods parity system in 1971 and its successor, the Smithsonian agreement, rapidly collapsed. The world became one of floating exchange rates with increased scope for profits and losses due to speculation. The convergence of OECD growth directions and common experiences of accelerating inflation caused an increased demand for commodities, both for use in production and as inflation hedges. The commodity price boom appears to have been worsened by movement trading (see Bird, 1981) and many companies got their fingers severely burned through futures trading in a state where past experiences provided little guidance as to the likely behaviour of commodity prices and relative exchange rates.

The scope for speculation was given a further twist by the OPEC oil price rise and energy crisis of 1974. The inability of OPEC countries to spend their increased earnings on consumption or the development of their thinly populated countries put a brake on the boom. With the dollar and sterling simultaneously the most common means of payment for oil and currencies of countries with the weakest balance of payments positions it was not at all clear which currencies and financial centres the OPEC members would use for lending back their oil revenues to the rest of the world to finance the oil-induced balance of payments deficits. Hence currency instability increased while the demands for new goods, property and commodities fell. Experts were not agreed as to whether or not the lack of a lender of last resort in the Eurocurrency market would prove a further complication given that LDCs, too, had to borrow large amounts to finance oil imports.

In addition to the international ingredients of this disaster recipe a Minskian would also examine growth trends in external and multi-layered financing, as well as, like a monetarist, the growth in the credit bases of economies. Some indications are provided by the following: in Holland internal financing fell from 45.9 per cent of total financing in 1965 to 33.8 per cent in 1973; in Italy the financial deficit of the corporate sector rose from 1.9 per cent of GNP. in 1964–5 to 7.6 per cent in 1971–4; in the US the debt–equity ratio rose from 47 per cent in 1964 to 121 per cent in 1974; in the UK net liquid assets were 19.1 per cent of total assets of quoted companies in 1948, but by 1971 this figure had fallen to minus 3.6 per cent. Also in the UK bank advances rose from £7535m in 1967 to £42,728m in 1974. The last statistic is a particularly significant one, reflecting the combined effects of the Heath government's monetary expansion and its introduction of a fundamental change in banking regulations known as Competition and Credit Control (C and CC).

A detailed account of the C and CC regulations is to be found in

Table 12.1 *League of Bank Losses (Source:* The Times, *Europa X, 7 January 1975)*

Bank	Balance Sheet total	Losses	Remarks
Hessische Landesbank Girozentrale (West Germany)	DM34,000m	DM1700 (possible)	Losses through subsidiary Investitions und Handelsbank and bad loans to companies
I. D. Herstatt (West Germany)	DM2100m	DM1200m (possible)	Losses in currency dealings
Banca Privata Italiana (Italy)	—	170,000m lire (expected)	Withdrawal of deposits after the collapse of the Franklin National Bank, whose main shareholder, Michele Sundona, also owns the Banca Privata
Bau-Kreditbank (West Germany)	DM600m	DM456m	Losses due to loans to bankrupt companies
Westdeutsche Landesbank Girozentrale (West Germany)	DM54,000	DM270m	Losses in currency dealings
US National Bank of San Diego (USA)	$1200m	$45–98m (possible)	Allegedly fraudulent credit transactions with associated companies
Lloyds Bank International (UK)	£7600m	£33m	Losses in currency dealings
Schweizerische Bankgesellschaft (Switzerland)	SFr.40,500m	SFr.142m	Losses in currency dealings
Norddeutsche Landesbank Girozentrale (West Germany)	DM24.7m	DM300m	Bad Loan to Rollei
Franklin National Bank (USA)	$5000m	$59m	Losses in currency dealings
J. H. Vavasseur (UK)	£51m	£17.9m	Liquidity squeeze, decline in investments in stocks and property

Bank			
Scottish Cooperative Wholesale Society (UK)	—	£3.6–£12.6m (possible)	Losses in forward dealings on sterling CD market
London and County Securities (UK)	£129m	£16m (possible)	Price decline in stocks and property led to withdrawal of interbank deposits
Chase Manhattan Bank (USA)	$36,000m	$34m	Over-valuing of securities trading portfolio
Triumph Investment Trust (UK)	£153m	£9.7m	Liquidity squeeze
Cedar Holdings (UK)	£147m	£0.19m–£8.6m	Liquidity squeeze
Banque de Bruxelles (Belgium)	BFr.302,000m	BFr.600–1500	Losses in currency dealings
Banco Halles (Brazil)	3900m cruz	Unknown	Liquidity squeeze
Banque de Credit Internationale (Switzerland)	SF.r651m	Unknown	Withdrawal of deposits due to uncertainty concerning the future of the bank
Cannon Street Acceptances (UK)	£62m	Unknown	Liquidity squeeze, investments falling in value
Allgemeine Wirtschaftbank (Austria)	1000m schillings	Unknown	Allegedly bad loans to associated companies
Israel British Bank London (UK)	£59m	Unknown	Collapse of Israel parent company
Israel British Bank (Israel)	£Is.524m	Unknown	International liquidity crisis after Herstatt
Cosmos Bank (Switzerland)	SFr.185m	Unknown	International liquidity crisis after Herstatt
Interbank House Group, including International Bank of Grand Cayman and Sterling Bank and Trust (Cayman Islands)	$45m	Unknown	International liquidity crisis after Herstatt
Bass and Herz (West Germany)	DM70m	Unknown	Liquidity squeeze, withdrawal of deposits
Bankhaus Wolff (West Germany)	DM55m	Unknown	Liquidity squeeze, withdrawal of deposits
Frankfurter Handelsbank (West Germany)	DM114m	Unknown	Liquidity squeeze, withdrawal of deposits

At this time exchange parities were approximately: £1 = $2.35, 6 Swiss francs, 5.6 Deutschmarks.

Revell (1973). The main points of relevance to the present discussion are as follows. Free entry into non-clearing bank business was introduced. There was also a unified and extended 12½ per cent reserve assets ratio (10 per cent for HP companies), supposedly to place all banks on the same competitive footing. Previously the non-clearing banks had been controlled by the Department of Trade and Industry, while there had been close supervision of the behaviour of the clearing banks by the Bank of England. Also, in place of direct Bank of England influence on interest rates in the gilt and short markets, Minimum Lending Rate was introduced as an indirect means of affecting interest rates. A Minskian would see these developments as reflecting a misguided confidence in the stability of the banking system, born of the experiences of the postwar boom of the 1950s and 1960s. In this earlier period, however, there was little layering of credit: banks lent directly to ultimate spenders on the basis of deposits with the supervision of the Bank of England causing them to seek asset portfolios with little risk and an acceptable return. Financial layering only began to develop owing to the division of supervision between the primary and secondary money markets weakening the controls over the entry and behaviour of financial intermediaries who had spotted market niches on the lending side and then looked around for ways of financing them (i.e. the reverse of staid clearing bank behaviour). Such innovations in the UK banking system were already under way by 1971 when C and CC was introduced but C and CC, and the boom in demand for finance associated with the government's expansion, gave them a great filip.

With these modern financial developments in mind we can now turn to consider how various banks got into trouble trying to cope with them. We have chosen to study these recent cases in order to highlight any implications they have for current policy design, but readers interested in examining Minsky's theory with a broader historical perspective will find excellent material in Friedman and Schwartz's (1963) *A Monetary History of the United States* (especially chapter 7 on The Great Contraction, as a study of the US banking system, 1929–33) and Kindleberger's (1978) *Manias, Panics and Crashes*.

12.3 FIVE CASES OF FINANCIAL FAILURE

(a) *Credit Suisse*

It was disclosed in mid-April 1977 that a loss, provisionally estimated at $100m, had been made by the Chiasso branch of Credit Suisse, one of Switzerland's top three banks. It later turned out that the loss was really $869m, whereas the bank's reserves, from which it claimed it could easily cover the bad debts, were only $690m. Three managers from the branch were suspended and then, when the losses had been examined, they were all charged with criminal mismanagement and falsification of documents. There followed an immediate crisis of confidence in the banking community which, ironically, was worsened as a result of an announcement by the Swiss Bank Corporation, Swiss National Bank and Union Bank of Switzerland that they were providing, should Credit Suisse need it, a backup fund equivalent to $1185m. Even with support from the other banks Credit Suisse shares fell by 25 per cent in a rush of panic selling. Share values of the other banks fell too, and the Swiss franc dropped to its lowest level for over a year.

The losses of the Chiasso branch came about as a result of investments it had made in Liechtenstein using money from its fiduciary accounts. Fiduciary accounts are those that a bank invests for commission as it chooses, with the account-owners taking both profits and risks. Investments in Liechtenstein were chosen because there was the possibility of a higher return and hence higher commission, with the added dubious (but legal) complication of overlapping directorships between branch managers of Credit Suisse and the Liechtenstein company Texon Finanz Anstalt which handled some of the investments. The bulk of the money was invested in the International Wine and Food Establishment, a holding company controlled by the International Wine and Food Company SPA (Winefood). The problem was that the firm was not solvent and it was failing to generate sufficient cash for its Liechtenstein company to be able to pay the high interest rates it had contracted to pay on the loans.

The weakness of the Winefood investment could nonetheless have gone unnoticed for some time, for the Chiasso managers had concealed it by using two sets of 'books'. However, it rapidly came to notice when the Italian government declared a general amnesty for those tax-dodgers who, before the end of the year, repatriated illegally exported 'black money'. Many Italians, including those who feared a communist takeover or wished to benefit from the depreciation of the lire, as well as tax-evaders, banked in Switzerland near the Italian border. As a result of the amnesty the equivalent of $700m flowed back into Italy, creating a liquidity problem for banks close to the border, one of which was the Chiasso branch of Credit Suisse. It was then that the mismanagement came to light and the crisis occurred.

(b) *Lloyd's Bank International*

The fact that the Lugano branch of LBI was small and employed only sixteen people did not prevent it from losing on foreign exchange speculation in early 1974 the massive sum of £32.7m. This did not spread a lack of confidence elsewhere as Lloyds were able to cover the branch's losses from their overall reserves. However, it provides a neat illustration of the dangers of misguided speculation and, like the Credit Suisse example, raises grave doubts about the ability of head offices or even branch managers to delegate responsibility with confidence, and about scope for accurate surveillance.

Lloyds had set up their Lugano branch after seeing the potential for high profits as a result of flows of Italian money coming across the border into Lugano (around £6300m between 1960 and 1974). Marc Colombo, a Luganese with impeccable references, was hired to manage the foreign exchange department in the bank. His main dealings were in forward exchange; i.e. he sold currency forward, buying it at the spot rate when the forward contracts became due in order to cover himself and making profits on the difference.

In November 1973 Colombo sold $34m, 3 months forward, on the expectation that the US dollar would fall against the European currencies in which he had been paid. Owing to the oil crisis dollars experienced a high demand and rose. Colombo bought back the dollars to prevent himself from getting deeper into trouble. In the process he lost SFr.7m but did not report this for reasons of pride. Instead he attempted to recoup the loss by buying, with Swiss francs and Deutschmarks, $100m for 3 months forward delivery on the expectation that the dollar would continue to rise. But it did not and even after he had repurchased European currency at speed he was SFr.50m down, and would clearly have lost his job had he reported this loss. In a desperate last bid he sold $550m forward, expecting the dollar to continue falling. He was wrong yet again and was left SFr.222m (£32.7m) down.

Colombo had got into such a bad mess as a result of breaking many of the rigid rules of his employers. Officially his job was merely to manage the foreign exchange department and he was not supposed to deal forward at all. He broke the daily transaction limit of SFr.5m; he dealt with banks other than those with whom he was authorized to deal, making longer-term transactions than he should have done; he failed to cover every deal with a spot transaction as he was supposed to in order to reduce risks, since this reduced profits; he failed to report his transactions in his daily telex to head office.

Such substantial rule-breaking should have been discovered in such a small branch by the manager, Egidio Mombelli. However, Mombelli was 'overburdened with other work' and allowed Colombo almost complete freedom from supervision. LBI only discovered Colombo's over-dealing as a result of information they received from other exchange dealers. In October 1974 Colombo and Mobelli were both found guilty of the violation of Swiss banking laws and given suspended sentences. Summing up in the trial Judge Luvini described their behaviour as 'speculation – gambling, mad gambling'.

(c) *The United States National Bank of San Diego*

In June 1973 the USNB had $1 billion in deposits and was the ninth largest bank in California, the 83rd largest in the US. On 18 October 1973 it became the largest bank crash in American banking history (since overtaken by the Franklin failure). It provides a good example of a bank which failed despite its weakness having been spotted by the *Wall Street Journal* in 1969, and of a failure which did not lead to a considerable financial multiplier effect owing to the active *intervention* of the authorities (cf. section 11.5).

The 1969 *Wall Street Journal* exposé of USNB alleged that it was involved in 'incestuous' dealings with concerns controlled by the President of USNB, Mr C. Arnholt Smith, who was also a major shareholder in the bank. After its collapse 4 years later federal court papers revealed that the bank had lent almost *half* of its $600m loan portfolio to interests controlled by, or related to, Mr Smith. A further $91m had been committed in letters of credit as collateral for loans made by other banks. As much as a third of the total was reckoned to be uncollectable. The main cause of USNB's downfall was that it had given unsound loans and had financed the sale of assets at inflated prices to Smith's own company, Westgate California. Effectively Smith was fraudently building up his own corporate enterprise at the expense of the bank.

One of the great problems in the regulation of financial structures is that the complexity of accounts means that even specialist auditors may fail to spot bad loans. In the US banks have to be examined by auditors at least three times every 2 years, so between the *Wall Street Journal* exposé and its classification as a serious problem bank in November 1972 the USNB would have been subjected to three or four acceptable audits. In January 1973 the Comptroller of the Currency began another investigation of USNB, and on 23 May ordered Smith to stand down as President and Board Chairman. In the course of the investigation many of USNB's loans which had previously been considered substantial were reclassified as doubtful or losses. In all it took 15 months from its *detection* as a problem bank before USNB was declared insolvent.

Since only the first $40,000 of any single deposit had to be covered by deposit insurance, over half of USNB's $940m deposits were not covered by the Federal Deposit Insurance Corporation and had the FDIC let the bank go bust substantial losses would have been made. Rather than allow this to happen the FDIC assumed all of the $400m loans to Smith's interests, while simultaneously lending the Crocker National Bank of San Francisco $50m in order that it might take over the deposits and sound loans, keeping all USNB's offices open. For this Crocker paid $89m, receiving also a cash injection of $160m from the FDIC. By these means the worst ravages of a Minskian financial multiplier were avoided.

(d) *The Franklin National Bank of New York*

On 8 October 1974 the Franklin Bank became the largest bank failure in American history. Only 9 months before it had been the 20th largest bank in the US. Its crash also caused the failure of the Banca Private Italiana in Italy: deposits were withdrawn in a panic because the Italian bank's main shareholder, Michele Sindona, had a large share in the ownership of the Franklin. A full account of these events and their aftermath is to be found in Spero's (1980) book. In this discussion we shall concentrate on the reasons why Franklin failed rather than on how the Federal Reserve Bank managed the crisis. The failure of the bank seems only partly Minskian, since although its collapse has much to do with speculation and unwise loans these can hardly be said to be the result of euphoria. The bank got into making such unsound investments as the result of an attempt to escape from the invasion of its traditional market by making inroads into the territory of its new rivals.

During the 1950s and 1960s Franklin was a very successful bank, benefiting tremedously from its Long Island location. In this period Long Island was enjoying very rapid growth and its banks were protected against competition from the new York City banks by statute. Franklin, which was to all intents and purposes run by one man, Phillip Roth, managed to increase its assets from $78m in 1950 to over $1 billion in 1962. However, between 1960 and 1965 Long Island became a less profitable location as some of the New York banks managed to obtain licences to trade there. Roth decided to counter this by moving into the potentially lucrative New York market.

His first move – the attempted purchase of a smallish New York bank, the Federation Bank and Trust – fell through, so Roth decided simply to open Franklin branches in New York. He then had to contend with the problem of acquiring customer goodwill as a new and relatively unknown bank, and opted to specialize in the exceedingly competitive wholesale (corporate rather than general public) loan market. In attempting to cope with the problem Franklin accepted high-risk customers which were attracted by offers of prime, or near-prime, rates normally reserved for the safest of borrowers. Assets grew rapidly through this tactic but the growth was heavily and expensively funded on the interbank market, by Certificates of Deposit, and Federal Reserve money.

By 1973 this strategy was eating heavily into profits, and matters were made worse by foreign exchange losses, though the latter were kept concealed by the mangement. As a major shareholder, the Italian financier Michele Sindona was becoming worried by the way things were going and suggested that the bank should be merged with a New York financial concern, the Talcott National Corporation. Franklin's tax loss carry-forward could then be put to good use to reduce the tax bill Talcott would otherwise have as a profitable company. While the deal was being negotiated Franklin increased the scale of its operations in the risky bond and foreign exchange markets. But before the merger went through it was revealed that Franklin had made very heavy losses in suspicious circumstances on the foreign exchange markets.

After a 4-month examination by the Comptroller's office, which ended in March 1974, it became clear to the Federal Reserve that Franklin was in deep trouble and the proposed merger with Talcott was vetoed. The veto caused a collapse of confidence in Franklin and the ensuing liquidity problems forced it to borrow $110m from the Federal Reserve Bank of New York. On 10 May 1974 Franklin announced that its quarterly dividend would not be paid, and soon after revealed that its foreign exchange losses were $14m. Many of its managers had already been suspended by the Federal Reserve and most of the rest were fired, but despite this and further heavy borrowing from the Federal Reserve the Franklin National Bank was declared insolvent early in October 1974.

Franklin's failure seems to have been due almost entirely to an incompetent managerial strategy and management of its foreign exchange dealings. It was not so much the move into the New York market that was wrong but the way it was handled in the rushed attempt to acquire goodwill – the Meadowbrook National Bank, now the National Bank of North America, made the same move from Long Island to New York with a fair degree of success under better management.

(e) *The UK Secondary Bank Crisis*

On 30 November 1973 the stock exchange quotation of the London and Counties Securities group was suspended, providing the curtain-raiser to a series of collapses of secondary banks and property companies which stand in sharp contrast to the stability of the previous two decades. Minsky's theory can be used to suggest, in fact, why the earlier stability might be expected to lead to such disasters. Stability implies that banks find their reserves are not being called upon very frequently. This will make them tend to neglect the need for reserves in excess of legal requirements and experiment with inherently more fragile portfolios. Past experiences, coupled with the expansionary policies of the Conservative Government and the introduction of the new C and CC regulations, seem, in the light of Minsky's theory, to be a recipe for disaster; particularly the last factor, for free entry into banking may allow the entry not only of expertly managed new financial intermediaries but also concerns run with scant regard for banking laws. The London and Counties group were just such a result of allowing free entry into banking: they had supported their share price by internal dealings and overstated their profits, inflating their liquidity position by dealings designed to give depositors a false impression. Criminal activities aside, however, the market still seems to have been inherently prone to the kind of instability predicted by Minsky's theory. The events leading up to the crash, and the crash itself, fit the theory much more closely than any of the cases previously discussed (if those cases are each considered in isolation).

The increase in the money supply at the same time as C and CC led to a boom in consumer goods and property with the prices of the latter rising rapidly, suggesting it was a good hedge against inflation. Lending by clearing banks on the interbank market increased by 40 per cent in the first 9 months of C and CC, while borrowing on this market by secondary banking institutions trebled from £3867m in October 1971 to £11,222m in May 1973. Much of this money was then lent to property developers: between 1971 and 1973 the amount of money banks were lending to the property sector quadrupled, reaching about £5000m by the end of 1973. Because of the rapid rise in property prices many developers borrowed short money confident that, in the event of refunding not being possible, their assets could be sold at a handsome profit.

But by July 1973 the growth in the money supply and in imports was beginning to worry foreign holders of sterling and they began to sell. To stop the fall in the pound the Bank of England raised Minimum Lending Rate from 7½ per cent to 11½ per cent: this made it much more expensive for the secondary banks to borrow on the interbank market. Building society interest rates became less competitive and the resulting withdrawals caused a mortgage squeeze, putting a brake on the rise in house prices. This, and the start of the fall in price of commercial property, put developers, who had been expecting price increases to continue, into serious trouble. The current yield from property was not sufficient to pay interest on the borrowed funds. In response to a further run on sterling Minimum Lending Rate was raised to 13 per cent in November 1973. At the same time the Chancellor announced the introduction of a development gains tax on the profits of property developers. This worsened the tendency for property prices to fall and developers began to default on their loans with disastrous repercussions for the secondary banks. London and Counties were rapidly followed into liquidiation by Cornhill Consolidated, Cannon Street Acceptances, Cedar Holdings, the Triumph Investment Trust, and others.

The Bank of England then launched its 'lifeboat' support operation, pumping money into the secondary banks via the clearing bank sector. While this was beginning even the clearing banks began to experience problems. The worst affected was National Westminster whose shares fell below par, something unheard of in such a bank, owing to involvement with London and Counties. Soon, however, the existence of the lifeboat operation caused a turnround in confidence. The provision of funds to the secondary banks prevented them from having to recall loans that would have forced the sale of property at knockdown prices. By January 1975 the tide turned and the *Financial Times* Ordinary Share Index rose from 150 to over 300 in a few weeks. Clearing up the debris took much longer. By the end of 1976 still half of the 'lifeboat loans' were outstanding. The Bank of England allowed properties to be sold off in an orderly way, permitting secondary bank loans, and hence lifeboat loans, to be paid off.

Subsequent investigation revealed some disturbing pieces of information. Supervision mechanisms which had worked well in the less complex environment of the 1950s had lagged behind changes in banking systems. The discount office of the Bank of England had been short-staffed and heavily dependent on published figures. It had been accustomed to direct contact with a small number of banks but in the 1970s the number increased suddenly. Many of the smaller concerns never had any dealings at all with the discount office, relying instead on the interbank market when they were short of funds. Even those concerns that were under the watchful eye of the Bank of England took it by surprise in the crisis. This was particularly the case with Slater Walker Securities. The Bank had failed to spot some of the doubtful activities of Slater's banking subsidiary even after examining its quarterly returns. These failed to show up unsound loans or the extent to which the banking section was lending to other arms of Slater's enterprise or to owners of equity in companies to which loans were also being made. The failure of the Bank of England to ask appropriate questions in many ways explains this but one is left wondering to what extent this was an _ad hoc_ accident or whether it is in the nature of finance that the supervisory authority will always be a step behind events as people innovate and discover new tricks.

12.4 POLICY LESSONS OF THE EVENTS OF THE MID-1970s

Given that the UK came closest in the 1970s to suffering from the worst ravages of the Minskian financial multiplier it is perhaps appropriate to see what lessons the UK monetary authorities themselves learned from the crisis. These lessons are to be found in two important documents: the article on the capital and liquidity adequacy of banks in the September 1975 Bank of England _Quarterly Bulletin_, and the (UK, 1976) White Paper on the licensing and supervision of deposit-taking institutions. Let us consider their main concerns in turn.

The Bank of England paper was concerned with the importance of the availability of adequate financial capital to banks. Capital is needed by banks for two reasons: firstly, for building up their infrastructure, i.e. their premises and equipment; and secondly, to protect their depositors against the risk of loss. The paper implied that the uniform reserve ratio philosophy of c and cc was unsound. Instead of judging the adequacy of a bank's liquidity position by looking at the ratio of free capital to deposits one should look at the risk structure of the bank's assets. This view is in striking contrast with the c and cc assumption that all banks are essentially the same, and recognizes that the volatility of asset values may undermine the use of precise rules of thumb. The Bank divided up assets into three broad risk categories.

(1) *Forced sale risks*: assets with certain interest yields but uncertain capital values, such as Treasury bills, local authority bills, gilts and other public sector stocks, certificates of deposit with UK listed banks. In the two decades before c and cc it would have been most unlikely that the first three kinds of assets would have been thought of in these terms because the Bank had been pursuing a passive monetary policy keeping interest rates stable. An active monetary policy requires banks to operate with greater reserves since it increases forced sale risks.

(2) *Credit risks*: balances with other banks, advances to customers in the private sector. Since different financial intermediaries operate in different market niches it is obviously mistaken to assume they will have identical credit risks and should therefore face identical reserve requirements.

(3) *Credit and forced sale risks*: assets such as certificates of deposit with other banks, trade bills, leased assets and other portfolio investments.

Credit risks and the likelihood of forced sales of assets will vary according to the composition of bank liabilities. The obvious implication is that if we *must* have a uniform reserve ratio it should be buttressed by regular examination of the liquidity positions of banks in the light of business done, but it would be better to develop different standards for institutions with different kinds of asset and liability structures. But the case studies of the previous section imply that it may be very difficult to keep an adequate watch over what banks are doing; even with strict controls banks have still managed to deceive the regulatory bodies, be they parent or central banks.

The need for stricter controls and recognition that the US system had many advantages over c and cc also comes across in the White Paper. It proposed that there should be a legal code for banks in the UK, to be administered by the Bank of England and to replace the Bank's informal 'moral authority'. A second proposal was for a two-tier structure of deposit-taking institutions categorized as either 'banks' or 'licensed deposit-takers'. The latter would include the UK branches of overseas banks but institutions in this category would not be allowed to describe themselves as 'banks'. The second group would be subject to less exacting controls over capital and reserves to encourage entry, though these would be reassessed in the light of past management performance.

The White Paper also proposed a deposit insurance scheme up to the first £10,000 of a person's deposits. This idea was strongly opposed by the London clearing banks who held 90 per cent of the insurable deposits. They claimed they were perfectly safe and that with the Bank of England as lender of last resort no such scheme was necessary. While the clearing banks' reluctance to finance such a scheme is perhaps understandable if they believe 'lifeboat' actions will reduce their risks when their weaker competitors collapse, they seem to be ignoring the fact that large losses *did* occur despite the existence of a lender of last resort because it did not act *sufficiently rapidly*. Deposit insurance discourages withdrawals when confidence in a bank fails, thereby reducing the likelihood of its collapse and the subsequent (actual or expected) sale of its assets. The threat that such events would pose to the portfolios of other banks is thus eliminated, along with the risk of a violent domino effect. In the US the smaller concentration of banks means that failures may be more likely to occur because branch losses are less easily offset elsewhere in the group (as was possible with Lloyds International). Hence in the US there is less opposition to deposit insurance and it is not surprising that it has been made compulsory despite the existence of lender of last resort facilities.

12.5 CONCLUSION

This chapter has found much that is consistent with Minsky's financial instability hypothesis concerning the likely effects of the free working of a financial system, and also much that is consistent with the moderating mechanism proposed in the previous chapter to devices which would stop any crash from getting completely out of hand. But it should be emphasized that what stopped crashes from spreading in many cases was *intervention* and that they occurred as they did often despite the existence of strict *rules* and supervision. In the case of the UK the removal of controls seems to have aided the appearance of the secondary bank crisis. It is difficult to assess the extent to which the financial chaos of the mid-1970s *of itself* affected productive activity and employment. Even without such problems, the uncertainties associated with the oil crisis (and demand effects of higher oil prices) and rapid inflation would make us expect a decline in producer and consumer confidence, followed by falling share prices and rising unemployment. We would be rather inclined to support the idea that in this case the system was fairly decomposable and that spillover effects of the financial crisis were rather small, noting the rapid recovery of the share index once the lifeboat operation had been launched, but this is only an inclination and not based on hard evidence.

If financial structures *do* have a Minskian tendency to instability then the regulatory and support role of the Central Bank is very important. In particular, to reduce forced sale risks and scope for speculation to a minimum, it should reduce instability in interest rates. A Minskian monetary policy will not try to create a boom by lowering interest rates nor, because of the effect on asset prices, will it try to restrain activity by raising interest rates. Instead the money stock will be determined endogenously, for unexpected attempts to restrain it will lead to financial failures that will *force*, via lender of last resort action, an expansion of the money stock to stop them from getting out of hand. They are much better avoided in the first place. The implication seems to be that monetary policy should not be used to control demand and that fiscal policy, with an accommodating monetary growth to keep interest rates stable, is the appropriate tool. Minsky's interpretation of Keynesian monetary theory drives us to this conclusion not because 'money does not matter' but because in a complex financial system money has a *powerful* force and is not a mere veil over real forces. Clearly, a single country would find it difficult to implement a policy of stable interest rates unless it also controlled currency flows across its borders. Any tendency of the interest rate of the rest of the world to diverge from the one chosen would lead to speculative currency flows and the kind of exchange rate instability that, as we have seen, encourages speculation and leads to bank failures.

13

Schools of Thought in
Monetary Economics

13.1 INTRODUCTION

This book abounds with examples of disagreements between economists over causal mechanisms and policy recommendations. When faced with such controversies we have made our Keynesian biases quite clear, showing that our theories do not seem inconsistent with data about the real world. But we have often had to point to ambiguities in empirical works, e.g. those concerning the stability of the consumption function. Since the three chapters following the present one concern the most important controversy, that between monetarists and Keynesians, it may be helpful if we outline the general characteristics of the main world views held by rival groups of monetary economists and explain why a single body of thought is usually unable to win a decisive victory over all the others.

The chapter is divided up as follows. Section 13.2 is an analysis of the main beliefs of five schools of thought that are commonly identified in macroeconomic and monetary theory. Section 13.3 examines the main problems with which the economic scientist has to cope and explains why decisive victories are difficult to win in scientific disputes. Section 13.4, which is followed by a brief conclusion, combines elements of the previous two sections to show how economists with different ways of thinking can all begin with the same avowed intention – a desire to understand what Keynes was attempting to argue in his (1936) *General Theory of Employment, Interest and Money,* and the policy implications of his arguments – yet come to very different conclusions.

13.2 FIVE WORLD VIEWS IN MONETARY AND MACROECONOMICS

When the work of any monetary economist is being read it is often helpful to be able to classify him or her as being a particular kind of monetary economist at an early stage. A label that implies a certain set of beliefs likely to be held by the economist will enable a more rapid assimilation of the direction and content of the arguments being proposed, though it must be added that sometimes the blinkering brought about by a misjudged labelling of someone may cause great confusion. To enable the classification of monetary economists into particular camps table 13.1 has been constructed, but not, it must be added, without some difficulty and doubts about certain generalizations. It is as well to raise some of these before simply letting the reader examine the figure and then passing straight on to consider why such divergent views can be held.

It should first be pointed out that the group whom we call Neo Ricardian Keynesians – we have in mind such economists as Eatwell, Garegnani, Pasinetti and, when he is writing about growth, Kaldor – are often elsewhere labelled Neo Keynesians and, sometimes, even Post Keynesians. An examination of some of their recent work (e.g. Eatwell (1979), Garegnani (1979)) suggests that their extreme concern with underlying long-run forces in economies and dismissal of the importance of money and uncertainty as being central to Keynesian theory implies that they hardly warrant the title 'Keynesian' at all. By Post Keynesians we mean those economists who have attempted to take account of the central importance of the need for agents to make advance *financial* commitments with uncertain payoffs before any productive activity and employment can take place, with an emphasis on the institutional settings in which such commitments are made. This group, including ourselves, Davidson, Minsky, Shackle, and Weintraub, view Keynes' work as an essential starting point, though not a complete work by any means.

Secondly, a number of very well-known economists are difficult to fit into single categories. Joan Robinson, for example, seems to fit at various times into the Radical, Neo Ricardian and Keynesian categories. Clower and Leijonhufvud's many writings have influenced the arguments in this book considerably yet their tendencies to use Walrasian modes of analysis in formal arguments rather imply that they cannot rest easily in the Post Keynesian camp alongside the

Table 13.1 An outline of the characteristics of main schools of thought in macroeconomics and monetary theory

	Radicals	Neo Ricardian Keynesians	Post Keynesians	Neoclassical Keynesians	Monetarists
Political stance of academic economists (a spectrum of views).	Extreme left	*But there are exceptions!*			Extreme right
Attitude to government intervention in economic affairs.	Government controls essential due to inadequacies of price signals as co-ordinating device in a system where market power is unevenly distributed.		Emphasis on macroeconomic failings of market system but considerable faith in allocative properties of microeconomic free market mechanism so long as sufficient aggregate demand has been generated. Need for strong controls over banking system to prevent instability.		Government intervention unnecessary so long as appropriate pattern of property rights is provided to generate incentives. Government activity positively harmful.
Usual mode of analysis (see section 13.4).	Holistic systemic approach if aggregates have an existence not readily to be inferred from parts considered in isolation			'Hydraulic' aggregate approach with no use of micro-foundations; or 'reconstituted reductionism' with emphasis on false-trading.	Reductionist.
Outcome of disturbance to system (a spectrum of views)	Cumulative departure from original position until some kind of crisis is reached.		Tendency towards cumulating processes depends on extent of system's buffering properties relative to size of disturbance.		A new position of equilibrium.
Control of money supply	Money supply is managed to suit interests of dominant group in capitalist élite. In the UK the dominant group are financial capitalists interested in international currency flows and speculation, and the secondary group, industrial capitalists, have	Money supply (in so far as it can be defined) is dependent on the demand for money; i.e. it is endogenous. Attempts to control supply of money defined according to one definition are dangerous for system stability to the extent that they are successful but will tend to fail due to offsetting changes in other money supply definitions unless they affect demand for money.		Money supply is determined (exogenously) by central banking authorities.	

Effects of changes in the money supply.	Long-run real effects vary according to expectational effects produced in the Phillips curve effects in any regular way. In a state of extreme pessimism a short-run real response in output may be difficult to achieve by monetary policy alone since 'you cannot push on a string'.	← – – – – – – → In the long run there will be no real effects if the Phillips curve is vertical but otherwise output and employment will be affected. In the short run output will be affected unless the economy is in the 'liquidity trap'. IS–LM diagrams usually used to demonstrate what will happen.		In the long run only money variables will be affected and there will be no real changes in the system. In the short run real variables may be affected temporarily due to confusion of expectations. In the long run money is little more than a 'veil' over real events.
Employment properties of unmanaged system.	Any level of employment possible but full employment is dangerous for system stability as it gives bargaining power to the working classes which does not exist when the reserve army of the unemployed is present.	No reason why the economy should tend to have zero involuntary unemployment even with no institutional barriers to wage changes. Wage stickiness helps the attainment and preservation of high employment levels by providing anchor for price level, thus aiding expectation formation and reducing the possibility of bankruptcies.	Tendency to assume full employment when constructing growth models; otherwise seem to imply that any level of employment might occur in short run while insisting on studying long-run properties of the system.	With flexible wages, even with a binding liquidity trap floor to interest rates, the economy will, with the aid of the real balance effect, tend towards a state of zero involuntary unemployment. This conclusion assumes that behaviour functions are stable. Without flexible wages unemployment equilibrium possible. Economy tends to the natural level of employment implied by the underlying 'Walrasian equations'. Rigidities will affect this natural level.
Attitude to fiscal stabilization policies.	← – – – – – – – – Expansionary policies needed over long period due to stagnationist tendencies associated with rising marginal propensity to save; but should be used with accommodating monetary policy, in event of any major aggregate demand failure.		Emphasis on difficulties of getting extent of fiscal intervention right due to expectational shifts; 'crowd behaviour'. Bottlenecks in various sectors mean that composition of expansionary expenditure matters.	← – – – – – – → In the long run fiscal intervention is not needed due to vertical Phillips curve/self-righting properties of the system. Fiscal expansion likely to be ineffectual in short run due to crowding out if money supply not expanded to finance it. Authorities are prone to be concerned with aggregate demand rather than sectoral composition and generate unsustainable positions.

Table 13.1 An outline of the characteristics of main schools of thought in macroeconomics and monetary theory

	Radicals	Neo Ricardian Keynesians	Post Keynesians	Neoclassical Keynesians	Monetarists
Income distribution.	Historical: emphasis on class struggle, shifts in bargaining strength of major groups.	In growth theories aggregate profit share depends on growth of labour force, technical progress and savings of capitalists. Otherwise hold Radical or Post Keynesian view (usually the former).	Quasi-rent (scarcity theory). Historically determined money wage and 'normal' interest rate. Emphasis on relatively concerns of workers.	Marginal productivity theory Aggregate production functions frequently used despite logical flaws exposed in 'Cambridge Capital Controversy'.	Marginal productivity theory Trade unions affect relative wages of worker groups but not share of wages in aggregate.
Inflation and its control	Inflation comes about mainly due to shifts in costs and profit margins			Inflation is mainly a monetary phenomenon in the long run	Inflation arises due to excessively rapid growth of money supply. In so far as this comes about due to trade union pressure on Government because of 'temporary' increases in unemployment when expectations have shown to be wrong, union power should be curbed.
			Indexation may spark off hyper-inflation if there is a shock to the system. Control inflation via a *permanent* incomes policy and relativities board. With costs under control competitive pressures will keep prices in line with costs.	Indexation is a useful tool in the control of inflation.	
	Inflation is an inherent flaw in a capitalist system where demands for shares in national income sum to more than 100 per cent of the total. Hence an incomes policy will be inadequate without a 'social contract' and price controls to keep capitalist power in check. Since it reduces output and raises average overheads, a reduction in demand will not contribute to reducing inflation unless it is associated with very high unemployment and a destruction of union bargaining power.			Incomes policies will be ineffectual in inflation control if money supply growth excessive, and unnecessary if it is not.	

purists, even though their emphasis on coordination problems and the failings of the IS–LM approach to macroeconomic theory also prevents them from full membership of the neoclassical Keynesian group. There is a world of difference between the neoclassical Keynesian 'quantity-constrained' and so-called 'disequilibrium' approaches to macroeconomics associated with Barro and Grossman (1976) or Malinvaud (1977), and the earlier work of Clower and Leijonhufvud from which the new approaches have clearly descended. Perhaps Clower and Leijonhufvud occupy a no-man's-land between neoclassical and Post Keynesians with attempts to force them into either camp doomed always to failure, yet never completely fruitless since they help illuminate the nature of the differences between the two groups.

Finally, it should be added that, although there are fundamental structural differences between monetarist and neoclassical Keynesian approaches to monetary economics, they have come increasingly to resemble each other in their conclusions in recent years with the incorporation of vertical Phillips curves into both approaches and the introduction of flexible price levels into neoclassical IS–LM models. Once the latter show economies tending automatically to some natural rate of output (as happens in Gordon (1979) and other leading US texts) they too barely deserve the label 'Keynesian'.

13.3 METHODOLOGICAL RULES OF THE GAME

In this section we provide a concise overview of the constraints that economists face as they use and choose between theories. Anyone wishing to explore the area of methodology further should find Katouzian's (1980) book *Ideology and Method in Economics* especially helpful as a guide. We illustrate our overview as far as possible with reference to one of the classic disputes in monetary economics, namely, the Friedman–Meiselman controversy. Using US data for the period 1896–1958 Friedman and Meiselman (henceforth FM) attempted to answer what they believed to be the crucial questions relevant for the choice between monetarism and Keynesianism. They asked (1963, p. 169):

(a) whether investment or the stock of money can better be regarded as subject to independent change, and to changes that have major effects on other variables; and

(b) whether the multiplier (the ratio of the flow of income or consumption to the flow of investment) or velocity (the ratio of the flow of income or consumption to the stock of money) is the more stable.

FM's calculations led them to conclude that, except for the early years of the Great Depression after 1929, the income velocity of circulation of money was decidedly and consistently more stable than the expenditure multiplier. This was so regardless of whether they dealt in nominal or real terms and whether they took the whole period or split the time series data into twelve periods, each of which contained at least one complete business cycle. Their relative stability criterion was the goodness of fit of regression equations for simple extreme 'Keynesian' and Quantity Theory models. Friedman (1962, p. 84) used their findings to justify an early exposition of his 100 per cent crowding out hypothesis. He also took them to imply that instead of complex attempts at macroeconomic management by fiscal means all that was needed was a steady growth of the money supply, at a rate slightly higher than the growth of capacity. The long-running controversy that the FM study immediately provoked illustrates neatly many of the characteristics of 'scientific' activity that we wish to highlight; where it does not we use examples from our earlier work (S. C. Dow (1980, 1981); Earl (1980); Dow and Earl (1981)).

Eight constraints on the activities of an economic scientist stand out as particularly worthy of attention.

(1) Economists may not have sufficient time to discover, read and adequately comprehend everything that has been written which might be relevant to their areas of interest. This forces them to evolve selective research strategies which enable them to make contributions without making too many oversights. They can never know in advance whether their chosen strategies will ultimately turn out to be time-wasting. The inevitably selective nature of research is what may make it possible for monetarist readers of this book simultaneously to be surprised by, say, our analysis of Minsky's work and yet feel that our conclusions would have been different had we spent more time researching work at the frontiers of monetarism. Our defence when accused of oversight is partly to counterattack, pointing out that monetarists might spend more time on the frontiers of Keynesian theory, and partly to blame our upbringings as economists, for these determine which authorities we have found useful guides and which journals we usually consult.

(2) As well as being based on selective research, scientific judgements are inevitably prone to ideological bias. When we form theories the types of concepts we attempt to relate out of the many that could conceivably be related are inextricably tied up with our own predispositions, whether innate or dependent on our past histories. For example, in the search for appropriate microfoundations for macroeconomics, the general equilibrium world view caused many theorists seemingly to be oblivious of the possibility of using disequilibrium behavioural microeconomics (such as are used in the present book) as a starting point. The problem of subjective bias also arises whenever evidence has to be interpreted. As the experiments of cognitive psychologists surveyed in chapter four of Steinbruner's (1974) book seem to show, people automatically filter out information which is at odds with their core precepts, or fudge interpretations to remove any inconsistencies.

(3) However it evolves, a theory has to be set of *causal* relationships rather than a mere statistical association between variables. The FM study was carried out before Friedman had properly developed his monetarist theories. FM's use of a crude 'Quantity Theory' rather smacked of measurement without theory, particularly to those who felt that a stable velocity of circulation might merely reflect a passive monetary stance by the Federal Reserve, accommodating the supply of money to shifts in demand in order to stabilize interest rates, rather than a stable demand for an exogenously determined money stock.

FM argued that the money supply was exogenous on the ground that if the level of activity and the rate of change of the money stock were plotted on a graph the latter showed a lead of about a quarter of the length of the business cycle. Solow and Kareken (1963) (henceforth SK) removed trends and showed that if the *size* of the money stock and the level of activity move roughly simultaneously, each tracing fluctuations rather like a sine wave, the rate of change of the money stock will, if also plotted, show an approximately quarter-cycle lead over business activity for purely arithmetical reasons. On the evidence they provided FM failed to convince SK that they were justified in taking the money stock as an independent variable and, therefore, in treating the Quantity Theory as anything other than a tautology. SK further suggested that FM had merely drawn conclusions without making some hypothesis of what the course of events would have been had the monetary authorities acted differently. Hence FM's argument about the determining role of money seemed no more sound to SK than the argument that investment is necessarily positively related to interest rates because both fall in depressions!

(4) The quality of predictions a theory generates may often be a function of the way the test of the theory is specified. De Prano and Mayer (1965) showed that the poor performance of FM's 'Keynesian' equation was transformed if gross, rather than net, investment figures were used in the calculation of autonomous expenditure (on the ground that depreciation measures are highly imperfect). They also demonstrated that if one excluded the period 1942–6 as being affected by wartime forced savings and their postwar release, the 'Keynesian' model actually out-performed the Quantity Theory for the period 1930–58. Ando and Modigliani (1965) further criticized FM's 'Keynesian' equa-tion, saying that it involved a grievous mis-specification of the consumption function because of an incorrect use of national income identities.

The most sophisticated critique of the FM test procedures was offered by Savin (1978). He used Leijonhufvud's (1969) sugges-tion that the size of the multiplier would vary according to the volume of buffer reserves of liquidity (that traders could use to keep spending if their incomes fell) to question whether or not FM were looking for the right thing. On this analysis the expenditure multiplier would increase in the trough of a recession as sources of liquidity became used up. Furthermore, fiscal policy would have very powerful pump-priming properties in the depths of a reces-sion, a time when an easy monetary policy might be somewhat ineffectual because transactors would be reluctant to expand their borrowing. On the surface the FM findings seemed to disprove this idea: they showed the value of the autonomous expenditure multi-plier to be no higher in the period 1929–39 than for other periods. But Savin then used the Durbin–Watson test to show that the FM results, which used the conventional ordinary least-squares tech-niques, suffered severely from positive autocorrelation and were not admissible. To get round this difficulty Savin re-estimated both FM equations using the maximum-likelihood technique and obtained results consistent with his theoretical analysis, i.e. high expenditure multipliers and low money multipliers in the 1930s. However, he was careful to point out that he had been forced to use very short sample periods to work out the multipliers without also being dogged by the autocorrelation problem. This meant he could not say his results were necessarily better than those achieved by FM, merely that the sample period used was not conducive to answering the questions FM had sought to ask.

(5) Theories can never be tested with regard to future events. Consequently, they can never be said to have been proved correct. Theories presently at odds with the facts as they are presently perceived may one day begin to perform rather well, while current good performers may suddenly start to do badly. Theories currently favoured should thus be used with caution, with a watchful eye for limitations to their likely ranges of convenience and a willingness to revise them should circumstances change. This is well shown by Poole and Kornblith's (1973) examination of the predictive properties of equations offered in the early stages of the FM controversy against observations for the later period 1959–70. They argued that their findings pointed to the futility of attempting to decide between monetarist and 'Keynesian' ideas on the basis of correlation coefficients. Beyond the original estimation period the relationships – including the revised 'Keynesian' ones proposed by De Prano and Mayer, Ando and Modigliani, and Hester (1964) – fell apart. None could predict the future very well.

(6) Scientists cannot subject single theories to testing; inevitably they have to test the interlinked component theories of what Lakatos (1970) has called scientific research programmes. Tests of modern monetarist ideas at the macro level apply simultaneously to monetarist theories of the behaviour of agents in labour-markets, of portfolio choice, of firm price-setting behaviour, of the working of financial markets and so on. If predictions leave something to be desired, the monetarist may have little idea where the trouble lies, even if she is fairly sure she has used the right econometric techniques. It could be due to no more than an inappropriate money supply definition. Yet, at the other extreme, one of her core ideas (e.g. that it is unnecessary to incorporate elements from sociology and psychology in economic models) might be wrong. But she cannot for ever keep returning to first principles. Progress seems to depend on it usually being safe to presume that core concepts are correct, and on the presence of a group of mavericks, not prepared to accept the core, who are attempting to develop other research programmes.

(7) Economic theories, if they can be tested at all, cannot meaningfully be tested in situations where other things can be held equal. In respect of the FM controversy Laidler (1975, p. 25) observed that

even if the critics of FM could obtain bigger correlation coefficients for 'Keynesian' models this would not necessarily prove that money was not important in the income-generation process. It is perfectly possible that both investment and consumption expenditures bear stable relationships with a third feature, such as money, and this gives the illusion that they are causally related in a 'Keynesian' way. But the impossibility of performing controlled experiments means that economists cannot, say, hold the money stock constant to see whether such an illusion has taken place. All they have at hand are the data of history. This is very damaging for Friedman's (1953) proposed positive approach to economics, which insists that we should look for theories which dominate in terms of predictive realism without worrying about *a priori* plausibility, the ground for the neglect of assumptive realism being the fact that any manageable theory is only a partial model. If systematic controlled testing is not possible almost any theory might seem to predict well or be able to offer an *ex post* rationalization with the addition of *ad hoc* assumptions.

(8) Although Friedman is quite correct to suggest that theories are descriptively false, there are several reasons why we should still profit from examining their assumptive structures for plausibility even if we are not faced with disagreements over *ad hoc* rationalizations, statistical methods, or what constitutes a plausible assumption. The first of these is that a research programme may still be in its early days in a particular area and so far have failed to yield any testable hypotheses. In such a situation the *a priori* plausibility of what she is doing, shaped as it may be by ideology, is the only guide the scientist has concerning the merits of persisting with the work.

A careful examination of the assumptive structure of a theory may reveal that it generates the kind of predictions it does because it suffers from a logical flaw. In her contribution to the FM controversy, for example, Chick (1977) took a careful look at the way FM set up their Quantity Theory equation to make it symmetrical with their 'Keynesian' equation. Chick showed that rather unwittingly FM had ended up implicitly assuming what they wanted to test. In effect they seemed to be assuming that total autonomous expenditure was constant. Hence a change in any of its components would displace another component to leave the total unchanged, implying a situation of total crowding out. Not only this, but the implicit assumption of constant autonomous expenditure in their Quantity Theory equation necessarily was at odds with FM's stated expectation of a positive correlation between monetary growth and autonomous expenditure.

Usually the discovery of a logical muddle after a careful examination of assumptions leads to attempts to test a corrected hypothesis. But not always. A clear example of economists breaching the rules of the game is the upshot of the Cambridge Capital Controversy. Neoclassical theorists conceded that their marginal productivity theory of aggregate income distribution only made sense in a one-commodity economy. But instead of abandoning it they now assume that the world behaves *as if* there is only one commodity. They continue to estimate production functions and such-like as if nothing had happened to destroy the notion that, in the real world, physical capital can be aggregated without reference to money rates of profit.

When rival theories are each systematically consistent with the same body of evidence it is necessary to look at assumptions to decide which is the least likely to be getting the right answer for the wrong reasons. Monetarists predict that the growth of expenditure and inflation usually comes about 2 years after a monetary expansion. Minskians would argue that lender-of-last-resort measures to reduce the extent of a collapse may increase the monetary base of an economy when activity is falling, and that if the intervention succeeds confidence (including confidence in wage bargaining) will be restored within a year or two. In the Minskian view the shift in confidence, not the growth of the money supply, causes expenditure and, ultimately, prices to increase, but both theories are consistent with a growth in the monetary base coming first.

The implication of points (1) to (8) taken together is that theories can only be accepted on faith. Economists disagree about which theories to use because there is no unambiguous way of judging a given theory. Different economists have different preferences and see different things in alternative approaches to the understanding of economic phenomena. Just as one product will not usually dominate in all dimensions in more mundane arguments about, say, the relative merits of different kinds of cars or clothes; so, too, a single theoretical approach will rarely stand out as superior in all the respects felt to be important. The two types of argument are not fundamentally different. Which theoretical approach an economist will believe to be best will depend on her academic upbringing, the circles within which she moves and the country whose affairs claim most of her attention, as well as her inbuilt predispositions. In many ways then, the success of a theoretical approach should be understood just as a marketing manager would attempt to understand the success of a consumer or industrial product. If it is launched at an inopportune moment, is poorly packaged, is too complex for the consumer to grasp, and fails to appeal to traditional values, then it will not find a market. Similarly, a skilful salesperson may be able to sell a veritable 'lemon' of a product or theory to the public.

13.4   INTERPRETATIONS OF WHAT KEYNES 'REALLY MEANT'

Keynes presented his *General Theory* as a work which called into question the existing mode of theorizing by revealing in it a fallacy of composition – the failure to see that one firm's wage cuts cause another firm's loss of sales – and a confusion concerning the relationship between stocks of money and flows of income, saving and investment. The kind of theorizing he attacked, which has nonetheless largely survived to form the underpinnings of modern monetarism and orthodox neoclassical versions of 'Keynesian' economics, is best described as being reductionist in form; that is to say, the focus of attention is directed at the choices of *individual* traders deciding whether or not to buy any individual commodities. (It should be recognized, however, that firms, households and commodities are themselves aggregate constructs, of workers, family members, and characteristics.)

In order that aggregate market phenomena can be inferred from the level of the individual trader and transaction without causing horrendous mathematical complications, reductionist theories usually treat the individual components as completely detached from each other (i.e. there is no room for interdependent preferences and other complementarities), and as if they are microcosmic representations of the aggregate features. Convex preference and production sets ensure that traders consume or produce some of each commodity, and the assumption that traders are identical, 'representative', agents enables aggregate phenomena to be inferred by multiplying what the individual firm or consumer does by the number of firms or consumers.

Modern reductionist theorists avoid making the mistake of economists before Keynes, who ignored income effects caused by an individual's reduction in spending because they were trivial, not realizing that when added together at the level of the economy they might be significant. However, such theorists have to confine their attention largely to equilibrium situations where all markets clear and macroeconomic problems do not exist; their tools of analysis are ill-equipped for use in situations where individuals attempt to do what is, in the aggregate, impossible. They have found it easier to discover ways of supposedly rehabilitating the classical view that an economy tends towards a position of zero involuntary unemployment if disturbed, than to abandon their cherished analytical techniques. To achieve such a rehabilitation they first concede that wage cuts reduce purchasing power and therefore cannot directly lead to a higher level of employment becoming profitable, and then argue that money wage flexibility can bring about the desired result indirectly since consequent changes in the price level will raise the real supply of finance and bring about the real balance effect. We have criticized this way of attempting to understand modern, intensely financial, economies in chapters 9 and 11 and will not repeat our arguments here.

Other economists have been more willing to accept that the price mechanism might be less than perfect, even in the long run, and have attempted to make Keynes' ideas more tractable. But no single version has been accepted as the obvious distillation of the essence of what he had in mind.

One interpretation of the message of the *General Theory* shifted attention away from the relative price concerns so central to reductionist theory and focused on aggregates of income and expenditure. If wages are downwardly sticky and expenditure is highly interest-inelastic it may be reasonable to assume that the price level for produced goods is sticky too, and that changes in monetary policy may have little effect on demand. On this view the main device for reducing unemployment is fiscal policy, with the size of necessary tax cuts or expenditure increases being calculated from econometrically observed consumption functions from which a value for the multiplier has been inferred. This was the 'Keynesian' theory that Friedman and Meiselman sought to confront with their Quantity Theory. Coddington (1976) has suggested that it is best described with the epithet 'hydraulic Keynesianism'. This seems a particularly apt idea when one recalls the hydraulic flow models of macroeconomic relationships built by Phillips and others before computers came into use. In the relatively stable 1950s and 1960s econometric models built according to the hydraulic philosophy achieved greater and greater refinement, but little attention was seemingly given to their possible limited usefulness if disturbances caused their underlying functions to shift around in an unpredictable manner.

An alternative interpretation of Keynesian ideas has grown out of work carried out by Clower and Leijonhufvud in the 1960s. Their research seems to have been provoked not by a feeling that the empirical contributions of the hydraulic Keynesians were inadequate but by a desire to see what theoretical innovation was contained in, or implied by, Keynes' work. They sought to understand this theoretical contribution in terms of their own Walrasian frameworks with an approach which Coddington has labelled 'reconstituted reductionism'. They practise reductionism in that they concentrate on the activities of individual traders and the role of relative prices. It is reconstituted reductionism, however, since it allows traders often to be in disequilibrium due to an inability (actual or expected) to sell as much as they would like at prevailing market prices.

Clower's (1965) Walrasian starting point caused him to attempt to understand effective demand failures in terms of a system of simultaneous equations for a one-period economy. His analysis thus compressed the future into the present, inevitably excluding saving and investment, and any ideas of a multiplier process unfolding through time, from the centre of the stage. As such it seems to concentrate on a very specialized kind of effective demand failure. Clower suggested that it is fruitful to distinguish between notional demands (what traders *would* be prepared to buy *if they could* sell, at particular prices, as much as they would like of what they have (e.g. labour services) or plan to produce) and effective demands (what traders *do* buy given their *actual* ability to sell what they have and conjectured ability to sell what they could produce at prevailing prices). Relative prices might be precisely those prices which would exist at full employment and yet firms might not hire all available workers because of a fear that they could not sell the output. A failure to be hired prevents workers from causing excess demand for the firms' products which would signal that more workers should be hired, even though *notionally* such excess demand exists.

The problem arises because wages are paid not in product but as money, which may be spent on anything, if it gets spent at all. Firms can see no necessary reason to believe that wage payments will automatically return to them, directly or indirectly, as product demand, so they may be unwilling to chance hiring workers. In a one-period model all transactions are finalized before any production takes place and there can be no saving or speculation. Hence, if firms *did* hire more workers *all* of the extra wages would return as demands for the extra output. There would also be excess effective demand, before trades were concluded and workers hired, if workers were given a larger initial endowment of spending power by some central authority.

Leijonhufvud's (1967, 1968, 1969, 1973) work adapts Clower's analysis into a multi-period system. It arose from his attempts to demonstrate that many economists, particularly those who developed the neoclassical synthesis by extending simple hydraulic models into IS–LM expositions, based their analyses on things that Keynes did not say or assume. In the *General Theory* the failure of an economy to achieve a position of equilibrium does not necessarily result from money wage rigidity, an absolutely interest-inelastic investment function, or a binding liquidity trap. The source of a persistent disequilibrium must be elsewhere if Keynes did not assume any of these factors were operative, unless Keynes was simply wrong. In chapter 9 we have proposed an alternative explanation of unemployment disquilibria which was partly inspired by Leijonhufvud's work on Keynes. But only partly. Leijonhufvud has performed a great service in showing how economists have often read Keynes' work in a very blinkered manner but we view *his* interpretation of Keynes with rather mixed feelings. His Walrasian blinkers have caused him to evolve a view of unemployment disequilibria and the multiplier which leaves out much that we see as important in Keynes' theory.

For Leijonhufvud, the spread of chaos has nothing to do with the instability of underlying behaviour functions in the face of falsified expectations and changes in the state of 'the news'; it has everything to do with inelastic expectations causing inertia in price adjustments. The multiplier is presented as the process whereby a mistake made in one part of the system gets amplified in subsequent periods because some traders do not change prices sufficiently rapidly to generate appropriate signals to others. For example, workers who lose their jobs do not know what the real state of the labour market is so they do not immediately offer to work for lower wages. Their lack of income prevents them from spending as they search for jobs at the 'normal' wage. This causes firms unexpectedly to pile up stocks and then cut production; and so on. Similarly, expectations of a 'normal' rate of interest delay the rate at which interest rates fall, and the inducement to invest rises, when a falling price level increases the real money supply.

Although he treats behaviour functions as stable, Leijonhufvud seems haunted by the spectre of an utterly explosive multiplier rather than the system eventually settling down either in a full-employment state or in the liquidity trap. If behaviour functions are stable one would have expected either of these outcomes to be the end result if no prices turn out ultimately to be rigid rather than merely sticky. Which outcome actually arose would depend on the power of real balance effects. Yet he continually writes as though the only thing which stops a worker's loss of earnings from causing an *equal* loss of expenditure, and hence an infinite multiplier contraction, is the possibility that the worker may be able to borrow or use up liquid reserves. In all of his descriptions of the multiplier he fails to mention that a worker who loses her income would otherwise probably have saved part of it. An ability and willingness to spend from liquid reserves *does* act as a buffer when an effective demand failure occurs, but in the *General Theory* it is a fractional marginal propensity to consume which acts as the main brake on the multiplier.

A final group of economists, whom we have labelled Post Keynesians and to whom Coddington gives the title 'fundamentalists', believe that they see the world through similar blinkers to Keynes. This group rejects both reductionist (reconstituted or otherwise) and holistic hydraulic approaches in favour of a systemic, hierarchical approach to macroeconomics and monetary theory of the kind used in the present book. They see individual decision-takers' expectations as interdependent and partly consequent on aggregate events. In an environment where choice has a flimsy foundation in expectations about an unknowable future, agents must take their behavioural cues from each other. Such beliefs as they have will, as Coddington (1976, p. 1260) puts it, 'be sustained by hopes and continually buffeted by "the news"'. The interdependence and potential for instability in behaviour functions militates against a reductionist, mathematical mode of theorizing. It also means that the properties of aggregates may be unstable, particularly in response to policies derived from hydraulic models which take behaviour functions as given. Simple hydraulic theorizing is also felt to be dangerous because it neglects the fact that the impact of any given expenditure injection is not independent of its composition or effect on relative prices.

Many economists view the fundamentalist position with horror, thinking that it implies that anything can happen at any moment, and then retreat into one of the other approaches. Certainly it is correct to follow Coddington (1976, p. 1263) and view fundamentalist Keynesianism as being 'concerned with the texture rather than the direction, as it were, of the economic process'. However this does not mean it is devoid of policy insights: we may not know the scale or timing of a shift in confidence but that does not prevent us from suggesting measures that may help prevent it from occurring or its sequel from being unnecessarily harmful.

13.5 CONCLUSION

This chapter has been concerned with the ways in which economists come to have different beliefs about economic relationships and the approaches to adopt in understanding them. 'Beliefs' is an appropriate term to use in this context, despite its somewhat non-scientific connotations, for we have shown that neither evidence nor an examination of the assumptions and internal logic of competing theories can provide a clear-cut reason for using one in preference to another which purports to explain the same phenomenon. Unrealistically simple theories may give very good results, but not always, and there is much scope for arguing about what constitutes a good set of results. Since economic theories are often untestable economists tend to argue about the choice of assumptions when trying to justify their theoretical frameworks; but often assumptions are also not beyond dispute as regards their realism since they too depend on the results of theorizing, albeit at another level in the research programme. With personal preferences and ideologies having the final say it is hardly surprising that economists from different backgrounds come to different conclusions about given contributions to knowledge or subscribe to different theoretical approaches with what amounts to a religious fervour, attempting to sell their ideas to others in a manner verging on the evangelical.

14

Monetarism – A Sympathetic Exposition

Given the overt Keynesian stance that this book has adopted its critical examination of the body of thought known as monetarism must do more than present a flimsy 'straw man' monetarist caricature and then kick it down. Instead it is necessary to present as convincing an exposition of monetarist ideas as possible, anticipating in advance many of the criticisms Keynesian economists often make of 'vulgar' monetarism and stealing their thunder by filling the theoretical holes they imply. In order that we are not accused of undue bias, then, we will not present a monetarist world view whose coherence depends on the presence of, for example, 'Central Bank helicopters', to increase the money supply, and the absence of trade unions, to provide a perfectly competetive labour market. And, to ensure that attention is not directed from the coherent picture which thoughtful monetarists can construct, we will save what we believe to be more refined objections for the next chapter.

In the previous chapter it was mentioned that, unlike much neoclassical 'Keynesian' theorizing which reaches similar conclusions, monetarism employs a reductionist methodology. It is for this reason that section 14.2 is concerned with a detailed examination of the kind of microfoundations which will generate the monetarist conclusion that in the long run changes in the money supply can only affect money variables, not the underlying real economy. Section 14.3 then examines the effects of changes in the rate of monetary growth, bearing in mind these microfoundations, and shows how the central monetarist conclusion is derived. In section 14.4, which is followed by a brief conclusion, there is a consideration of how monetarists would expect economies to behave in the face of externally imposed cost increases such as those of oil in 1973, and why some 'Austrian' monetarists such as Hayek appear to want to reduce trade union power, as well as monetary growth, in times of inflation.

14.2   MONETARIST MICROFOUNDATIONS

This section is itself divided into four subsections to concentrate attention on the fact that to discuss the effects of a change in the rate of growth of the money supply on output, unemployment and the price level it is necessary to understand what determines (a) the willingness of transactors to spend money from their income flows and borrow money for spending purposes, (b) the willingness of transactors to hold their wealth as money instead of buying financial or physical assets, (c) firm price and output choices, and (d) the responses of wage rates to changes in the demand for labour.

(a)   *The Determination of Private Expenditure*

If they are not to go bankrupt over the long run, consumers and firms will be able to spend no more than the limit set by their income flows (wages, unearned income and profits) and what they can realize by selling their initial endowments of non-human wealth, if these are not better used to generate income flows. With a given income flow and prices, borrowing cannot be used to increase the long-run command over goods – indeed, with a fixed price level, interest charges mean that the consumer could purchase more if she waited instead of borrowing – but it permits a temporal reallocation of command over goods. Consumers who expect their incomes to be higher in future may wish to increase their current rates of consumption. By doing this they will avoid the bunching of consumption later on and reduce present boredom. A lower rate of interest means that the sacrifice of future consumption for the present exploration of the properties of commodities is reduced so a fall in the rate of interest associated with an increase in the money supply should be expected to lead to more borrowing and current demand for goods.

Borrowing also permits the augmentation of income flows. A student who is smart enough to win a place at, say, Harvard Business School will usually be able to borrow the money to finance her studies and lack of current income because the greatly increased earning power she will enjoy after obtaining her MBA makes her seem a safe bet and not likely to be unable to repay the loan. With a lower rate of interest more students seeking to augment their human capital will attempt to obtain loans as the net present value of more loan-financed courses will become positive. Similarly we should expect businesses to expand their activities if interest rates fall causing more marginal schemes to appear worth undertaking. So long as interest rates are not expected to rise and make any refunding of short- and medium-term loans more costly firms will be prepared to expand their gearing ratios when interest rates come down. Even in countries such as the UK, where manufacturing business is often reluctant to finance fixed capital by borrowing and prefers to use internally generated funds, lower interest rates may still lead to an expanded scale of stock-holding and, by raising expectations of loan-financed product demand, to increased investment from retentions. However, firms and consumers will only increase borrowing with a view to augmenting their income flows if interest rates are expected to remain lower than they have been, until their projects come to maturity.

When an increased supply of money enters the system, someone's borrowing will raise someone else's income. Monetarists suggest that increases in income will only be spent on current consumption if they are expected to be permanent; i.e. if they seem to represent a new trend in income streams rather than merely part of expected random fluctuations around an existing trend. Friedman's (1957) study produced evidence consistent with this 'Permanent Income Hypothesis'. Firms may be expected to adopt a similar attitude towards profits increases – there is, after all, little point in engaging in the costly activity of putting together a skilled management team to cope with a 'permanently' higher rate of corporate expansion if it turns out to be possible for only a year or two. Where consumers and firms are not spending additions to income on current flows of goods and services they have still to decide what to do with their newly received money wealth, which leads to our next section.

(b) *Portfolio Choice: the Demand for Money*

The leading monetarist view of the demand for money, i.e. that associated with Milton Friedman (1970, p. 202–6), seems closely to resemble the Keynesian analysis presented in chapter 8, except for some disagreement over the relative importance and stability of the parameters. Friedman suggests that the demand for money is a function of the following variables:

(1) *Total wealth*, for which useful surrogates are formed by (permanent) income flows. Friedman provides no reason why wealthier people should wish to hold more money than poor people, but the following Keynesian justification may be what he has in mind. Since consumption is related to wealth in human or non-human form we should expect cash balances (in the pocket or in financial institutions) to bear some relationship to wealth: greater consumption expenditures will be associated with greater holdings of liquid reserves for *transactions purposes*. Richer individuals may tend proportionately to use cheque payments to a greater extent and thus keep a bigger part of their reserves in financial institutions. The division of wealth between human and non-human wealth may also affect the demand for money at a given level of wealth: dividend payments, for example, are often only made at half-yearly intervals, so wealth-holders who rely on unearned income to support a given regular flow of consumption may be expected to hold larger cash balances than those who do not.

(2) *The expected rates of return on money and other assets*. Like Keynes, Friedman recognizes that the existence of yields on assets other than cash and bank deposits will often provide an incentive to economize on money-holdings from a given level of wealth. He points out that asset yields are affected by carrying costs and price movements as well as currently paid components such as interest and dividends. His only difference from Keynes in this area is in the importance he accords to the scope for instability in yield expectations consequent on changes in people's hopes and fears about future relative money values of assets. But such instability turns out to be allowed for in the component we consider next; namely, his final, catch-all, 'portmanteau' variable.

(3) *Other variables determining the utility attached to the services rendered by money relative to those tendered by other assets – in Keynesian terminology, determining the value attached to liquidity proper*. Friedman (1970, pp. 203–4) provides two examples of what he has in mind, the second of which is truly Keynesian. He suggests, first, that the greater the volume of transfers between existing capital assets wealth-holders make, the greater the fraction of their total assets they may find it worth holding as cash. Presumably a higher (average) cash holding is worth having in such circumstances because it will often be advantageous to have slight mismatches between purchase and sale timings and/or to meet irregular stockbrokers' bills. He then argues, conceding the

problems it will cause for statistical testing, that demands for cash will vary according to the degree of instability expected in the economy: an outbreak of war, for example, will usually be accompanied by an increase in holdings of cash balances.

(c) *Price and Output Choices of Firms*

If an increase in the growth of the money supply is to cause increases in output in the short run but only in prices in the long run, with output then falling to its original level, an exposition of monetarism cannot be complete without an analysis of how firms set their prices and outputs, and how they respond to changes in demand for their products. In all markets except those for custom-built capital goods there typically will be stocks which can be run down when demand increases. Also, firms may usually allow for some expansion of output through over-time or adjusting the pace of production lines with the existing labour force before they will concern themselves with hiring new employees. As a result, some slack exists in the system which will permit an expansion of output without any changes in price if sales increase. Firms thereby avoid the risk that price changes will confuse customers and lose goodwill. Consumers may be prepared to queue for goods or, rather, will have to queue for goods if a large demand shift takes place relative to the slack in the system, since it is not they who set the prices. Firms will try to avoid having queues longer than their rivals to prevent long-term loss of custom, and they will not expect to keep their workforces working at full pace indefinitely. Sooner or later they will take delivery of new plant and/or wish to hire new workers.

The monetarist view of the labour market – see section (d) below – implies that additional workers will not be available for the average firm unless it offers a higher wage rate. The higher wage rate will not be paid merely to the new employees but to all employees of a similar grade. Likewise, in a situation where the average firm wishes to shed labour, worker turnover will be encouraged by offering *all* employees of a certain grade a lower rate of wage increase than the increase in prices. A firm's average wage costs, then, are going to be positively related to the level of output due to the nature of the labour market. Average wage costs may also rise when output increases if the extra employees are set to work on older vintages of machinery, with higher unit labour requirements, which would otherwise have lain idle (cf. Salter, 1966). With an expansion of final product demand raw material costs will also be expected to rise, once stocks have been used up, as marginal sources of supply are called upon. Hence firms will have upward-sloping average total cost curves even if their production functions, expressed in engineering terms, exhibit constant returns to scale.

On conventional perfect competition grounds – a common 'as if' assumption of monetarist theorizing – the supply curve of an industry is upward sloping as a result of the upward-sloping supply curves of factors, so a rise in industrial output will be associated with a rise in prices. We would prefer to see the argument taking account of the more realistic assumption of competitive oligopoly with easy entry by existing firms with similar production and/or selling bases. In such a market situation firms will tend to adopt some kind of non-marginalist, full-cost/mark-up method of pricing to ward off entry and maximize long-run profits. In this case, too, rising output will be accompanied by rising prices if firms find their average cost curves shifting upwards as they expand employment. Such firms may say their prices are cost-determined but the positions of their cost curves depend on the level of industrial demand. If all their rivals are experiencing cost increases they can raise their prices without any fear of attracting entry as they expand output so long as they keep them in line with their average costs (which will be commonly used as a proxy for the costs of potential producers).

(d) *The Labour Market*

In monetarist theories of the labour market there are no involuntarily unemployed workers amongst those members of the labour force who do not have jobs. People are unemployed because they are searching round for better jobs than the low-grade jobs they expect they could obtain and for which they have already discovered vacancies. Instead of taking the first job they see after being made redundant they will only consider seriously those jobs which offer roughly their previous real wages. If they are unsuccessful in obtaining these then gradually they will reduce their target real wages and begin to attempt to obtain those jobs whose money wages have fallen back relative to the price level; or, if they were previously employed at their real transfer-fee wage (i.e. they enjoyed no slack/consumer surplus payment), will prefer a life on the dole, hoping that they are not offered any jobs by their employment office unless these offer their real transfer wages. The reason why they do not bother to get the first job they see, and carry on searching for something better while doing the job and obtaining income, is that they expect that ultimately they will get a better job if they engage in search as a full-time activity, supporting themselves from their savings and state benefits until they do. Thus they are trading current income for the prospect of higher future income.

The thinking behind the search theory approach to unemployment appears to be as follows. If you are searching for a job it is an institutional fact of life that you can only search during normal working hours and it will thus be necessary to be absent from work, sacrificing pay and incurring the wrath of the employer. To try to search for a large number of jobs simultaneously will, if one is successful in obtaining interviews and if they involve overnight stays in distant areas, mean that one will have to be absent from work practically all the time. State employement offices, on the other hand, will not reduce dole payments or demand justifications for absenteeism of the kind that would have to be offered to maintain credibility with the 'temporary' employer. A key assumption is that it will be necessary to apply for many jobs of the desired kind within a limited time period before an offer is received at the advertised wage since many other people will be doing the same thing. To show that this may not be an unrealistic view of how the labour market possibly works all we need do is recall the behaviour of final-year undergraduates neglecting their studies while attending interviews for vast numbers of jobs, only one of which they expect to take up after graduation.

Clearly this search theory view of the behaviour of the unemployed on the supply side of the labour market is completely independent on the existence of trade unions who may affect the wages of jobs on offer. All it requires is the existence of some low-grade job vacancies and the expectation that, in the near future, job vacancies of the desired kind will be discovered which workers feel they have a sufficiently high probability of being offered. If low-grade job vacancies do not exist then we can appeal to the presence of high unemployment benefits to explain why workers are not attempting to bargain individually with employers for lower wages. But it is not usually necessary to make such appeals. The labour market is in a constant state of disequilibrium owing to people retiring or moving to jobs in expanding companies even if many companies are making workers redundant. Hence there will always be vacancies, or the likelihood of vacancies in the near future, at all levels of the labour market.

Given the existence of job vacancies, actual or expected, at the target real wage there is no point in trying to bargain for wage reductions to make sure one gets the kind of job one wants. When reservation wages are lowered, because the probability of obtaining the desired real wage within a given time period appears to have been over-estimated, it is easier to obtain the lower wage by applying for jobs already offering the lower wage. The reason for this is that even if interviews gave the opportunity for workers to bid for lower wages than those advertised they would be aware that employers would not usually accept such bids because they would then require them to reduce wages to *all* workers in the same job slot. The expectation that employers would not wish to do this because of the disruption it might cause, and the general anxiety that arises from the prospect of engaging in an attempt at bargaining that breaks with conventional practices, will usually result in the would-be employee taking the advertised price as a datum. The same reasoning can be applied to explain why *individuals* will not usually offer to work for lower wages when faced with redundancy notices. The task of attempting to change real wages by changing money wages (or their rate of increase) will thus rest with the trade unions or with the employers, not with individual workers.

Leaving aside the effects of trade unions for the moment, consider the behaviour of firms when they face increases or decreases in product demand. If demand rises and they attempt to hire workers they will initially succeed at the existing wage, but it will soon become apparent to workers searching for jobs at any particular level of the labour market that the probability of employment being offered from a given number of applications has increased. This will deter them from lowering their reservation wages when otherwise they might have done. To the extent that workers who *would* have lowered their reservation wages are of superior quality to those offering themselves at what would have been the new reservation wage, firms will find the productivity of workers hired at existing wages tending to fall. They will thus have an incentive to offer higher wages even though they still get at least one applicant for each job slot advertised. In times of falling product demand the reduced demand for labour brings about the reverse process. In economies where inflation is already occurring monetarists contend that, unless there are militant trade unions in *all* sectors, there will be a general slowdown in the rate of increase of money wages rather than an actual cut. Firms will be hiring additional workers less frequently and hence the number of good applicants for particular job slots will tend to rise, given the initial number of searchers for jobs. They will thus feel less inclined to raise wages by as much as they otherwise would have felt to be necessary to preserve the quality of their workforces in the face of natural wastage.

If some sectors of the labour market are affected by the behaviour of recalcitrant trade unions firms may find wages rising faster than they otherwise would have done. This will mean, in the case of a state of expanding demand, they they hire fewer additional workers. As a result, in other sectors of the labour market firms will not find the quality of job applicants at given wages tending to decline as much as it would have done and, in these sectors, wages, and hence firm costs, will not tend to rise rapidly. The argument is the same on a falling market, except that firms will have to make workers redundant to reduce their labour forces because union action prevents the desired slowdown in the rate at which money wages increase. Redundant workers searching for jobs reduce the need of firms with weakly unionized labour forces to raise wages while maintaining desired employment levels. The activities of strong trade unions do not, on this view, raise *average* wage costs; they merely affect the *sectoral* structure of wages.

14.3 THE EFFECT OF A CHANGE IN THE RATE
OF MONETARY GROWTH

In this section the monetarist microfoundations are used to examine what happens in the short and long runs when there is a change in the rate of growth of the money supply. To keep matters simple we shall confine attention to the discussion of a closed economy, such as the world as a whole, leaving the discussion of an open economy until chapter 16. It should be noted at the outset that, since there are many definitions of the money supply and monetarists usually concentrate their attention on the monetary base, the ability to predict changes in expenditure from a knowledge of the demand for money and expenditure functions is heavily dependent on there being a well-defined relationship between the monetary base and broader definitions of the money supply. This requires that the monetary system corresponds fairly closely on the supply side to the multiplier concept rather than the portfolio theory, and that banking and financial intermediation enjoy more or less constant returns to scale.

If the economy is to be in equilibrium with a constant level of output (to abstract from the complications of economic growth) and employment then no-one must be finding their money balances to be of a different real value than the desired one, nor real wages falling below the transfer fee level, and estimations of permanent income must not be changing. Real wages must not be such, given the expected level of demand, as to cause firms to be wanting to change their volume of employment. Such an equilibrium can occur with constant prices and no growth of the money supply, or with a constant rate of inflation and an equal, constant, rate of growth of the money supply.

If the money supply is increased at a faster rate that in the past banks will lower their nominal interest rates in order to expand the volume of loans. A fall in interest rates will provide consumers with the possibility for expanding their lifetime consumption, given their temporal consumption preferences, and they will increase their loan-financed expenditure. They will also tend to hold smaller money balances and increase their holdings of other assets, driving up their prices and reducing their effective returns. This will encourage firms to expand their equity issues and loan-financed investment since, for a given set of expectations, some marginal schemes will now seem viable. Expectations will shift, too, because of the increasing rate of expenditure of consumers: this will imply a greater need for capacity.

The increased spending of some agents in the economy will lead to increased incomes for others but the latter will not wish to increase their money balances unless their permanent incomes are rising or the yield on other assets is falling. The extra money is, so to speak, like a hot potato which no-one wants to hold and which will not cool down until something happens to raise the demand for it. Initially, firms will have responded to the increased demand by increasing overtime working, running down stocks and expanding waiting lists, but they will then wish to increase employment as they experience a continuing high level of demand. To do this they will, after a short period before they perceive that the average quality of applicants for jobs is falling, need to offer higher wages to new (and existing) workers. This will represent a higher average cost of production and they will be planning to raise their prices. To workers being given higher wages in advance of production it will seem as though a higher real wage is being offered: wages are rising faster than the expected increase in the price level. In the short to medium term output and employment will expand and there will be fewer workers searching for jobs.

But this position will not be sustainable in the long run. Workers will discover that only money wages have risen. Unexpected rises in the price level mean that real wages have not increased. Because of the higher price level they will find their money balances inadequate for their usual transaction activities. Money permanent income has increased, real permanent income has not, but the same real money balances will be desired. These can only be built up by reducing expenditure for a time or selling other assets. A fall in asset prices and reduced expenditure will involve the disappointment of expectations and firms will wish to cut back their output. There will be two other reasons for firms to reduce output and push the real side of the economy back towards its original position. Rising prices and wages will be raising the demand for loans to finance stock holdings and wage advances. This will tend to raise the rate of interest as the banks make loans to firms rather than to consumers. Real demand for output will thus be reduced unless the money supply is expanded at a faster rate. The rise in the rate of interest offered by banks also encourages agents to switch their portfolios out of bonds and equities and into bank deposits. Workers who are dissatisfied with their real wages will tend increasingly to prefer to search for jobs which offer their target real wages. As they all move up-market the quality of job applicants will be falling and firms will need to offer a higher rate of pay to attract applicants of a given calibre. Higher real wage costs will mean that firms will be wishing to reduce their output.

The end result of this is that all real variables in the system fall to their original values and, so long as the rate of monetary growth remains at its new rate, the economy will experience a higher rate of inflation than before, corresponding to the higher excess growth of the money supply. The inflation brings actual money balances into equality with desired *real* money balances and people have no tendency to increase expenditure. Hence so long as actual rates of change correspond to expected rates of change the economy will be at what is known as the natural rate of output and unemployment. In the short run increases in the rate of change of money wages lead to reduced search unemployment. In the long run they do not, unless the increases continually run ahead of increases in the rate of inflation. But if inflation accelerates this will be brought into expectations. Any attempt to run the system at a higher rate of output than the natural rate at which expectations are in equiibrium must lead to hyperinflation and the destruction of the existing currency. The long-run Phillips curve is thus vertical and if policy-makers do not like the volume of unemployment associated with equilibrium they can only change it by affecting workers' inclinations and abilities to search.

The reverse of the process described above can bring the economy from a state of perfectly anticipated inflation to a position of zero inflation if there is a cessation in the growth of the money supply. This will involve shattering expectations and a temporary rise in unemployment above the natural level, but, eventually, prices and wages will cease to rise and unemployment will fall to its natural rate. The monetarist conclusion quite clearly is that inflation is always and everywhere a monetary phenomenon and that, in the long run, a monetary change cannot affect real variables: in this sense money does not matter.

14.4 MONETARISTS, OPEC AND TRADE UNIONS

When the Organization of Petroleum Exporting Countries increased the price of oil dramatically at the end of 1973 inflation rates increased in many countries in the next 2 years. Keynesians usually interpret this is cost-push terms. Monetarists, however, argue that if the money supply expansions of the 1972–73 boom period had not occurred, the increases in oil prices would not have seemed to be associated with higher long-run rates of inflation. All that otherwise would have happened, the monetarists suggest, would have been a change in relative prices. Oil-intensive commodities would have risen in price faster than they otherwise would have done with other products rising less. Rises in petrol prices would have left consumers with less of their incomes to spend on other things. The lower demand would have led to a smaller demand for labour, so wages, and hence prices, would have risen less in the non-petrol sector. As a result, wage costs in the petrol sector would also have increased less rapidly than they did. Real incomes of non-owners of oil resources would fall to offset the rise in real incomes of oil-producers. If there were no distributional effects the volume of employment would not have changed. However, it is plausible to suggest that oil-producers might tend to have a higher demand for money and that some workers in the rest of the world might prefer not to work at the lower real wage. These two factors combined would tend to cause unemployment to rise to a new, higher, natural level and the rate of inflation to have a lower equilibrium rate than previously.

While monetarists have thus denied the ability of autonomous increases in one kind of cost to cause a rise in the general price level in the absence of an expansionary monetary policy, and, as we have seen, have used a similar argument to suggest that wage increases obtained by some trade unions cannot cause inflation, a minority of monetarists led by Hayek (1972) have suggested that trade union powers should be curbed. Their case for arguing this starts with the view that the adjustment of relative wages will take some time to achieve when unions in some sectors price some of their own members out of jobs. In the short period *structural* unemployment rises and the trade unions then lobby the government for a *general* Keynesian reflation which in turn leads to inflation by the usual monetarist process. Groups with strong bargaining power will find their real wages threatened and attempt to restore their positions by strike action. If they are successful the process will be started again and the natural level of unemployment and real wage configuration consistent with the underlying real forces is never attained. What will be observed instead will be increasingly high rates of inflation. The government's willingness to reflate in the usual Keynesian manner will be high if unemployment threatens its popularity and it will also look forward to the extra tax revenues that inflation will generate. Increasingly high rates of inflation will subsequently make it become unpopular and it may, for a period, attempt to reduce inflation by monetarist means. Since these involve a shattering of expectations there will inevitably be a temporary increase in unemployment till the new equilibrium is obtained. But, again, union lobbying will often cause the monetarist medicine to be abandoned before it has had time to cure the problem.

14.5   CONCLUSION

This chapter has attempted to present an exposition of the main threads of monetarist thinking, avoiding any distractions from Keynesian objections. Particular attention has been given to the labour market to show that monetarist analyses are based on a careful consideration of the difficulties of job search when information is restricted and job interviews, if attained, may be time-consuming affairs. We have also noted how similar monetarist and Keynesian views of the determinants of the demand for money seem to be. Despite the similarities, however, the monetarist model leads to conclusions about the determination of the level of employment and ultimate role of money and monetary policy which we, as Keynesians, find decidedly unpalatable. This distaste with monetarism arises not from an unwillingness to accept their conclusions despite their logical coherence, but because even this genuine attempt at a convincing exposition of monetarist ideas contains a number of potentially serious flaws. The next chapter brings them out into the open.

15

Monetarism – A Keynesian Critique

15.1 INTRODUCTION

In this chapter the internal logic of monetarist theories and policies comes under strict scrutiny and is found to be flawed. It is suggested that, when mounting unemployment is observed in a period of inflation, the appropriate policy is not continued monetary restraint but a carefully designed Keynesian reflation coupled with a permanent incomes policy. We shall not concern ourselves over-much with empirical findings which appear to support monetarist theories. It has already been argued in chapter 13 that data consistent with monetarist approaches are often perfectly consistent with a Keynesian explanation of the observed phenomena.

The critique is divided up into three main parts, followed by a brief conclusion. Section 15.2 examines the monetarist view of the transmission mechanisms of monetary changes. In section 15.3 it is argued that unemployment is not entirely due to voluntary search activity and that what is often being observed in large part is really Keynesian involuntary unemployment. Finally, in section 15.4 there is an examination of possible forms of non-inflationary Keynesian reflation policies. However, before proceeding to the critique it is perhaps worth observing the attitude of advanced equilibrium theorists to the application of monetarist ideas to the real world, and see precisely what the proponents of monetarism have been able to sell to some politicians and why they have bought it.

Modern monetarism is firmly rooted in Walrasian general equilibrium theory. This much is quite clear from Friedman's original definition of the natural unemployment rate to which he believes an economy will converge in the absence of monetary disturbances, and which is consistent with equilibrium in the structure of real wage rates. Friedman (1968, p. 8) suggests that the natural level of unemployment is the level that would be ground out by the Walrasian system of general equilibrium equations, provided there is embedded in them the actual structural characteristics of the labour and commodity markets, including market imperfections, stochastic variability in demands and supplies, the costs of gathering information about job vacancies and labour availabilities, the costs of mobility and so on.

General equilibrium theorists such as Arrow and Hahn (1971), working at the frontiers of their subject, have been careful to warn that such systems only converge towards equilibrium positions with convenient stability properties in special circumstances. Such theorists make no presumption that the real world approximates to such a system. Monetarists have chosen not to heed the warnings of these high theorists and have instead attempted to sell their ideas to the governments of many countries. In this they have been very successful.

The monetarist view that inflation is always a monetary phenomenon to be controlled by monetary means has an attraction for governments that wish to avoid confrontations of the kind that usually arise when incomes policies are temporarily imposed on an unwilling trade union movement. Politicians who never understood Keynes' work and believe that governments, like individuals, cannot in the long run spend more than their incomes find convenient the idea that the economy always converges towards some equilibrium level of output and employment if left undisturbed, and that continued attempts to achieve higher employment are doomed to end in ever-accelerating inflation. It provides them with an excuse for not carrying out Keynesian expansionary policies when unemployment is rising. The other major selling point of monetarist theories, for those not versed in methodology or the kind of critique proposed in this chapter, is the abundance of empirical evidence which is consistent with what the theories say about inflation and monetary growth.

For many countries very good correlation coefficients are to be found between the 'excess' growth in the 'money supply' and inflation rates six to eight quarters later. This lag in price-level response is explained by the monetarist theory and is entirely consistent with the proposed direction of causation. Examination of the relevant regression equations will provide naïve policy-makers with a very tempting conclusion of what must be done to control inflation. They may imply, say, that a slowdown in the annual rate of monetary growth to 10 per cent this year will lead to a lower rate of inflation of 10 per cent in 2 years' time. They do not imply that an incomes policy or particular kinds of taxation policy could be required too.

Deviations from the predicted value will be largely explained by a failure of economic actors to adjust their expectations correctly and will be associated, also, with fluctuations in employment. If a steady rate of inflation greater than 10 per cent continues to be expected by firms and workers the real money supply, and hence demand, will be contracting. Firms will find their sales expectations falsified if they try to raise prices by more than 10 per cent after wages have risen by more than 10 per cent, and will be forced to lay off workers. Such unemployment as is thus observed in 2 years' time will, however, only be a temporary phenomenon. In time the extra unemployed workers in any market segment, and their increasing quality as reservation wages fall, will cause firms to realize that to get and keep workers of a given calibre they can offer much lower wage increases than in the past. Lower wage and price increases will cause a rise in the real money supply and lower interest rates, permitting convergence to the original level of employment and a 10 per cent steady-state inflation rate.

In the above example matters would be so much simpler, say the monetarists, if the government announced that its new monetary target would bring inflation down to 10 per cent in 2 years' time without rasing unemployment. If, as a result, everyone in the economy formed 'rational expectations' of a 10 per cent future rate of inflation then, sure enough, it would be achieved at the expected time without any nasty rise in unemployment. Appropriate government announcements to an audience who all appreciated the monetarist model would lead, as it were, to 'disinflation by magic'. Keynesian economists, trade union leaders, enlightened industrialists, and others, who declare the monetarist model is not correct and act according to other expectations, will prevent such a smooth transition but, so the monetarists suggest, they cannot prevent an unflinching policy of monetary restraint from succeeding in the long run. Such is the package which many politicians have bought and which is now subjected to critical examination.

15.2 WEAKNESSES IN THE TRANSMISSION MECHANISM

It will be convenient to divide the arguments of this section into three subsections. First we shall examine the rational expectations argument. Secondly, we shall consider whether, assuming the money supply can be controlled, changes in monetary growth need inevitably be closely related to changes in expenditure. Thirdly, and in the light of the work of Cramp (1970), Roe (1973) and Minsky (1975), we shall consider whether or not governments can control monetary growth without bringing about financial catastrophes.

Agents in the economy will not form rational expectations in response to a government announcement of projected money supply growth and inflation rates if they do not have grounds for believing the projections to be sensible. Even if there is a direct link between monetary growth and inflation agents will only start expecting the proposed inflation rate if they believe the government will adhere to its money supply targets. Past experience tends to support Hayek's (1972) view that governments give in to political pressure during the transition period of rising unemployment and abandon their monetary targets. When governments continue to borrow at fixed interest rates greater than the projected rate of inflation instead of making index-linked bonds generally available at a zero real rate of return it inevitably gives rise to the suspicion that the authorities do not believe their own projections.

In a dynamic economy, where the structure of relative wages and prices is changing through time, the announcement of a different inflation projection *may* affect expectations (despite the above objections) but there is no guarantee that it will affect them in a way which adds up to the projection. Firms and workers do not work out the future structure of prices and wages all at once in some Walrasian auction. As a result they cannot merely mark up money prices or wages by a different amount across the board leaving future relative magnitudes unchanged. Instead, participants do not know what relative magnitudes ought to be, and adjust them period by period at the same time as coping with past and expected inflationary forces. Since wages and prices are not all changed simultaneously it is not easy to separate out the two effects. Wages and profit margins are changed partly after having been eroded by inflation and partly after relative real demands and supplies have shifted, as well as in the light of expectations of general inflation rates. Even if trade unions are concerned about the possibility of some of their members losing their jobs as a result of an excessive wage bargain, they may accidentally bring about redundancies during the period of their wage contracts because they have misjudged what constitutes a rational wage demand and their employers have failed to hold out for the appropriate value because of the costs of a strike or because they did not know what the value was.

As Matthews and Reddaway (1980, p. 12) argue, wage bargaining will tend to be done not on the basis of uncertain expectations but with regard to the actual experience of past price increases which have eroded previous settlements. Workers are always trying to catch up with the real wage they thought they had obtained last time. A lower rate of actual inflation will cause lower wage targets in the next wage round but a lower expected rate may not. If this is the case then a monetary squeeze works not by its effect on expectations but by its effect on supply and demand in the labour market. Unemployment frightens groups of workers into accepting lower rates of growth of money wages. A substantial growth of unemployment as firms find insufficient demand for their products may cause firms to bargain more keenly, and reservation wages of workers who lose their jobs to be lowered more rapidly as the probability of re-employment at the old real wage seems less. It is only then that expectations will tend to influence wage bargains.

If a monetary contraction reduces the rate of inflation by frightening workers, rather than by directly reducing inflationary expectations, then there is no guarantee that workers will not tend to use their bargaining power once more as the economy begins to expand en route for equilibrium at the natural rate of unemployment. The result is that it never gets there and lurches instead between different rates of inflation and unemployment if the government stands fast with its monetary policy and does not attempt to introduce an incomes policy or restrict trade union power.

In a Keynesian analysis of inflation the wage level and the price level are inextricably tied together. If there is an excess demand inflationary gap (such as Keynes discussed in his (1940) pamphlet *How To Pay For The War*) wages are bid up as firms attempt to expand, seeing rising profit margins. The excess demand persists because higher wages increase purchasing power and, as a result, firms *still* find profit margins higher than expected. In a cost inflation autonomous increases in costs, which firms attempt to pass on by proportionate price rises, are validated by a rise in aggregate demand due to the higher income payments. In both scenarios the only brake to the process comes about via a rise in interest rates causing a reduction of real expenditure. In the demand inflation this eliminates the excess demand and firms cease bidding for labour against each other. In the cost inflation this brings into play the fear mechanism described above. For Keynes the analysis of wage inflation was the reverse of the process of wage deflation, which only worked via its effect on interest rates and not directly by a real wage effect. However, Keynes suggested that there was no neccessary reason why either process should converge. The change in interest rates might not occur and, even if it did, it might not be effective.

To put the Keynesian theory into monetarist language we need note simply that the velocity of circulation may shift to accommodate an increased demand for money or to nullify the effect of an increased real supply of money. The possibility that the velocity of circulation is not stable opens up serious doubts about the likelihood of a given change in the rate of growth of the money supply bringing about a particular response on the rate of inflation in a subsequent period. To the extent that a demand contraction is an appropriate way of controlling infla- tion – a view to which we cannot subscribe because of its employment effects – what must be controlled is *expenditure*, for which the rate of growth of the money supply is only a good proxy if velocity is stable. The components of Friedman's demand for money function, discussed in the previous chapter, only imply a stable velocity if expectations about the stability of the economy and relative yields on assets are stable, and if, when interest rates change, money has a low interest- elasticity of demand.

The scope for shifts in velocity is higher the greater the volume of discretionary loans and expenditure in an economy and the greater the volume of money balances being held at any moment for speculative as opposed to transactions purposes. The Walrasian mode of analysis diverts attention from the possibility that, in the absence of cor- responding shifts in the money supply, the velocity of circulation can be unstable, since it is always cast in terms of individuals constrained by their budgets. It excludes speculative aspects of consumption of the kind discussed in chapters 8 and 9. If demand depends on willingness to spend as well as ability to pay, consumers can increase the velocity of circulation if they suddenly decide to buy things. By writing out cheques to pay for them they do not necessarily reduce the ability of banks to lend: money simply shifts between bank accounts if they run down their deposits rather than extending their overdrafts. Monetarists also fail to make clear precisely who are the 'individuals' who figure in the empirical studies which, they claim, show the de- mand for money is not very sensitive to interest rates and depends mainly on permanent income levels. As Kaldor (1970, p. 5) asks:

> Are they the wage- and salary-earners, who, between them account for 70% of the national income, but hold, at any one time, a much lesser proportion, perhaps 10 to 20% of the total money supply? Or

are they the 'rentiers' whose 'portfolio selection' and 'portfolio shifts' are much influenced at any time by short term expectations, as well as by the relative yields of various types of financial assets? Or are they businesses, for which holding money is just one of a number of ways of securing liquidity – unexploited borrowing power, un-used overdraft limits and so on being many other ways – and for which the state of liquidity is only one of a number of factors that influence current expenditure decisions?

The demands for money of the corporate or financial sectors must necessarily be highly interest-elastic. Otherwise the Central Bank could never adjust the monetary base via open market operations without producing extreme shifts in the rate of interest on government stocks. Small changes in the rate of interest will thus have a consider-able effect on the supply of finance for expenditure. In so far as confidence is rising (in which case the supply of finance may increase without any necessary rise in interest rates at all – see chapter 11), or would-be borrowers usually rationed by quantity rather than cost of finance, there is no reason why a demand for finance in an inflationary environment should not be accommodated with no reduction in real expenditure.

The discussions so far have assumed that the monetary base is exogenously determined by the authorities. Control over the monetary base will give policy-makers little leverage over demand if velocity shifts occur with regard to the base definition of the money supply, as a result of a high interest elasticity of demand for financial assets causing rises in the money supply by other definitions (events thus approximat-ing over the short run to the portfolio rather than the multiplier approach to money supply determination). However, a ruthless monetarist would no doubt suggest that a sufficiently tough monetary policy with regard to the base could bring the volume of loan finance under control so that the economy was, thereafter, going to approxi-mate to the monetarist model of monetary transmission.

The experience of the UK authorities in 1979–80 suggests that this is not an easy thing to do. Their task was hampered by the removal of foreign exchange controls which meant that rises in interest rates led to a rapid inflow of foreign funds. However, even if they had not suffered from this problem the arguments which we have examined in previous chapters suggest that single-minded attempts to control expenditure by monetary means are likely to be doomed to fail. An intensely financial economic structure cannot survive sharp rises in interest rates which have not been anticipated. They will cause asset prices to fall and leave parties who have borrowed on a short-term basis to finance long-term projects unable safely to refund their debts. To the extent they succeed in reducing real expenditure they will cause bankruptcies on top of those caused by the collapse of asset prices and refunding problems. And, in a world of layered finance, one collapse may lead to others even before the income multiplier has got to work through newly unemployed workers reducing their expenditure. Once such a process has started it can only be stopped quickly by large-scale lender-of-last-resort action and the abandonment of the policy of monetary restraint.

To summarize, insufficiently ruthless or unsuccessful attempts to control the monetary base only cause reduced expenditure by their effects on confidence, i.e. on the demand for loans. A large amount of unemployment may have to emerge as a result of reduced expenditure before any reduction in the rate of wage and price increases occurs.

15.3 NOT ALL UNEMPLOYMENT IS VOLUNTARY

The key assumption underlying the monetarists' theory of the labour market is that when unemployment rises above the 'natural' rate its return to that rate depends on the willingness of individual unemployed workers to lower their target real wages and seek employment in an inferior part of the labour market. They hold to this even when the number of unemployed workers supposedly searching voluntarily for jobs is vastly in excess of the number of vacancies. The lowering of reservation wages would lead to a fall in the rate of growth of money wages and price increases, raising real balances and demand until all those who wanted to work were employed. Stickiness in real wage targets is thus held to be the cause of unemployment.

For workers to be voluntarily unemployed in the monetarists' sense, however, a number of subsidiary assumptions are needed. Let us consider them in turn.

(1) *Full-time job search is more efficient than search while employed in a low-grade job.* Three objections to this may be proposed. First, prospective employers may, as Goodhart (1975, p. 197) has observed, judge the quality of workers by whether or not they currently have jobs. Unemployed workers may have been selected for redundancy because they are idle or less efficient than their workmates in similar job slots. Second, when unemployment is very high the number of applicants for every job will be high too

and the probability of getting an interview will be low. Hence there will be few interviews for which workers in what they regard as 'temporary' jobs will need to be absent; it will be easy to disguise such absence on job search as 'going to the dentist' or 'domestic problems'. Third, when a worker loses employment she gets socially out of touch. Not only may it be worth a real wage cut to avoid this, but as Hines (in Worswick, ed. (1973)) has pointed out, the worker may miss out on useful information about where job vacancies are coming up that would enable her to make early applications. Nobody is an island, one might say, except in reductionist economic theory.

(2) *If they went 'down-market' relatively skilled workers could successfully obtain jobs at the expense of those who are failing to move 'down-market'.* Exceptionally qualified candidates may fail to get jobs because prospective employers expect that they will constantly be on the lookout for something better and will soon leave. It would thus be foolish to hire them, train them and integrate them and then have to pay the costs of advertising for, and interviewing, replacements shortly after.

(3) *There exists a non-unionized sector of the labour market able to soak up workers displaced as a result of the excessive wage increases obtained by the exertion of market power by their industries' trade unions.* This may be a reasonable assumption as far as, say, the USA is concerned. For the UK, however, the long-run persistence of inter-industry wage differentials and struggles over relativities seemingly regardless of the level of unemployment, which are consistent with the behavioural and Keynesian analyses of Baxter (1980) and Trevithick (1976), make it seem an unwise approximation.

(4) *There is no such thing as wage stickiness from the demand side. It is always rational for firms to attempt to obtain lower rates of increase in money wages as labour markets become slack.* This assumption has been subjected to critical examination from a theoretical standpoint by Earl and Glaister (1979, 1980) and has been shown to hold only in economies where workers are employed according to contracts which spell out in complete detail *all* of their input aids and outputs. If jobs have task idiosyncrasies and the performance of a worker depends on other workers passing on to her information which cannot be written down in contracts owing to its idiosyncratic nature, it will be profitable for firms to leave employment contracts somewhat

loosely specified. Output levels may then benefit from inter-worker co-operation because workers recognize that the size of the corporate pie from which they are paid depends on their willingness to volunteer assistance to each other beyond the minimum that the employer would find acceptable. If employees leave and have to be replaced their replacements' abilities to perform at a similar level will be restricted by the extent of their on-the-job learning, part of which comes about as a result of the voluntary help from their colleagues. It is in the nature of this learning that it cannot be written into the employment contracts.

With incompletely detailed employment contracts existing holders of particular job slots will thus have a superior productivity for which they are not being paid more than raw recruits would receive. Their reward comes via promotion in the firm's internal labour markets after a lengthy period during which the employer has enjoyed the benefits of their excess productivity (to the extent that workers' bargaining powers have not reclaimed it). A failure to be promoted sufficiently rapidly or a relative fall-back in the rate of remuneration will accelerate natural wastage from the firm. If those workers who do not leave remove their coopera-tion and behave in a perfunctory manner their productivity may fall and, because they fail to pass on information to new recruits, the productivity of the replacements may stay vastly below that of those who have left. As a result, attempts by firms to lower the relative wages of their employees as labour markets become slack will reduce profits. Thus firms will keep their rates of wage increases in line with those of their competitors in the labour market to avoid losing skilled workers. If they need to shed labour, redundancy notices can be given to those workers conjectured to be among the least productive in a given job slot. To lower the rate of growth of money wages would reduce control over which workers departed. The more firms that behave in this way the less attractive it would be for any one firm unilaterally to reduce the rate at which it increases wages.

Where wage stickiness arises from the demand side, because firms are afraid that attempts to reduce the rate of increase of money wages unilaterally will lead to reduced profits, it is neces-sary for *trade unions* across the relevant part of the labour market to attempt to bargain collectively for economy-wide slower wage growth. Otherwise there will be no possibility of convergence towards the natural rate of unemployment.

In the light of these objections to the assumptions underlying the monetarist model of the labour market we conclude that there is no presumption that all observed unemployment is voluntary, resulting from an unwillingness of workers to lower their target real wages. Attempts of individual workers to price themselves into poorer-quality jobs are not necessarily irrational from the point of view of efficient search, but there is no guarantee that they will be successful. Involuntarily unemployed workers are perfectly prepared to work even if there is a higher increase in prices than in money wages (i.e. if real wages fall) but they have no direct means of pricing themselves into jobs. The best they can do is to carry on applying for whatever jobs there are and become self-employed as window-cleaners and cab-drivers or subsist on inadequate state benefits.

It should be added that, in so far as a lowering of the reservation wages of would-be workers actually leads to a reduction in the rate of increase of money wages, a lasting increase in employment in the economy is not the result of lower wage inflation directly bringing about a reduction in real wages. If the marginal propensity to spend income in the economy is less than unity the sustainable increase in employment arises only as a result of lower money wage increases cutting the rate of growth of purchasing power and hence reducing the price level below what it otherwise would have been. This *may* increase the real supply of loan finance and thus increase real expenditure sufficiently to offset any marginal tendency to save from current income (but it must not be forgotten that shifts in the velocity of circulation may prevent even this indirect effect from working). As will become evident in the next section, this result, and any other means of increasing employment, need not involve a reduction in *real* wages at all.

15.4   REFLATION WITHOUT INFLATION

If involuntary unemployment exists an increase in aggregate demand will only cause wages to increase at a faster rate than they otherwise would have done if trade unions become less afraid that high wage settlements will force firms to make their members redundant, or if there are bottlenecks in some segments of the labour market. The latter may lead to a bidding-up of wages which, if unions are conscious of relativities in bargaining, may have more general effects on wage increases. To prevent the first kind of acceleration of wage increases it is necessary to curb trade union bargaining powers or to introduce an effective incomes policy. To prevent the bottleneck effect it is necessary to avoid indiscriminate increases in demand when a reflation is carried out. The sectoral composition of demand should be purposefully influenced by the direction of public expenditure increases and tax cuts, and via directives to the banking system on where loans should be made available (cf. also chapter 10 on crowding out).

When wage increases are controlled in the above manner the only need for a rise in the price level when demand is increased at a time of involuntary unemployment is as a result of diminishing returns to labour (as marginal machinery is brought back into use, marginal supplies of natural resources are used, or a depreciation of the exchange rate raises import prices). With wages firmly controlled, these effects on the price level, if they occur, should be very much in the nature of one-off events. If involuntary unemployment exists individual workers will be quite prepared to suffer a reduction in living standards to get back into employment. But it is not inherent in an economic system that when aggregate demand increases real wages will necessarily fall.

If firms adopt the kind of 'normal cost' pricing policy discussed by Andrews (1949) and Neild (1963) they will not raise their prices as they bring lower productivity machinery back into operation or employ less experienced workers at a given wage in particular job slots. They will simply raise output. Their prices will be set with regard to the costs of producing at the average level of output they hope to be able to get through the business cycle. For many firms with highly integrated production tracks there will be no older vintage machines to be brought back into operation at a higher unit variable cost. Rather, they will enjoy *lower* average total costs as demand expands and, if they price according to normal costs, will simply expand capacity utilization at the same price and take increased profits per unit sold. If such firms do not use normal cost pricing but relate their prices to short-run average costs, in an attempt to maximize sales volumes and inconvenience rivals, a rise in orders will lead to a fall in prices.

It is perfectly possible that the same argument applies in the case of raw materials. Increases in their prices will only be passed on in finished output prices if they are expected to be permanent. But, if raw materials costs are not normalized in this way, a reflation should not be delayed for fear that it will drive up costs of commodity inputs. A single country's increase in demand will not have a substantial effect on world commodity prices. Although the same will not be true for a world-wide increase in demand it should be noted that the longer demand remains stagnant in commodity markets the more marginal suppliers will have dismantled their operations and stocks will have been reduced. Thus, as Kahn and Posner (1977) point out, the less reflation is delayed the smaller its effect on commodity prices will be. It will also be less likely that movement traders will enter commodity markets and cause speculative exacerbations of price rises. A similar argument can be used to suggest that a country which delays reflation is more likely eventually to suffer an inflationary exchange rate depreciation. The more demand is held down the greater the scrapping of plant and the more its productivity levels fall behind those of countries which have a greater incentive to innovate and invest because of relatively more buoyant demand. Thus its underlying competitive position, and ability to meet demand increases when they do occur, will be declining.

Even if an incomes policy and *ad hoc* demand-increasing measures are less than perfectly effective in preventing increases in wage rates on a greater scale than would have occurred in the absence of reflation, and if other input costs rise while firms do not pursue normal cost pricing policies, it is *still* possible to increase demand without increasing the price level. If reflation takes the form of subsidies to industrial costs or indirect tax reductions, financed by monetary expansion, firm supply curves will be shifted downwards. If reflation takes the form of income tax cuts (financed by monetary expansion rather than bond sales if crowding out, and hence rising mortgage rates, are felt possible) workers will need smaller money wage increases to meet given real wage targets and, again, firm supply curves will be shifted downwards.

The above collection of arguments suggests that, if there is involuntary unemployment, an increase in demand need have no upward effect on the price level if properly managed and could permit an expansion of output and employment with no reduction in real wages. The crucial factor in determining the non-inflationary success of a demand expansion is the ability of the authorities to prevent a lower threat of unemployment from causing unions to ask for and obtain wage increases that, gross of tax, are more costly to their employers than they otherwise would have been. If the authorities are unable to prevent this, by means of a permanent incomes policy and relativities board or more direct legal restraints on the power of trade unions, then the problem of involuntary unemployment facing individual workers is a purely political one. Economic analysis is of no further help in alleviating it.

Monetarists regard the natural rate as something inherently impossible to observe, and suggest it is only possible to alter it by introducing improved labour exchanges, cutting taxes and unemployment benefits, or reducing the abilities of trade unions to obstruct structural change. Now, suppose that all unemployment really *is* voluntary, but the government is not sure whether this is the case and, anyway, does not find it acceptable. In such a situation it will be perfectly safe to attempt to increase employment with a policy package that adds to aggregate demand so long as it is of the kind discussed in the previous paragraph. That is to say, it should not only raise the incentive for firms to hire workers, by increasing demand, but must also increase the incentive for workers to increase the labour force, using tax cuts and industrial subsidies to permit non-inflationary real wage increases that only partly deter firms from increasing employment. The only situation in which such a reflation will misfire, if there are no involuntarily unemployed workers, is where the aggregate supply curve for labour is backward-bending. It is well known that monetarists do not believe the supply of labour to behave in this way.

Since indexation is a central component in the monetarists' kit of devices for reducing inflationary expectations (see Friedman (1974), for example) we cannot proceed to our conclusion without presenting a brief warning about it from the Keynesian standpoint. Keynesians see indexation not as a device which helps reduce inflationary expectations but as something prone to generate disastrous instability. They hold this view because flexibility in the velocity of circulation makes them believe that the key determinant of the rise in the general price level for produced goods is the rate of change of money wages, not the rate of growth of the money supply. The German hyperinflation of 1923 was made much worse by daily wage increases which effectively amounted to a system of wage indexation. As the money supply lagged behind, velocity increases were able to accommodate the exploding price level.

Davidson (1978a, p. 399) has presented a succinct theoretical explanation of why Keynesians believe that indexation may eventually lead to hyperinflation:

> In any perfectly indexed economy, any increase in the price index would start a process of continually shifting the flow supply curves of all goods upwards, causing people to fly from currency (i.e. there is a dramatic fall in the liquidity of money) as people will prefer to hold liquid goods (whose future spot price is expected to be inflation proof).

An indexed economy is thus perched on a knife edge from which it can be tipped by anything which sparks off changes in current prices, even a commodity boom which comes about as a result of mere expectations of price changes. UK Keynesians thus regard as very fortunate the abandonment of Edward Heath's final incomes policy by the incoming Labour Government in 1974. In this policy workers were to receive £0.40 for every 1 per cent increase in the retail price index beyond a threshold amount and just as it was coming into operation the OPEC oil price rise began to make an impact on the price level.

15.5 CONCLUSION

A good critique is surely one which is based upon an understanding of that which is being criticized, and which presents an alternative way of analysing a problem which is constructive rather than nihilistic. In this chapter we have had cause to challenge the monetarists' theory of output and inflation control, of the nature of unemployment, and their theory of the natural rate of unemployment. Attempts to control the 'money supply' by acting upon one particular definition will therefore only reduce the rate of growth of expenditure if they reduce the demand for money and are not simply accommodated by shifts in velocity or the expansion of other definitions of the money supply. Reductions in expenditure, if labour markets are highly unionized and involuntary unemployment exists, only lower inflation rates by frightening workers into accepting lower rates of wage increase in pay bargaining. As a result, inflation is only restrained by monetary measures so long as unemployment is high and may tend to accelerate as the latter falls unless cuts in unemployment are accompanied by the introduction of powerful incomes policies, or engineered by reflationary measures which involve a lowering of firm supply curves. Monetary measures of the kind usually advocated by monetarists – i.e. a fixed target for the rate of growth of the monetary base – are not sufficient for obtaining the long-run reduction of inflation and unemployment, and they may not even be necessary either.

16

DCE and the Monetary Approach to the Balance of Payments

16.1 INTRODUCTION

This chapter is concerned with the international dimension of the debate between monetarists and Keynesians over monetary theory and policy. On the theoretical level the debate has focused on the monetary approach to the balance of payments. This is a modern revival of ideas that date back over two centuries to David Hume. Its present main proponents are members of the notoriously monetarist faculty of economics at the University of Chicago. Frenkel and Johnson (eds) (1976) is a collection of some of their major contributions. On the policy level there has been considerable disagreement over the merits of alternative means of managing balance of payments problems, particularly those used by the IMF when granting loans to countries with balance of payments deficits. Even where countries do not suffer from a trade imbalance the international aspects of their monetary systems are of interest for the difficulties they can pose for governments trying to control interest rates, exchange rates or monetary growth. This is particularly the case now that fixed exchange rates have largely been abandoned and companies are increasingly multinational or of a size sufficient to be able to borrow on international money markets and engage in currency speculation.

The structure of the rest of the chapter is as follows. In section 16.2 there is a lengthy examination of how domestic money supplies can be affected by international imbalances. It will be shown that in particular circumstances governments may be able to isolate their economies from such effects. Because the overseas sector can often affect the amount of finance available to domestic participants in an economic system it has increasingly been felt necessary to distinguish between total monetary growth and changes caused directly by domestic monetary policies, the latter aggregate being known as Domestic

Credit Expansion. Part of the interest in DCE arises because the IMF often imposes DCE limits on countries with balance of payments deficits to whom it is lending foreign currency. Section 16.3 considers the rationale for, and likely consequences of, such DCE restrictions. Having argued that the IMF's policies are often both short-run and short-sighted we move on to consider the monetary approach to the balance of payments in the last two sections. This will be outlined in section 16.4, with special attention being paid to the assumptions it involves. In section 16.5 criticisms of the monetary approach to the balance of payments will be offered where they do not duplicate those already given in the critique of IMF attitudes. In particular, we will emphasize the long-run nature of this theory since it seems to have found favour with IMF economists who insist on short-run corrective policies. By implication they seem to be acting in their policy-making as though the long run comes very rapidly.

16.2 STERILIZATION AND THE OVERSEAS ORIGINS OF DOMESTIC MONEY SUPPLIES

In both fixed and floating exchange rate regimes imbalances on a country's current or capital flow accounts with the rest of the world can have monetary implications. If such monetary effects are success-fully eliminated by the monetary authorities a sterilization of currency flows is said to have been achieved. Monetarists typically believe that sterilization is not possible but later in this section some examples of how successful sterilizations might be achieved will be outlined. In examining the basic mechanisms it is helpful to decompose the present usual exchange rate regime of managed floating into two artificial extreme cases: first, completely flexible exchange rates; and second, completely fixed exchange rates.

In the absence of speculative flows and holdings of foreign currency by domestic traders a country would effectively be like a closed economy if exchange rates were completely freely floating. Any tendency for an excess relative demand for imports would cause the exchange rate to fall. This would both raise the demand for exports and choke off demand for imports until the supplies and demands for domestic and overseas currencies were back in equilibrium. In such a situation there would be no question of currency outflows and trade conditions could not directly affect the money supply. This is not the case if domestic residents can hold foreign currency deposits. This they may well wish to do if exchange rates are expected to change and/or if they can earn a higher rate of interest by banking in another country. Recalling the analysis of asset yields in chapter 8, we would class the yield components of holdings of foreign currency associated with the possibility of changes in the exchange rate as their liquidity premiums. These are not observable, unlike interest payments or, in the case of countries such as Switzerland where interest is negative for foreign depositors, carrying costs. The existence of these non-observable liquidity premium yield components means that interest rates can differ between countries without precluding the equalization of marginal yields on asset holdings.

Suppose that holders of domestic currency decide they would like to hold Deutschmarks. Unless there is an offsetting shift in import and export functions they will tend to cause the exchange rate to fall as they purchase their Deutschmarks with domestic currency. What happens next depends on whether they deposit their newly acquired Deutschmark holdings in domestic or foreign banks. Even if the exchange rate is free to float exchange control regulations may prevent the holding in domestic banks of foreign currency deposits not already earmarked for import or overseas investment payments. If foreign currency deposits *are* allowed in domestic banks and are attractive, the credit base of the economy will be unaffected by the domestically owned Deutschmarks being deposited in them unless the banks adjust their reserve asset ratios because they think that holdings of foreign currency have a different probability of being withdrawn. This aside, the only change may be in some money supply definitions – e.g. in the UK sterling M_3 would fall, but M_3 would not.

In the latter case there will clearly be a reduction in domestic bank deposits and an offsetting rise in bank deposits somewhere else in the world. The speculative shift would thus affect the domestic money supply. In so far as a reduced money supply affected demand adversely by raising interest rates, the exchange rate would tend to rise as imports fell, as well as due to the interest rate attraction of domestic bank deposits. The willingness of holders of foreign balances to make deposits in the domestic currency would depend on their expectations of the future behaviour of exchange rates. There is thus no reason for inflows to restore exchange and interest rates to their original levels. Furthermore, an additional speculative outflow could be sparked off by the initial fall in the exchange rate providing cues for movement traders to adjust their portfolios.

In a fixed exchange rate system the Central Bank uses changes in the size of its gold and currency reserves as a buffer to balance out domestic supplies and demands for foreign currency. Leaving aside capital flows for simplicity, consider what happens when exporters receive payment in foreign currency. They will prefer to have this converted into domestic currency to pay their workers or buy home-produced goods. Their banks can do this by accepting the currency entitlement and holding it as a reserve asset, creating a domestic currency deposit against it. The conversion can be carried out by the Central Bank if the clearing banks do not wish to hold foreign currency. In this case additions to foreign currency reserves can either be used directly to support an increase in the money supply or, as is the case in some countries, there is a more complex process involving the Bank's Exchange Equalization Account (EEA).

An EEA consists of a country's foreign exchange reserves and stocks of government securities. When an exporting company or its bank presents foreign exchange to the EEA the latter obtains it by selling government securities on the open market (or, in the UK, offering to purchase fewer Treasury bills to replace those that have matured than it otherwise would have done) and adds the foreign exchange to its holdings. This does not involve any increase in the money supply; it may take the form of a simple transfer of bank deposits to the exporters from the accounts of the purchasers of securities. However, unless something has happened to raise the demand for securities, the EEA's sale must cause security prices to fall and the rate of interest to rise. A rise in the rate of interest will encourage currency inflows from abroad. These will either be deposited directly in domestic banks, raising the money supply, or will pass via the EEA with the same end result. If the Central Bank attempts to sterilize such inflows by open market operations, its sales of bonds will simply restore the upward pressure on the rate of interest and encourage further inflows.

This vicious circle of currency inflows and spiralling interest rates has trapped a number of governments since the Second World War. In early 1950 the Canadian authorities tried to sterilize the inflows associated with a strong balance of trade surplus with the US and found themselves overwhelmed by speculative inflows. Rather than simply abandon attempts at sterilization they decided to float the Canadian dollar. In the 1960s many OECD countries experienced the problem again as the balance of payments deficit of the US grew with its commitment to the Vietnam War. These countries were reluctant to revalue against the dollar and had instead to tolerate increases in their money supplies following unsuccessful attempts at sterilization. (See

Kouri (1975) for an analysis of the German experience in the 1960s. It should be noted, however, that not all writers agree with his findings and that recent work by Alexakis (1981) shows that the Germans were fairly successful at sterilizing currency flows in the 1970s.) However, all the time this was happening the US did not seem to be experiencing a shrinking money supply despite its balance of payments problems. Rather, money continued to flow out of the US to augment the world money supply (and give rise to the 'global monetarists' ' view of inflation) at the same time as domestic credit was expanded. This suggests that, as far as the US was concerned, a massive sterilization process was going on. This process was doubtless partly aided by exchange controls and imperfect international capital markets but may also have been possible due to the existence of some inherent features of modern financial structures.

When a country is suffering from a declining position of competi-tiveness, which manifests itself as a balance of payments deficit, this will rapidly cause unemployment unless the private sector runs down its net wealth (dis-hoards) or the government increases its net spend-ing. If firms making losses sell off assets or make rights issues they can be adding to the supply of securities at just the same time as the EEA is adding to its demand for them as it runs down its foreign exchange holdings to permit payments for imports. Thus despite the deficit there may be no tendency for bond prices to rise and interest rates to fall.

Evidently, the private sector will not wish to run down its net wealth and make losses indefinitely. After a certain point it will prefer to cut employment unless aggregate demand increases. However, so long as official reserves or its overseas borrowing power have not been exhausted there is no reason why the government should not expand its deficit and thus augment the supply of bonds. It will find its defi-cit growing automatically as growing unemployment causes dole payments to rise and tax receipts to fall. Alternatively, and more efficiently, it can prevent the unemployment from emerging by increas-ing industrial subsidies, its own direct expenditure, or by cutting taxes. These devices will reduce the size of the private sector deficit associated with a given level of employment but need not entail a greater public sector deficit than would the dole payments/do nothing strategy.

Deficit-financed arms expenditure of the kind carried out by the US government in the 1960s can be seen, in the light of the above discus-sion, as an aid to both the preservation of employment and the sterilization of the monetary implications of the US balance of pay-ments deficit. It should be added that so long as the rest of the world was prepared to accept export payments in dollars there was no need for the US to reduce its deficit by deflation, devaluation or import controls. So long as dollars were felt convertible into gold, governments were quite prepared to build up extensive dollar holdings in their official reserves; there was no fear that they might be eroded in value by a devaluation of the dollar (cf. Magdoff (1969)). The trouble came when the French government noticed that the US deficit had accumulated way beyond the value of the contents of Fort Knox and asked for its reserves of dollars to be converted. Then followed in 1971 the collapse of the Bretton Woods parity system, a devaluation of the dollar and a rise in the dollar price of gold.

In the US example – which, as Cramp (1971) shows, could be applied with reversed signs to currency inflows – sterilization was possible owing to a divergence of the rates of growth in the money supply and domestic credit. We now conclude this section of the chapter by examining in some detail the concept of Domestic Credit Expansion (DCE). This can be terribly confusing but the idea behind it is, in essence, very simple. In a modern economy, the bulk of the money supply consists of credit; that is to say, loans made by people and institutions. But not all of the supply of credit need come from domestic agencies and individuals. The part that does we call domestic credit; the rest comes from overseas. When a country's money stock grows its growth can come from an expansion of domestic credit (by open market operations; by 'printing money' to finance the public sector deficit; by a greater willingness of the non-bank private sector to make deposits in financial institutions) or from a net expansion in the rate of inflows from overseas of the kind we have been describing above. Changes in the net rate of foreign inflows thus affect the amount of domestic credit expansion needed to get a given expansion of the money stock by any definition. For example, if a German makes a sterling deposit with a London bank she is lending money to the UK (or there is a net reduction in loans to Germany by UK banks). The UK money supply thus rises more than it otherwise would have done for a given expansion of domestic credit. Similarly, if an American bomber manufacturer buys British ejector seats the US money supply growth will be smaller than it otherwise would have been since US reserves and bank deposits will have fallen. However, when the US government 'prints money' to purchase the finished bombers the growth of money balances will be restored by this increase in US domestic credit expansion.

The simplest approach to the definition of DCE is as follows:

$$\text{DCE} \equiv \varDelta M - \varDelta R$$

In this identity, $\varDelta M$ is the growth of the money stock and $\varDelta R$ is the increase in reserves a country experiences as a result of a balance of payments surplus. For a country with a foreign deficit it may be the case that there is an increase in net government borrowing overseas. This is normally counted as a decrease in reserves since, without such borrowing, official reserves would otherwise have fallen. Although not all official borrowing overseas is made expressly for this purpose it is always recorded as a fall in reserves since the *ceteris paribus* effect on reserves is the same whatever the intention of the government that accepts the loan.

Official definitions of DCE bring out more explicitly the links between the public sector and the overseas capital account. If the PSBR is not financed by purchases of debt by the non-bank domestic private sector it must either be funded abroad or involve the purchase of debt by the banking system ('printing money'). Official definitions of DCE, being concerned with credit, are constructed with regard to the assets side of banks' balance sheets, unlike money supply definitions. These features can be seen clearly in the definitions of DCE introduced by the UK government in 1977. Both yield the same result:

(a) DCE $\equiv$ The change in non-bank holdings of notes and coin
  plus the increase in lending by UK banks to public, private and overseas sectors;
  plus overseas lending to the public sector and bank lending to the public sector in foreign currencies.
(b) DCE $\equiv$ The Public Sector Borrowing Requirement
  less purchases of public sector debt by the non-bank private sector;
  plus the increase in bank lending in sterling to the private sector and the overseas sector.

Some authors have tended to cause confusion by treating these relationships as other than mere identities, speaking of 'corrected' or '*ex post*' money supply (cf. Artis and Nobay (1969), pp. 44–6). No causal relationship is necessarily implied. A change in the growth rate of exports may be associated with a change in the rate of DCE or in $\varDelta M$, depending on the actions of the monetary authorities. If they do not attempt to sterilize the effects of the greater currency outflow then $\varDelta M$ will fall. A successful sterilization results in an expansion of DCE and this prevents ΔM from being other than it would have been had exports not fallen. For a balance of payments surplus the same argument applies but with the signs reversed.

16.3 DCE TARGETS AND IMF LOANS

The DCE identities of the previous section would be of little more than definitional significance were it not for the fact that countries borrowing from the IMF are often forced to agree to DCE limits as a precondition of being granted loans. The operational importance of the distinction between DCE and usual money supply definitions becomes clear when the IMF policies are scrutinized for their underlying rationale and likely significance.

The IMF seems an unwilling lender of last resort to countries suffering from balance of payments problems. It displays a very conservative attitude on the occasions when it acts in this role. It requires rapid payment and does not expect to be asked to expand the size of the loans it has reluctantly given. Countries borrowing from the IMF are thus obliged to eliminate their deficits at speed and turn them into surpluses so that they can repay their loans. Given such attitudes it is not surprising that countries needing loans have increasingly preferred to avoid IMF funds even at the cost of more expensive credit from the Eurodollar market, which has fewer conditions attached. Particularly unpalatable are the credit limits the IMF typically demands in cases where a balance of payments problem goes hand-in-hand with rapid inflation. Hirschman (1963, p. 233) provides an example of the IMF's attitude, quoting their 1950 report to Chile:

> A credit restriction, to be effective, must force businessmen to sell goods at prices lower than they had anticipated, often times at a loss; it must make it financially impossible for them to increase wage rates and it must cause a certain minimum amount of unemployment.

In usually insisting on DCE limits rather than controls on the growth of the borrower's money supply the IMF displays still further its reluctance to take chances. Reference to the simple definition of DCE makes it clear that, so long as a country has a balance of payments problem causing an outflow of reserves, a DCE limit is more restrictive than one on the growth rate of the money supply. A money supply target would mean that a government which did not care about further harming its reserves position (feeling, say, that it could extract a further loan from the IMF) could simply expand domestic credit to offset the tendency of the money supply to fall as a result of a continuing balance of payments deficit. With only a money supply limit active sterilization policies could be applied unless thwarted by an IMF restriction on the size of the public sector deficit. When a DCE limit is applied (and is typically accompanied by a PSBR limit as a failsafe) a continuing balance of payments deficit leads towards the exhaustion of domestic money balances. As in the monetary approach to the balance of payments, discussed in section 16.4, the IMF assumes that people will not allow a permanent fall in the ratio of their money balances to their permanent incomes. With a binding DCE limit the implication of this assumption is that expenditure will fall as people attempt to preserve their money balances. Hence both the rundown of reserves and the balances of payments deficit will cease.

The IMF need to have some idea of the relationship between the rate of credit expansion and the balance of payments before they can choose DCE limits that are no more than *ad hoc* and possibly dangerously inappropriate magnitudes. Following Polak (1957) and Polak and Boissoneault (1960) we see that the relevant linkages for the IMF are thus: (a) a rise in domestic credit leads to (b) increased aggregate demand, associated with (c) an increase in imports, which must be accompanied by (d) a rundown in reserves or greater borrowing from the overseas sector, in the absence of private overseas borrowing or inflows of overseas capital.

The usefulness of a DCE target depends heavily on the stability/predictability of these linkages, and on the ability of the monetary authorities to adhere to the target. The two key relationships are the income velocity of circulation of money and the marginal propensity to import. An examination of the history of these relationships for the UK immediately prior to the UK loan from the IMF in 1976 does not inspire confidence in the DCE limits that were attached to it as being anything other than some arbitrarily chosen figures. The ratio of GNP to the M_3 money supply definition fell around 2½ per cent a year from 1961 to 1968 after experiencing a large rise in the 1950s. From 1970 onwards it was less predictable, with values of 2.17 in 1973, 2.15 in 1975 and 2.35 in 1975. There was thus a 10 per cent increase between 1974 and 1975 alone. The propensity to import had also fluctuated sharply, having values of 24.8 per cent in 1973, 31.4 per cent in 1974 and 28.9 per cent in 1975.

The variability in these ratios would not strike a Keynesian as being at all strange. The marginal propensity to import will depend on the composition of expenditure (which may have been thrown into a state of change by the energy crisis), relative prices, and changes in non-price factors. The last will be affected by the level of employment in so far as this determines the availability of import substitutes. It should be added that the rate of growth of export sales can fluctuate for the same reasons, and it is the overall balance of payments position that decides whether or not a DCE target becomes a binding limit. A slump in world trade which forces a DCE limit to grip an economy tighter than otherwise forces that economy to deflate and add to the overall recession.

Whether or not a cut in credit expansion according to one definition merely leads to a compensating expansion of the extra components of a wider definition has been questioned in earlier chapters. Even if it does not, we have also noted that the income velocity of circulation of money in a particular period will not be independent of shifts in confidence. Much also depends on the way the money enters the system and the composition of its initial expenditure, since this will determine what happens in subsequent rounds. There is, for example, a conspicuous difference in the early effects on import demands of an increase in the money supply by open market operations used initially to buy property, and expanding the money supply to finance government expenditure on foreign-produced military hardware.

As part of the terms of the UK's loan from the IMF in 1976 the then Chancellor of the Exchequer, Mr Denis Healey, proposed to reduce the UK's PSBR by between £2 billion and £3 billion per annum in the subsequent years. Given the restriction on DCE it was felt that the PSBR levels originally planned would have implied rising interest rates and the crowding out of private expenditure due to the greater volume of bonds being sold to the non-bank private sector. Higher interest rates would have attracted foreign currency inflows, making the DCE targets easier to meet but at the cost of a higher exchange rate. Such foreign capital inflows could just as easily be withdrawn in future and could, in the meantime, merely conceal a declining underlying position of trade competitiveness. High interest rates and exchange rates were felt likely to hinder the growth of output and employment, but the adverse employment effects of a reduced PSBR received scant attention from non-Keynesians increasingly sold on the '100 per cent crowding out' idea. Warnings that various possible methods of cutting the PSBR – such as the introduction of a wealth tax or a cut in old age pensions – could have very different demand effects came from Keynesian economists (see, for example, Chapter 3 of the February 1977 *National Institute Economic Review*) but they were largely unheeded.

This critique of the use of restrictive DCE targets by the IMF as a condition of loan provision to countries with balance of payments problems has so far centred on the contingent nature and instability of the linkages between credit expansions and currency flows. We conclude it by suggesting that its whole philosophy is misplaced and short-sighted. A cut in demand, which is what a DCE restriction implies if it is to have any effect on the balance of payments, both reduces the incentive and the ability of a country's firms to invest. They will thus slip further behind their competitors overseas and, for a given exchange parity, the full employment trade balance of the country will thus get worse and worse, not better. Wealth which otherwise would have been created will not exist. Furthermore, to the extent that the country's balance of payments does improve at the cost of rising unemployment, demand in the rest of the world will be lower (but not by the multiple suffered in the deflating economy because of its fractional marginal propensity to import). Everyone, even the IMF in the long run, loses when such a policy is implemented.

16.4 THE MONETARY APPROACH TO THE BALANCE OF PAYMENTS

The most cogent theoretical underpinning of the IMF's approach to the management of balance of payments disequilibria consists in the monetary approach to the balance of payments. Since we have just criticized the IMF for being excessively short-sighted it is ironic, even disturbing, to find that the monetary approach to the balance of payments is a theory of the long-run equilibrium positions which countries will attain so long as they are not subjected to continuous monetary disturbances. In essence it is an adaptation of the monetarist view that inflation is always and everywhere a monetary phenomenon to read 'a balance of payments deficit is always and everywhere a monetary phenomenon'. As such, therefore, it can only be corrected by monetary means. Just as incomes policies or curbs on free collective bargaining by trade unions are felt by monetarists to be irrelevant to the control of inflation, so they see devaluation or import controls as irrelevant to the permanent elimination of a balance of payments deficit.

The monetarists' result depends upon four key assumptions or, rather, upon the world operating 'as if' the four assumptions hold when empirical work is being done. The first is that arbitrage rapidly ensures that the 'law of one price' holds for identical goods sold in different countries, after allowing for transport costs. If, after adjusting for the exchange parity, the price of a particular country's output of a commodity is below the world price, traders will buy up the product and sell it on the world market. This will bid up the domestic price until it is the same as the world price. The addition of a small country's output to the world supply will not, however, alter the world price. If exchange rates are fixed and this mechanism works quickly one country cannot have an inflation rate greater than that of the rest of the world. Any tendency for it to do so for reasons of declining competitiveness will produce higher unemployment in the short run until inflationary expectations are revised and the inflation and unemployment rates fall by the mechanisms described in chapter 14.

For some markets, particularly those for primary commodities and manufactured inputs, this assumption does not seem too far-fetched. Furthermore, even if countries produce different finished products, it may work pretty well at the industry level so long as the products are close substitutes, which is the case in many oligopolistic markets. Proponents of the theory (e.g. Genberg, in Frenkel and Johnson, 1976) claim they have found good empirical support for the notion that prices in a small country (including the rate of interest – the price of money) are tied up very closely to world prices.

The second assumption is that all countries are fully employed. For this reason, increases in demand in a country cannot be met by a rise in domestic output. Nor, because of the law of one price, can they be soaked up by higher domestic prices except in the short run. All demand excesses thus escape via the balance of payments. Frenkel and Johnson (1976, p. 25) offer a quite extraordinary justification for their employment assumption:

> [In the long run] either employment expands into the full employment range, or it contracts and people either starve to death and go back to full employment numbers, or there is a revolution on Marxist lines, or more likely the public simply votes for the other political party than the one in power since all of them promise to maintain full employment and the public expects them to do it.

Amongst other things, this view completely neglects the existence of state benefits or extended family support for the unemployed and does not specify quite how long it might take for the long run to be reached.

The experience of the world in the Great Depression of the 1930s, and since 1974, rather suggests that the long run is a long time coming and not just the 2 or 3 years that the IMF policies seem to have in mind.

As a third assumption it is suggested that with fixed exchange rates the sterilization of currency flows is not possible. This is the result of the law of one price being assumed to hold in international money markets under a fixed exchange rate regime. (With flexible exchange rates and speculation there would, as we argued earlier, be no necessary equalization of interest rates between countries.) It should be clear, in the light of section 16.2, that this assumption will not always be appropriate, even if exchange rates are fixed. A balance of payments deficit need not lead to reduced money balances so long as domestic credit is expanded and this can be done without any fall in the rate of interest being necessary and causing further outflows. All that is required is for the supply of financial assets to rise in line with domestic credit. If the IMF really believed that currency flows could not be sterilized in the long run it would be indifferent between imposing DCE and money supply limits on deficit countries to whom it was lending.

Lastly, it is assumed that the growth of domestic credit, on some appropriate definition, can be controlled by the central authorities and that there is a stable demand for money. This, according to Frenkel and Johnson (1976, p. 24), is a function of a 'small number of aggregate economic variables'. Usually the only variable that gets mentioned is wealth, or its flow proxy, permanent income. There seems little point in repeating our objections to the monetarists' view of the supply and demand for money yet again; we shall simply note that *were* it not misleading to analyse the world in terms of long-run equilibrium we would gladly withdraw our objections to this mode of theorizing.

Given these assumptions, an increase in the money supply of an individual country must be associated with a balance of payments deficit between that country and the rest of the world if the international monetary system is one where exchange rates are fixed. Unless monetary growth comes about via a reduction in the bond-financed component of the public deficit (which causes problems for the 'no sterilization' assumption) or by helicopter drops of money sanctioned by the Central Bank, the monetary expansion must initially be associated with a fall in the rate of interest. For this to happen international capital markets must be somewhat imperfect in the short run, since otherwise domestic monetary expansion would leak out to the rest of the world immediately by a capital flow before any trade deficit had time to emerge. A lower rate of interest leads to more borrowing and more expenditure on current output. New borrowers who succeed in buying domestic output force other transactors to buy imports since output is fixed. Prices cannot be bid up instead owing to the one price assumption. Hence excess demand has no escape except via the balance of payments, taking with it the excess money balances until equilibrium is restored.

Devaluation or import controls will not lead to other than a temporary improvement in a balance of payments deficit unless accompanied by a reduction in the rate of growth of the deficit country's money supply. But a restriction of monetary growth would have the same effect *without* devaluation or import controls; it would also have the added advantage of not suffering from the '*J*-curve' effects associated with devaluations (where the change in currency parities causes the problem to get worse in the short run owing to import contracts being denominated in foreign currencies before the parity change), or from the distortions that are supposed to accompany import controls in a fully employed economy. Devaluation and import controls fail to improve balance of payments deficits in the long run owing to the law of one price. A devaluation cannot affect the world price of commodities so domestic production, now being relatively cheap, will be bid up in price. Output cannot be increased if the full-employment assumption holds. The best that can happen will be a temporary improvement owing to the initial inflation of import prices eroding the real value of money balances and leading to a temporary cutback in expenditure while they are being restored. If tariffs are imposed on imports rises in their prices also reduce real money balances and lead to expenditure cutbacks, reducing the leakage rate of the excess money supply until real money balances have been restored to their desired levels.

Although, with fixed exchange rates, excess money supply growth in an individual country cannot push its price level above that of the rest of the world (after conversion for currency parities and transport costs), by adding to the global money supply via its balance of payments deficit a country can help generate a rise in the world price level. Only in this way would a single country in a fixed exchange rate system expect to find any relationship between its money supply growth and its price level movements, and then only if the behaviour of the rest of the world followed a consistent pattern. Furthermore, a small country would not be likely to make much of an impact on the world money supply through its balance of payments deficits. This 'global monetarist' view can be extended to attribute the worldwide acceleration of inflation around 1968–9 to the significant effects on the world money supply of the balance of payments deficit of the US at a time when the Bretton Woods system of fixed exchange rates was still in use.

If, with fixed exchange rates, a small country tries to enjoy a lower rate of inflation than the rest of the world by restricting its rate of domestic credit expansion, the monetarists hold that it will not succeed. Rather, it will, so long as it persists in the policy, simply generate a balance of payments surplus. Any tendency for demand to fall below the full employment level (in advance of wage adjustments) and moderate inflation will be offset by extra export orders and an inflow of currency. Since, by assumption, this cannot be sterilized, it will tend to get respent and correct the balance of payments surplus unless the government reduces domestic credit creation still further – which will only cause the process to be repeated.

The monetary approach to the balance of payments thus leads to the following conclusion. Policy-makers in small countries have no control at all over their domestic price levels unless they float their exchange rates. However, they have as a consolation the advantage that their balance of payments positions need not be a permanent problem unless they choose to mismanage their rates of domestic credit expansion.

16.5   OBJECTIONS TO THE MONETARY APPROACH
TO THE BALANCE OF PAYMENTS

Since our objections to monetarist theorizing in general have been spelt out at length elsewhere in this book, especially in the previous chapter, we shall not trouble here to comment again on our reasons for viewing with scepticism the assumptions about employment and the stability of demand for money. If there is involuntary unemployment increases in demand need not all leak out of the system via higher imports. If the demand for money is unstable and unpredictable it is not at all clear what constitutes an appropriate rate of domestic credit expansion. Having made these basic points we concentrate in this section on issues related, in so far as is possible, to the balance of payments-specific portion of the theory.

First, if non-traded goods form a significant volume of purchases within a country then rises in their prices could occur even if the law of one price held for traded goods. Frenkel and Johnson claim that this argument is invalid because excess demand for non-traded output will spill over into reduced supplies of traded goods (and hence higher imports) as factors of production are drawn into sectors producing non-traded goods. They only allow this point to be of importance, as something of which empirical researchers should be aware, as a transitory phenomenon liable to disturb the correspondence between price indices and the predictions of purchasing power parity calculations. The central question here must surely concern the length of time it takes before sectoral resource shifts occur and a long-run equilibrium is reached. The persistence of regional problems in countries where a structural shift in demand has occurred, and the fact the capital is not some malleable putty-like substance, but highly specific and long-lived once turned from finance into a machine, suggests that transitions may take a very long time. Also, trade union resistance to changes in the structure of wage differentials may be very effective over a long period.

Second, market imperfections may prevent the law of one price from working properly in many markets for traded goods, which also means that domestic price levels are not entirely at the mercy of world events in fixed exchange rate systems. Car makers, for example, can allow their dealers franchises on the condition that cars cannot be exchanged between dealers in different countries and still be sold as 'new'. Price differentials may also persist due to the lack of information about overseas prices and trade regulations faced by non-specialist traders and their lower economies in transport. The market for books, even books by monetarists, is another obvious example of a structure in which prices can differ substantially between countries.

Third, to reiterate the arguments of section 16.2, sterilization of currency flows is entirely possible if the private sector is willing to adjust the composition of its wealth portfolio with regard to the relative importance of bonds and money balances, or if the public sector is prepared to run a higher budget deficit whenever it has a balance of payments deficit with which to contend.

Finally, and perhaps most importantly, doubts need to be expressed about the notion that it is appropriate to view the international economic system as if it is tending towards a predetermined long-run equilibrium. There is a growing body of literature which argues that the world is often a place of deviation-amplifying, rather than deviation-counteracting, forces, a world where cumulative causation is the dominant process (cf. Myrdal (1957) and Singh (1977)). If the underlying real structures of economic systems are diverging at a faster rate than can be offset by adjustments in labour and capital markets, and if devaluations are met by substantial real wage resistance by workers, then it is perfectly possible to explain the failure of devaluations to correct balance of payments problems without recourse to the monetarists' theory. To the extent that demand is restricted a full-employment balance of payments deficit may be concealed at the cost of growing unemployment. But, as was emphasized at the end of section 16.3, this can just make matters worse by reducing the competitive power of the economy. Unemployment may frighten workers into accepting wage reductions in the long run – possibly at the cost of a disastrous Minskian debt deflation – or the hidden hand may, to borrow a quip from Joan Robinson, 'do its work by strangulation' as in the world of Frenkel and Johnson, but this hardly seems to be an efficient form of economic management.

Policy-makers who follow the monetary approach to the balance of payments are thus in danger of neglecting the lengthy transition of the short and medium terms – during which the exhaustion of reserves and international borrowing power or the emergence of unemployment could be causing crises – for a long run which does not exist. If credit restriction measures take a long time to have any effect it will be no use telling speculative sellers of the domestic currency that a devaluation will not be necessary to eliminate a trade deficit; a devaluation may be necessary merely to remove pressure on the exchange rate even if the theory might conceivably work in the long run. Such problems will only be avoided if the adjustment process is fairly rapid or if holders of foreign currency have 'rational expectations' and believe in monetarist theories and the authorities' projections.

16.6   CONCLUSION

It is rather ironic that the monetarists turned their attention from closed to open economies at the time of the demise of the Bretton Woods system of fixed exchange rates and the rise of Eurocurrency markets. Floating exchange rates make it much harder to decide to what extent balance of payments problems can be corrected by monetary means, while the developments in international financial markets raise grave doubts about the ability of policy-makers to control activity by manipulating their rates of domestic credit expansion.

The possibility that companies may finance their purchases from overseas and from each other by borrowing in offshore currency markets is the final twist in the discussions of the impossibility of controlling the supply of monetary aggregates in an orderly way without first restricting the demand for loans. Without exchange controls a restriction of DCE may fail to halt money supply growth if there is a large inflow of deposits from abroad in response to a small change in the interest rate. Alternatively, or if there are exchange controls, the domestic money supply may be restricted but fail to cause a reduction in expenditure by domestic companies; dealings will simply be conducted between offshore accounts. With flexible exchange rates attempts to control domestic money balances by increasing interest rates and restrictions in DCE can also generate highly inappropriate exchange rates if speculation in currency markets is of the movement trading rather than the classical variety. For example, attempts to finance a greater part of the PSBR by bond sales to the non-bank private sector instead of DCE may drive up the rate of interest and provoke an upwards shift in the exchange rate. This will increase the demand for loans still further as companies with strong ties with export markets will be forced to engage in distress borrowing to maintain their levels of activity. If they cut employment instead the demand for loans will *still* rise – the PSBR increases due to falling tax receipts and rising unemployment benefits. Hence unless DCE or overseas borrowing is increased a ruthlessly monetarist government may find itself trapped in a vicious circle of rising unemployment, interest and exchange rates.

On all of these matters the monetarists have nothing to offer except exhortations to stand firm because it will all turn out all right in the long run. A Keynesian would suggest that monetary restrictions would do little to eliminate a country's tendency to have a full-employment balance of payments deficit. However, devaluations, unless accompanied by measures to reduce their impact on the domestic price level (see section 15.4), will make an incomes policy difficult to handle. A Keynesian is thus driven to advocate cost subsidies or import restrictions (in so far as retaliation can be avoided), with active Central Bank and liberal IMF support for the exchange rate to eliminate any tendency for it to fall due to a temporary excess of imports of goods or export of capital (due to a lack of competitiveness or adherence to an interest rate lower than that of the rest of the world in the cause of domestic monetary stability for the reasons outlined at the end of chapter 12).

Just as a Keynesian advocates industrial subsidies and a passive attitude towards money supply growth to prevent destabilizing wealth effects and the emergence of unemployment in a closed system, an extension of the same logic necessarily implies industrial subsidies to preserve competitiveness, and lender-of-last-resort action (by the IMF) in the foreign exchange markets to stabilize the exchange rate. In both cases inflation must be controlled by a permanent incomes policy and relativities board rather than monetary means. The latter are too dangerous to attempt to use should genuine control of the 'money supply' be possible. Furthermore, the existence of offshore currency markets means that this is highly unlikely without strict regulations on the means of exchange which domestic companies can use in their dealings with each other. Such regulations would be inconsistent with the monetarists' would view of the benefits of universal market freedom.

17

Monetary Policy:
Some General Principles

17.1 INTRODUCTION

We have now considered in detail how a monetary economy works, and the various theories as to how it should be analysed. It is now time to take stock and consider the conclusions to be drawn as to how monetary authorities should act. How should monetary policy be set? Or, indeed, should there be a policy at all?

In the first chapter the policy issue was expressed in terms of the effect of changes in the money supply and interest rates on aggregate output and the general price level. Given national goals with respect to income, employment and inflation, how could monetary authorities use their influence to promote these goals?

It has become clear, however, that the matter is not so simple that it can be expressed as the size of $\Delta Y/\Delta M$ or $\Delta P/\Delta M$; this is a dangerous shorthand for economists to employ. We have seen that the nature of money, as well as the demand for it, changes both in the long run and the short run in response to a complex of factors, including the behaviour of the monetary authorities. The demand for money is inextricably tied up with the demand for all other assets, whose valuation is also affected by the behaviour of the monetary authorities. Further, since the liabilities of the government underwrite the financial system, as well as determining the composition of assets, the demand for, and supply of, money are inextricably tied up with the financial activities of the government.

The purpose of this chapter is to formulate some general principles for the design of monetary policy. This formulation will be conducted in the light of, rather than in spite of, the fact that monetary conditions are set very much in historical time. It will be assumed throughout that the underlying goals of the monetary authority are to use what influence they have to promote growth of income and employment and discourage inflation; the balance of payments position may be a subsidiary goal, given its influence both on income and employment, and on inflation.

In section 17.2 these goals are translated into two general principles by which monetary policy should be guided: provision of finance for real activity, together with discouragement of speculative uses of money. Section 17.3 examines the role of monetary policy as one of the instruments employed to achieve what may be conflicting targets. This leads on to an examination of the interrelationships between monetary and fiscal policy, including reference to the balance of payments.

Section 17.4 considers the form which monetary policy might take: the dominant issues here are whether to concentrate on controlling the money supply or interest rates; if the first, which money supply concept, and if the second, which interest rate? This leads us into the whole question of techniques of control and the technical difficulties involved.

Section 17.5 considers the important question of how any method of control may change the nature of money and financial markets and how the prudential aspects of control relate to the 'macroeconomic' aspects. Finally, section 17.6 fills out the policy prescriptions of section 17.2 in light of the later sections.

17.2 TWO GUIDING PRINCIPLES FOR MONETARY POLICY

In view of what we have earlier concluded about monetary economics, the general means of promoting the goals of high employment and low inflation can be expressed as consisting of two policies:

(1) Encourage the full development of financial intermediation so that the supply of finance is forthcoming when required for real expenditure plans. This policy involves not only the growth of the supply of money and other financial assets just sufficient for investment demand to generate its own means of finance, but also the prudential control which prevents the undermining of money by inflation, bank failures or foreign exchange crises.

(2) Discourage the diversion of money into those speculative eddies which inhibit the availability of finance for investment plans. While all decisions may be described as speculative, they need only lead to a massive shift into money assets when there is widespread fear of capital losses due to economic recession or financial collapse.

This is a tall order. As financial systems develop, becoming more and more efficient in the intermediation process, they also provide more opportunities for speculation in the sense that financial capital gains and losses can arise quite independently of 'real' developments. Yet the consequence of such activity is very real in that it determines the prices of real assets as well as financial assets. One of the central tenets of Keynes' *General Theory* is that speculative activity in financial markets – and all activity in financial markets is by definition speculative – can prevent interest rates from falling sufficiently to induce investors to implement new projects, even when there is unemployed labour.

For developing countries, the task of monetary policy is particularly difficult. Where domestic financial institutions are at an early stage of development, it is relatively costly in terms of monetary base to provide finance for investment, and also relatively difficult given the narrow range of financial instruments and market segmentation. At the same time, because there is access, particularly in the export enclave, to sophisticated foreign financial markets, there is scope for speculative activity. Thus the scarcity of funds is exacerbated if speculation diverts part of the monetary base into foreign markets. Return of funds from these markets to finance domestic investment occurs, but requires particularly strong inducements.

Confining our attention now to developed economies, it is useful to consider further the significance and implications of the two principles suggested above. On the face of it they bear some similarity to monetarist policy guidelines: maintain the growth of money supply at a rate equal to the long-run rate of growth of output; in so doing, monetary authorities will be prevented from taking any unexpected action which will upset expectations and lead to speculative activity in the short run. (In fact, as we show below, a rigid growth rate for monetary aggregates in spite of cyclical changes in the rest of the economy will disrupt financial markets, violating the second principle.)

Given the fact that there are cyclical swings in the short run, that long-run growth projections may be mistaken, and that economies are periodically subject to external shocks, the monetarist policy will mean periods of monetary tightness. We have already seen that the supply of money is endogenous to a considerable degree, not only in the short run but also in terms of long-run institutional change. Thus the nature of what is being controlled changes as the consequence of attempts to enforce that control, reducing the meaningfulness of the policy in the long run. Further, an *absence* of reaction by the authorities to short-run events (because of the exclusiveness of the long-run policy) gives full play to the activity of speculators and destabilizing trends in expectations. In turn, when aggregate demand is weak the monetary authorities may not be able to keep up with the planned monetary growth; attempts to pump more money into an unwilling system will further dislocate expectations.

What do we mean, then, by 'just enough' money to allow investment to be financed? And *should* all investment plans be financed? The conventional rationing device is the rate of interest; only those invest- ment projects promising a rate of return greater than the return on financial assets will be effected. But the crucial factor is the *expected* rate of return on the investment, which is a financial return in so far as effective demand for output and the cost of capital are affected by financial markets. Thus, a particular investment project will come on stream at a particular market rate of interest when expectations are buoyant, but only at a much lower rate of interest when expectations are pessimistic. In turn that investment project is less desirable (relative to the underlying goals of high employment and low inflation) when expectations are buoyant but the capital goods sector is at full capacity than when expectations are weak but there is spare capacity. The expectations of returns are nevertheless correct in that they are finan- cial returns as opposed to real returns (whatever that means); when conditions are buoyant firms can raise the prices of the output of the new investment, while returns on financial assets may not keep up with inflation. The cost of allowing these expectations to be self-fulfilling will be higher inflation.

The rate of expansion of money assets, then, should be such as to produce the correct interest rate and expectations combination to encourage investment in downturns and discourage it if it runs ahead of capacity in upturns. This differs from the monetarist steady-growth rate rule in allowing some change in monetary growth rates through the cycle in order to achieve a stabilizing pattern of interest rates without disrupting expectations.

The more sophisticated the financial system, the better able it is to produce finance for investment during upturns regardless of what the authorities do. This accommodating process of increased financial intermediation may carry with it the seeds of its own destruction. As we saw in the history of Scottish banking, and with the banking crises of the 1970s, euphoric markets become very precarious. Unless there is some 'safety limit' on bank lending, and on forward contracts in foreign exchange or securities, then the collapse of the institutions involved can undermine the entire financial structure. That structure is based on the confidence of the participants in the basic 'money' assets, particularly the liabilities of financial institutions. If that structure is to continue to oil the 'real economy' machine, then confidence in these assets must be maintained. A crucial feature of monetary policy, then, is prudential control which stipulates conditions on the composition of financial institutions' assets, and sets up buffers in the system to prevent the failure of one institution spreading to other parts of the system.

The monetary authorities themselves also contribute to the availability of liquid financial assets by issuing government securities. These indeed are the basis of most modern financial systems: it is the confidence in the government's ability to back its security issues with taxation powers which allows bank reserves to consist largely of liabilities of the public sector. Thus the public sector, just like private financial institutions, can only expand finance indefinitely on the basis of that taxing power at the risk of undermining the confidence held in those liabilities. *If* fiscal policy financed by bond issues is inflationary, as it would be if it hit capacity constraints, then money and fixed-interest securities become less attractive as resting places for liquidity. While other assets take their place – gold, old masters, etc. – the financial system thus loses some of its ability to finance expenditure.

Thus, while financial systems are capable of financing expenditure growth by their own internal dynamic, there are also some safeguards against 'excessive' growth. Because of the dominance of public sector securities in financial markets, the monetary authorities are in a good position to put brakes on the generation of finance.

But, in downturns, it is much more difficult to inject liquidity into the system in such a way that it is made available to potential investors. 'You cannot push on a string.' Similarly, it is more difficult for the authorities to reverse pessimistic expectations simply by lowering interest rates. If the expected return on real investment is low because of collapsing effective demand, the expected value of real assets will be low and also their liquidity will be low because of thinness of markets. It is not surprising that potential investors would prefer to hold liquid financial assets, even at a low interest rate.

To address this problem, we must turn now to the second policy measure regarding the role of speculation. Since all decisions are made on the basis of expectations of the prices of an array of assets, all economic agents are in some sense speculators. But because speculation in financial markets is conducted purely in terms of expected asset prices, not with a view to ultimate expenditure, it must be singled out (see Keynes (1936), chapter 12).

The foreign exchange market is a classic case of a speculator's market. The monetary theory of the balance of payments postulates that exchange rates are determined such that purchasing power parity and interest rate parity are maintained. But the high value of the pound in 1980, for example, belied the relatively very high domestic inflation rate; in turn, while real interest rates domestically were thus very low, they were, in terms of the purchasing power of other currencies, very high. Most commentators asserted that the 'real' exchange value of the pound should have meant a much lower exchange rate. But as long as it is 'too high' for any reason, it is only rational for transactors to pay scant attention to the underlying 'real' factors. The capital account is just as important a determinant of exchange rates as the trade account, although exchange rates in turn have very 'real' effects in terms of export demand. In direct parallel, financial markets have a life of their own, with prices changing independently of 'real' causes, but with 'real' effects.

Keynes, in his plan for what became the IMF, wanted to outlaw speculative transactions in foreign exchange (see de Cecco (1979)). Some countries attempt at least to separate them into a 'financial' market, although it is difficult to effect complete control. In Belgium, for example, capital transactions with other countries must be conducted in the 'franc financier', whose exchange rate can move freely relative to the Belgian franc used for trade in goods and services.

There is always a trade-off involved when considering such direct controls. There is a fine line between financial transactions which allow a high degree of intermediation and those which prevent finance actually reaching the real expenditure demand at the other end. The very process of intermediation invites speculation. It is extremely difficult to design controls which reduce the harmful elements of speculation without actually causing costly 'disintermediation'.

It is expectations of asset prices which drive speculation. In particular, it is expectations of falls in asset values which encourage holders of financial assets to 'go liquid' just at the time when entrepreneurial investors need most encouragement in the form of available finance. When we consider the role of fiscal policy, we shall see the role to be played in directing expectations. In terms of monetary policy, the authorities should act in such a way as to avoid dislocating financial markets and upsetting expectations. As long as speculators are sufficiently confident in their expectations that a financial collapse will *not* occur, then they will be prepared to 'go illiquid', thus inadvertently providing the greatest assistance to entrepreneurial investors. As we shall see when we consider the means of achieving this end, the *last* type of policy required is a rigid short- and long-run target for the growth of any one monetary aggregate.

17.3   TARGETS AND INSTRUMENTS

There is a body of literature (see, for example, Goodhart (1975), chapter 12) which considers the goals (targets) of government and the policy instruments at their disposal. The main tenet of this literature is that, given that the goals may be incompatible, then each target must have its own instrument. In simple terms, fiscal policy to reduce unemployment may at the same time be inflationary; so monetary policy should be assigned to controlling inflation.

This literature is useful in pointing out the implications of incompatible goals, and further when it suggests that some instruments are more suited to some targets than others. But beyond these common-sense points, it is rather misleading in its emphasis on the separability of targets, and of instruments. In particular, a zero balance of payments is often included as one of the goals, although it seems to play more an instrumental role. It is difficult to distinguish the balance of payments situation from either the causes or consequences of a given inflation/ unemployment nexus. In turn, the goals of low inflation and unemployment are much more likely actually to feature in individual residents' utility functions than is the balance of payments.

Further, it is difficult in practice to consider monetary policy in isolation from fiscal policy, independently of the balance of payments situation. Fiscal policy involving a change in the government's budgetary position must be financed (or involve a reduction in financing). Deficit financing by borrowing from the banks or the non-bank public does not in general affect the money supply; the cash drain is returned to the financial system when the government spends it. But the composition of assets has changed, and attempts by the banks and non-bank public to adjust to the injection of government securities will have repercussions for international asset purchases and sales, and thus the balance of payments.

Together, the 'crowding out' literature and the monetary theory of the balance of payments have made a very useful contribution in highlighting these interdependencies. But we have here, in earlier chapters, suggested that portfolio decisions are arrived at in a rather different way, with rather different adjustment mechanisms. In particular, interdependencies go beyond those which are conventionally expressed in an IS–LM framework, i.e. beyond the influence of income levels and the interest rate in more than one market. *Anything which affects expectations about asset prices also affects the impact of monetary policy, fiscal policy and balance of payments policy on employment, inflation and the balance of payments.*

In order to illustrate this point, let us consider again the two polar cases: first, pervasive optimism, and then pervasive pessimism. When spending is rising too rapidly relative to capacity, due to optimistic expectations, the role of monetary policy is to attempt to choke off investment demand with a combination of high interest rates and a modification of expectations. This involves forcing up loan rates charged by banks and forcing down the prices of private sector securities. Both are reinforced if lenders as well as borrowers revise their expectations of continuing expansion.

Suppose, however, that the expansion mentality is hard to break, so that asset prices are expected to maintain their value. Velocity of circulation rises, domestic and foreign speculators continue to buy private-sector assets, and so investment plans can still go ahead. The anticipated balance of payments deterioration may not occur, and government securities are not purchased in the expected amounts because further attempts at monetary tightening (and thus further falls in government security prices) and further demand pressure in financial markets are expected.

Much depends on expectations about the balance of payments position and the government budgetary position. If exchange rates are fixed, and balance of payments deterioration is expected to occur, due to reduced competitiveness of exports, once inflationary processes set in, then there will be a tendency (modified by sterilization) for the domestic money supply to be reduced. Short-term capital inflows would still be attracted by the continued rise in interest rates, but long-term capital inflows would be discouraged by expected falls in asset prices. If, on the other hand, exchange rates are flexible, and if inflation is likely to drive the exchange rate down, then the interest rate attraction would be correspondingly reduced and there would again be downward pressure on the domestic money supply. But, as discussed earlier, the balance of payments (or exchange rate) can go either way depending on the relative strength and direction of capital flows.

Much also depends on fiscal policy and the budgetary deficit. If banks prefer to lend to business investors rather than buy government securities, any given fiscal deficit is more likely to have to be financed by money creation (borrowing from the monetary authorities), further fuelling the expansion. On the other hand, greater than anticipated private sector expansion will tend to reduce a budgetary deficit, through the endogeneity of much of taxation and government expenditure. The government's fiscal policy can be very influential in determining expectations about the timing of a cyclical peak. A sharp fall in expenditure and/or increase in tax burden aimed at the sectors with capacity constraints could reinforce the monetary policy efforts at reversing expectations. By discouraging capital inflows, such fiscal action would add further to the scope of the monetary authorities to exercise control.

In the obverse situation of a recession, the success of monetary policy again depends on fiscal policy to produce an adequate reversal of expectations, as well as on the expectations of foreign investors. Suppose the authorities attempt to bring down interest rates and generate expectations of expansion, yet expectations persist of falling private sector security prices, but of rising interest rates. Then, no matter how much money the authorities manage to inject into the system, interest rates do not fall, and there is no demand for private sector securities. This is the extreme liquidity trap case. Interest rates on short-dated government debt cannot fall further, and high liquidity preference impedes the substitutability between all other assets which would force other interest rates to fall. (Keynes considered this extreme form of 'liquidity trapness' fanciful (see A. Dow (1980)), although the process of real rates of return falling faster than financial rates is central to Keynes' theory.) The behaviour of capital flows again is based on a circular process: if capital flows are viewed as being able to dominate exchange rate movements, or the need for intervention to maintain a fixed rate, then speculators' behaviour depends on how they expect each other to behave.

Again, fiscal policy plays an important role in determining expectations regarding the real sector, which can filter through financial markets. An expansionary tax and expenditure mix aimed at the worst pockets of inactivity can inject optimism into the stock market, reinforcing the expansionary monetary policy. Such a mix could consist of financial backing for a large industry in temporary financial straits, together with taxation of excess profits of a healthy industry (such as oil or banking). Indeed the only way of injecting more liquidity into the system in such conditions may be as new money, financing an increased budget deficit. In turn, confident expectations of an appreciating currency as well as increasing bond and share prices as expansion gets under way may be sufficient to encourage further financing through capital inflows.

These are only some of the possible outcomes of such situations – there is a wide range of permutations and combinations of expectations among the various economic agents involved. Rather than providing a few simple scenarios, with universal applicability, this expectations analysis suggests that the context of any given monetary policy is exceedingly complex; that context is nevertheless crucial to the success of that policy. It can only be concluded at this stage that each case must be treated on its own merits, since institutional conditions and arrays of expectations are continually shifting.

We can complete this discussion with an example of how in practice monetary policy does not produce textbook outcomes. When minimum lending rate was eventually reduced by a long-awaited two percentage points in the UK in November 1980, it was part of a budgetary package. As a result, the exchange rate scarcely faltered on account of optimistic expectations on the part of foreign investors, while the stock market fell on account of pessimistic expectations on the part of domestic investors – quite the reverse of what conventional theory would lead us to expect.

17.4 MECHANISMS OF MONETARY CONTROL

The main choice facing makers of monetary policy is whether to concentrate on controlling the money supply or on controlling interest rates. The two tend to move inversely; a contraction in the money supply pushes up interest rates to squeeze out excess demand, while an interest rate increase is generally achieved by means of changing the money supply. But the relationship is more stable in the long run than the short run. Thus an attempt to maintain the money supply at a particular level causes day-to-day fluctuations in interest rates as financial conditions fluctuate. If it is the interest rate which must be kept stable, it is the money supply which must bear the brunt of market instability. The choice depends on two factors: whether the relationship between the money supply and output and prices is more direct than between interest rates and output and prices, and whether it is technically more difficult to control one rather than the other.

In general terms, the money supply instrument is preferred by monetarists and the interest rate by Keynesians, on two counts. First, monetarists view the transmission mechanism, whereby monetary policy affects expenditure, as operating directly from the money stock; excess money holdings are substituted for real assets or consumer goods (as well as variety of financial assets). Instability in the money supply would simple confuse that mechanism in the short run by confusing expectations. Keynesians, on the other hand, view the trans- mission mechanisms as operating through the direct influence of interest rates (as the price of liquidity) on investment expenditure. Velocity of circulation is sufficiently variable that variations in the money supply do not unsettle expenditure plans, but stable asset price expectations require stable interest rates. The representation of monetarism in chapter 14 did demonstrate the effect of money supply changes on expenditure as being transmitted by interest rates (particu- larly bank loan rates). But as long as velocity is viewed by most monetarists as being stable, the money supply remains the key variable.

The additional rationale relates to the stability of the money market and goods market relationships (see Poole (1970)). Because the demand for money function is believed to be the most stable relation- ship in the monetarist economy, and the interest rate does not feature strongly in this relationship, controlling the money supply ensures minimal variability of income. The Keynesian model is normally (albeit erroneously; see chapter 13) characterized as having a more stable expenditure function than demand for money function, so that income is less subject to variability if interest rates are controlled. The issue is, however, clouded to the extent that the authorities may not have good information on either relationship, far less their degree of stability.

In fact, the Keynesian rationale for emphasis on interest rates relates less to their direct effect on expenditure than to their effect on expecta- tions of the prices of *all* assets, and thus to their effect on *both* real expenditure and the demand for money. Nervousness of any kind in financial markets induces a shift into liquidity and shortage of finance for real expenditure. Control of the money supply by any one defini- tion like M_1 or M_3 is viewed as being a weak measure because either its supply is endogenous from non-government sources, or alternative money assets emerge, when conditions are tightened; the effectiveness of a policy of monetary expansion in a recession, in turn, is made difficult by the ease with which money can be added to idle balances when liquidity preference is high.

Interest rates, on the other hand, are regarded as the best indicator of liquidity tightness or slack, *whatever* is currently serving the function of liquidity. Thus it is interest rates which should be monitored to ensure that liquidity is at the appropriate level; action to adjust the availability of liquidity must, however, be taken in a sedate manner since sharp changes unsettle expectations and drive up liquidity preference. Fiscal policy is more appropriate for taking 'emergency' action. This policy stance was explained most fully in the UK Radcliffe Report (1959).

This view of monetary policy questions the ability of the authorities to control the supply of money in any case. There are technical difficulties, for example, in generating day-to-day information on banks' reserve positions, in designing financial institutions in such a way that banks have complete control over assets (no overdraft facilities), and in predicting the rate of cash drain to the general public, to take only a few examples.

These 'technical difficulties' become fundamental problems if strict requirements impede the functioning of the financial system. This is particularly true if banks could have no recourse to a lender-of-last-resort facility, whose use adds to the monetary base.

But since the very fact of control of a monetary aggregate, as well as long-run financial development, increased the moneyness of assets outside that aggregate, the value of that control is correspondingly reduced. The money supply definitions used for monetary control tend to become more and more broad over time, reflecting the broadening of the range of money assets. But the very fact of control speeds up the process by which money changes. Thus, it can be argued that interest rate control and money supply control are not two sides of the same coin, if the form of monetary control actually changes the financial structure, inducing the use of alternative forms of money. (In chapter 6, the portfolio theorists were described as treating a reduction in interest rates as being equivalent in effect to an increase in the money supply, because the analysis is all conducted in terms of a *given* financial structure.)

While ideally the monetary authorities would presumably like to be able to control the entire interest rate structure, they are limited to those markets in which they can deal. These are the money market and the market for medium- and long-term government securities. The monetary authorities already operate in these markets as a borrower and lender, on behalf of the government. In the long-term market, funds are raised to finance government expenditure. The money market provides funds to cover day-to-day fluctuations in government liquidity. But it is also the vehicle whereby the authorities adjust the liquidity position of the financial system, particularly if there is a lender-of-last-resort facility.

The authorities must thus deal with the conflict between the government's borrowing requirement and the interest rate levels required by monetary policy. The two of course are interdependent in that the government's borrowing finances expenditure which itself may change liquidity preference. But, if the control of interest rates is given primacy, then government borrowing may be restricted to borrowing from the monetary authority ('printing money') if the asset structure of the private sector is not to be disturbed.

Clearly the authority takes account of the effect of government borrowing on longer-term rates, but it is generally a short-term rate which is selected as the signal of monetary policy. The presumption is that portfolio adjustments ensure that interest rate changes at the short end of the liquidity spectrum filter through to expenditure plans. There are, however, several impediments in the way:

(1) financial transactors may have 'preferred market habitats', so that the markets in various instruments are not closely connected and interest rate differentials (given term, risk, etc.) may persist;
(2) banks may not adjust their lending and deposit rates with each market fluctuation, in the interests of stability, so that satisfied demand is determined by rationing rather than price;
(3) uncertainty surrounding the long-term valuation of assets may outweigh short-term interest rate fluctuations.

Again we have returned to the dual significance of interest rates and expectations of future asset prices. A successful attempt at reducing short-term interest rates may not succeed in increasing effective investment demand if banks persist in cautious lending practices, if other lenders confine themselves to the short end of the spectrum and particularly if investment demand is held down by pessimistic expectations over the time horizon relevant to getting an investment project on-stream. Long-term rates could remain high in spite of the fall in short rates. To succeed in the objective of encouraging expenditure, then, the fall in short rates must be associated with measures to increase confidence among investors, both in real assets and in long-term financial assets. Public assurances that this low short rate is to be maintained for some time would be particularly helpful in this regard.

In developing countries, we have seen that there is less scope for evading monetary controls because of the relative absence of money-substitutes. But developed financial systems have become progressively more adept at devising new financial instruments which will maximize profits. In fact, banks tend to fare relatively well in periods of high interest rates; because of rigidities in their rate structures and in the behaviour of their customers, bank revenue grows faster than costs when market interest rates are high. The US banks have been particularly adept at designing new means of borrowing and lending.

We have already discussed how innovations within institutions and the emergence of new non-bank institutions allow evasion of monetary controls, when demand for liquidity to finance expenditure or purchase of financial assets is high. Not only must the authorities take account of these developments in designing their 'macroeconomic' policy, but also in designing their prudential monetary policy.

If the financial structure is to remain stable, with confidence that money assets will retain their value, then some prudential limit must be placed on the expansion of monetary aggregates. If that limit is inadequate relative to planned expenditure, then the emergence of alternative money assets will be induced in the private sector. The role of the monetary authority is to ensure that these new assets are also subject to prudential controls.

Prudential control is not separable from 'macroeconomic' control. The purpose is to influence the valuation of the entire structure of assets. That valuation is affected by the authorities' efforts to influence some interest rates, and it is most affected at turning points, particularly cyclical peaks. Similarly, over-extension of financial institutions relative to some base will not cause undue concern until turning points are reached and these institutions are at their most vulnerable.

The primary function of monetary control is to provide a stable financial environment for real expenditure. This requires that there be impediments to liquidity flooding into long-dated securities in such volumes that the euphoric bubble bursts with attendant huge capital losses. Similarly it requires that liquidity be impeded from flooding into backwaters when there is unsatisfied demand for investment financing. Prudential controls, together with stable interest rates, promote this end.

17.6 CONCLUSION

In this chapter it has been suggested that monetary policy, on its own, is not appropriate for stabilization policy. Rather, monetary policy is at its most effective when designed to complement fiscal policy. This means ensuring that the availability of liquid assets and their price are consistent with the expenditure patterns which fiscal policy tries to promote. Use of monetary mechanisms by themselves to stabilize expansions induce institutional change which allows the control to be avoided or else threatens the stability of the financial system. Monetary policy stabilize a downturn cannot by itself turn around pessimistic expectations as to the market value of real assets.

18

The Keynesian Revolution Mark II?

18.1 INTRODUCTION

> Now, as I have often pointed out to my students, some of whom have been brought up in sporting circles, high-brow opinion is like a hunted hare; if you stand in the same place, or nearly the same place, it can be relied upon to come round to you in a circle.

With this quotation from Dennis Robertson (1956, p. 81) Paul Davidson (1978b) introduces his analysis of Why Money Matters. The image of the 'hunted hare' is used to illustrate the way in which monetary theory has been going round in a circle over the last 50 years, with the monetarist ideas of the 1930s currently holding sway, but coming under attack from a 'fundamentalist' Keynesian perspective, similar to that contained in Keynes' *General Theory*.

The experience of the last few decades has shown that monetary policy goes round in more rapid circles. It is less easy for monetary authorities to persist with an inadequate policy in the face of financial crisis than for economic theorists to persist with inadequate theories. Thus attempts to control monetary aggregates or interest rates, while inconsistent expectations were being generated by fiscal policy or international developments, had to be supplemented quickly by direct controls. As a result, the nature of the variables which were intended to be controlled changed, requiring further revision of policy prescriptions.

But in a more fundamental sense, monetary policy at the start of the 1980s has returned to the distant era of the gold standard. Base money, M_0, is regarded, as was gold, as the fulcrum of the monetary system. Monetary aggregates are regarded as being stable multiples of that base, and expenditure in turn as a stable multiple of monetary aggregates. Further, the global monetarists see the supply of the money base governed by international capital flows which respond to relative competitiveness, and to any short-term interest rate disparities which emerge, only to be eliminated by the capital flows themselves.

While this concept of the monetary economy underlay much of monetary policy until the Second World War, the primary instrument of monetary policy was generally interest rates. The shift in thinking in both the US and the UK towards control of the monetary base itself represents a major historical departure.

Can we expect a second Keynesian Revolution? Will the hunted hare pursue the same course this time round? Certainly a groundswell of fundamentalist Keynesian thinking has been given a strong impetus by the clarity and forcefulness of the monetarist revival. The neoclassical synthesis, under a Keynesian label, had presented too amorphous and adaptable a paradigm with which to take effective issue. One of Friedman's greatest contributions to economic theory has been the way he has forced Keynesians to examine the underpinning of their theories.

In this final chapter we consider what lies in store for monetary theory and policy. In section 18.2 we consider the two major developments in economic theory which might divert the hare onto another course before it reaches the equivalent of 1936, the year of publications of Keynes' *General Theory*: general equilibrium theory (GE) and rational expectations theory (RE). Section 18.3 develops the particular form which monetary theory and policy would take in a framework which eschewed GE and RE: a 1980s General Theory. Keynes' *General Theory* represented the outcome of a 'long struggle to escape' from the neoclassicism of his time; the 1980s version would represent the outcome of a long struggle to escape from a GE and RE neoclassicism. Section 18.4 identifies a crucial element of Keynes' approach which was submerged by the scale of the Depression of the time: the importance of the *composition* of aggregates. The full development of this concept would ensure a longer-lasting Keynesian Revolution Mark II if it ever got off the ground.

18.2 GENERAL EQUILIBRIUM AND RATIONAL EXPECTATIONS

The concept of general equilibrium is central to the neoclassical synthesis and its monetarist relation, just as it was to the marginalists who preceded Keynes. GE theory portrays an economy as a collection of markets which simultaneously clear as a result of the marginalist optimizing behaviour of individual economic agents; general equilibrium differs from the partial equilibrium, represented by only one market clearing, in that it takes account of interactions between markets. If the economy is not in GE, then this must be due either to an exogenous shock which has not yet worked its way through the system, or to some impediment to free market forces. The equilibrium is viewed as being stable; market forces all generate a return to equilibrium if allowed to work freely.

This conceptualization of economies was more implicit then explicit in the economic orthodoxy of Keynes' day. It supported a particular stance against government intervention and was itself supported by Walrasian analysis which gave it a theoretical underpinning; and indeed it provided the means for belittling Keynes' contribution. Unemployment, the absence of clearing in the labour market, could only be the result of the absence of free market forces in that market. The other rationales were either perfectly inelastic demand for money, which was 'refuted' by the Pigou effect, or by interest-inelastic investment demand, a possibility which could not be explained away and was thus quietly ignored. Keynes' theory was thus interpreted as a special case of a particular form of market failure. Keynes, on the other hand, had presented his theory as being entirely general; it was a situation of general market clearing which was the very special case.

Indeed, the neoclassical synthesis, starting with Hicks' IS–LM representation, forced the *General Theory* into a GE framework in order to comprehend it in terms of prevailing modes of thought. But the essence of the Keynesian message was that it is not helpful to model the economy as a GE system. Some markets may clear at some points in time, but the general case is of markets not clearing. Entrepreneurs make decisions to change production on the basis of expectations of sales which may or may not prove to be correct. Labour bargains for wages whose value in real terms over the period of the contract cannot be predicted. Consumers make decisions in the absence of full information about prices. Savers acquire assets which suit the needs of their own particular plans, or absence of plans, for future expenditure. Even the institutional arrangements by which these decisions take effect change over time.

Perhaps if market forces were 'free' then the outcome of this form of decision-making would be disequilibrating, in the sense of driving the system further and further from some equilibrium. But economies do not in general behave in such a manner. Nor do they tend to converge on some general equilibrium. Rather it is the 'imperfection' of markets, and the adaptability of institutions, which promote stability (see Hirschman (1970), Keynes (1936, p. 253), Richardson (1953, 1960)). Because wages are sticky, because international capital flows are not infinitely interest-elastic, because loyalty of bank customers inhibits massive shifts of accounts from one bank to another, the 'mistakes' which economic agents frequently and inevitably make are not generally amplified. Further, the adaptability of financial institutions often averts crises. The term 'crisis situation' now seems an exaggeration when applied to the IMF in 1971–2 or the problem of financing oil deficits later in the 1970s, because the degree of adaptability had been under-anticipated.

But it may now be even more difficult than in Keynes' day to shake economists out of GE habits. The development of computer technology and massive data-collection efforts have changed the nature, not only of the subject, but of economists themselves. There is so much human capital tied up in GE theorizing and model-building and testing, that it would take a major crisis indeed to diminish its influence. The type of economy Keynes described cannot be analysed with GE methods.

This is not to deny the value of quantitative work; far from it. There is certainly a role for quantitative partial equilibrium analysis as part of a wider effort directed at understanding economic developments at any one point in time. Nor is it to deny the importance of interactions between markets; rather it is to emphasize that these interactions take place in an economy which is normally out of equilibrium. Indeed 'equilibrium' is a rather unhelpful concept in the Keynesian framework.

We have stressed the importance of expectations as being fundamental to the Keynesian approach. And indeed the monetarists again are to be praised for challenging the neoclassical synthesis for its inattention to expectations. But their method of introducing expectations, first as adaptive expectations, then as rational expectations, was designed to make sure that they could be modelled in a GE framework, rather than to reflect 'reality'.

To suggest that all agents' expectations are based on a particular functional form of past experience (adaptive expectations) or that they are based on a uniform interpretation of the current (common) stock of information on data and forecasting models (the usual application of rational expectations), is to adopt a very peculiar view of human behaviour. The way in which we have talked about expectations in financial markets has been to suggest *either* that expectations are different for different people at different points in time and over time, so that they are usually proved wrong, *or* that if they are sufficiently strong in one direction they will be self-fulfilling.

Certainly there is a great deal of truth in the proposition that expectations are formed on the basis of past experience and on knowledge about the future. But to enshrine this principle in a mathematical formulation – which is applied uniformly to all economic relationships both before and after a move from one GE position to another – is taking the proposition too far. The gyrations of exchange rates provide testimony to the fact that not only do expectations themselves determine the outcome, but that in general expectations are wrong; if there is a *widespread* conviction that an appreciation will occur, most expectations will be proved right, but only *because* they were held by most people and thus self-fulfilling. (There must of course be a willing seller of the appreciating currency – often the government, attempting to dampen the upward movement of the currency.)

'Real' investors are no less immune to this phenomenon. In a recession the expectations of the majority prevail, whatever they are. If most businesses postpone investment because of low expected returns, then continued stagnation of aggregate demand proves wrong the few businesses who decide to go ahead with investment plans. The reverse is the case if most businesses are optimistic.

But the word 'expectations' is no longer sufficient to make GE theorists feel inadequate. The fact that RE can be incorporated painlessly in GE models appears to be more persuasive for GE theorists than the suggestion that it is blatantly unrealistic as a general treatment of expectations as far as Post Keynesians are concerned. (The concepts of 'usefulness' and 'realism' take on a different meaning depending on the paradigm in question; see chapter 13.)

The tremendous hold which GE has on the economics profession, bolstered by the discovery that expectations can be brought into the fold, poses a daunting barrier to the spread of Post Keynesian ideas in the wake of monetarism. For this reason it is not at all clear that the hunted hare will continue on its circle. Not only may it be diverted from its course by GE + RE, but it is in great danger of being replaced by a mechanical, battery-operated hare running round a quite different course.

18.3   MONEY IN THE KEYNESIAN REVOLUTION MARK II

The most fundamental lack in GE theory is that it does not describe a *monetary* economy. Indeed, a vast proportion of economics ignores the significance of money. Money is treated as if it were *any* commodity, which acts as a means of exchange; it is not countenanced as a receptacle for uncertainty, since uncertainty is viewed as being captured in a probability distribution. Even those who spearheaded the back-to-Keynes movement, Clower and Leijonhufvud, only view money as important as a vehicle for expression of purchasing power.

But without money, uncertainty about the future would have no means of expression. If all savings are held in illiquid assets, such as company shares, then investment, which generates savings, generates its own means of finance. In a barter economy, as depicted in chapter 8, there need be no involuntary unemployment. It is no wonder that GE theory can only explain voluntary unemployment, and that is explained by market failure where the role of money is suppressed.

Keynes demonstrated that it is inherent in a monetary economy that a 'general equilibrium' will not normally occur. Monetary economics is thus synonymous with economics. It may seem paradoxical, then, that Keynes emphasized fiscal policy rather than monetary policy:

> it seems unlikely that the influence of banking policy on the rate of interest will be sufficient by itself to determine an optimum rate of investment. I conceive, therefore, that a somewhat comprehensive socialisation of investment will prove the only means of securing an approximation to full employment (Keynes (1936), p. 378).

Keynes had demonstrated that unemployment has its causes in the way in which monetary transactions are conducted, and in the way in which investors choose between real assets and any number of financial assets. Because unemployment is in this sense a 'monetary' phenomenon does not, however, mean that *monetary* policy will provide its cure.

The limited scope of monetary policy was discussed and demonstrated in chapter 17, particularly in generating an expansion. Rather the primary purpose of monetary policy should be to promote stability in financial markets. Stability involves growth of monetary aggregates commensurate with expenditure requirements. Stability discourages 'excessive' speculative activity, which in turn protects the financial system from crises of confidence which would erode the acceptability of conventional money assets. This approach also requires that the financing of budgetary deficits be conducted in such a way that the confidence in the monetary base, the liabilities in effect of the government, not be eroded. Since the valuation of all assets depends on expected levels of aggregate demand, it is fiscal policy which is the primary instrument of government policy.

In a monetary economy, the way in which transactions are conducted and expectations formed are crucial institutional factors. For a variety of reasons, not the least of which is the implementation of monetarist policies, institutions are currently undergoing rapid change. It was suggested earlier that the source of stability in monetary economies is more an institutional than a strictly 'economic' phenomenon. As a corollary, unsettling institutional change may reduce this buffering effect. Thus a Post Keynesian approach, which is built around the changing role of economic institutions, is much better equipped to analyse current economic conditions than GE theory, which presumes a given institutional structure.

The response of financial institutions to monetary tightness provides an excellent example of how the object of control can shift ground as a direct result of that control. In addition, monetary tightness irrespective of stages in the cycle, with a view to controlling inflation, is bound to have long-lasting effects on industrial structure. Financial stringency during a recession can be expected to hit small firms harder than large firms, and domestic firms rather than multinational branch plants. The successful re-emergence of small firms in a recovery will be impeded by the changed competitive structure. Industrial structure in turn determines how prices are generated and how wages are determined, and how far they are influenced by wage and price developments in other economies. If controlling inflation is the central policy goal, then an understanding of these processes, and how they may be changing, is crucial.

In turn, the degree of self-financing of investment is itself influenced by the size of firms and their relationships with banks, which could be fundamentally altered if overdraft facilities are curtailed in the interests of monetary control. The responsiveness of business expenditure to monetary conditions is less marked when self-finance is prevalent. It is also less marked the more firms seek finance elsewhere, e.g. on the Eurocurrency market, or from parent companies and their banks, in other countries. Controlling domestic currency monetary aggregates has less and less the predicted monetarist effects the more institutions diverge from the perfectly competitive economy isolated by floating exchange rates.

18.4 COMPOSITION OF AGGREGATES

The conventional criticism of Keynesian policies after the Second World War is that, by concentrating on fiscal expansion, the authorities lost control of monetary variables, and thus inflation. This outcome was influenced by the absence of attention paid to the monetary and international implications of fiscal policy; a successful strategy would have been based on their interdependence. It is also conventional to explain this over-expansionist zeal on the weakness of politicians. And indeed there is a lot of truth in the judgement that Keynes' message of 'spend, spend, spend', while valid for a recession, should not have been followed after the Second World War regardless of cyclical conditions.

But the main missing factor was attention to the composition of aggregates. In chapter 21 of the *General Theory*, in a letter to *The Times*, in 1937, as well as in correspondence, Keynes pointed out that increasing expenditure in sectors or regions already at full capacity would be inflationary, while in sectors or regions with spare capacity output could increase without inflationary effect. Similarly, funds distributed to businesses with pessimistic expectations about the future value of output would be held liquid, whereas an optimistic business would use the funds for additional expenditure. Thus the *composition* of fiscal expansion and monetary expansion is as important for the outcome for output and prices as the size of the expansion. Only when *all* sectors and regions are under-employed and pessimistic is the composition relatively unimportant, i.e. in a deep recession. Even then, the propensity for the particular sector chosen to import and to divert funds to other countries, or attract funds from other countries, will determine the aggregate outcome of the expenditure.

It was unfortunate that, in order to make a strong case for fiscal policy, Keynes said that spending public money to hire labour to dig holes and fill them in again would be better than nothing. This may sometimes be true, but unfortunately detracts from the fact that hiring the labour to build roads, say, using local materials and thus generating further employment, would be even better. But the convention has persisted of thinking of government expenditure and the money supply as amorphous lumps, G and M.

Even Friedman's attempt to portray a neutral money supply increase as resulting from a helicopter drop of banknotes cannot abstract from composition; the helicopter must be flying over a very specific area when the notes are dropped. In a monetarist world the composition of the money supply does not in fact matter (in terms of who holds it) since all above a fixed amount is spent. But once we allow individuals to vary in their liquidity preferences, in response to their own individual expectations as to the value of their own individual assets and liabilities, then it matters very much who receives the banknotes. It is equally possible that they could be hoarded in a sock, saved in a bank, spent on imports or spent on local goods and services.

Civil servants and bankers are very well aware of these facts. In selecting firms for fiscal aid or bank loans, practical common sense steers the choice in favour of those planning to increase output and employment. But overall fiscal and monetary guidelines aimed at limiting total expenditure can override such considerations. It is hard to comprehend, for example, how reducing government expenditure in particularly depressed regions helps to control inflation. Increased expenditure, chosen for its high local linkage effects, increases local output and employment and tax revenue and reduces unemployment benefits. There need be no net effect at all on the government's borrowing requirement.

Discretionary monetary policy is more difficult unless the banks are directed specifically to limit lending in inflationary areas and extend it in depressed areas. However, the best means of persuading the banks to follow such practices is a fiscal policy which concentrates expenditure on depressed regions and sectors, thus turning around expectations in their favour. Clearly, it is very difficult in practice to 'fine-tune' the economy in this way. Nevertheless, a shift in emphasis from aggregates to their composition would go a long way to avoiding unnecessary inflation and unemployment.

18.5 CONCLUSION

Our conclusion is thus of the 'bad news–good news' variety. First the bad news. General equilibrium economics has become even more deeply entrenched than in Keynes' day. Technological and technical advances have allowed it to take on a life of its own, with the recently added protection provided by incorporating expectations into the analysis. The GE concept and the RE representation of expectations are the antithesis of the way we as Post Keynesians interpret Keynes. Such a view is difficult to convey persuasively using the GE framework. That framework itself denies the validity of Keynes' fundamental analysis, particularly with respect to the role of money.

The fact that the current orthodoxy is monetarist, an outlier in the neoclassical synthesis, at least sharpens the debate, and more clearly differentiates the Post Keynesian view. Because monetarism is such an extreme version of the neoclassical synthesis it may actually generate crisis economic conditions, without which, sadly, the Post Keynesian view may not be allowed to emerge as an acceptable alternative.

The good news is that Keynesians have learnt a lot of lessons, both from the misapplications of Keynes' policy prescriptions and from the misinterpretations to which his theory has been subjected. If Keynesians can succeed in their long struggle to escape from GE, it will be clear that context-specific policy-making is the correct approach. Policies must continually be redesigned to take account of changing economic conditions in different regions and sectors, and of changing economic and financial structure. This redesign in turn must be conditioned by attention to promoting institutional stability, as a fertile ground for economic growth.

The central feature of the Keynesian Revolution Mark II, if it succeeds, will be the restoration of emphasis on the monetary features of a monetary economy. Money and financial institutions can be used to promote growth or to impede it. It is important that this power be given its due recognition.

References

Adekunle, J. O. (1968) The Demand for Money: Evidence from Developed and Less Developed Economies. *IMF Staff Papers*, 15 (July), 220–65.

Akerlof, G. (1970) The Market for 'Lemons': Quality Uncertainty and the Market Mechanism. *Quarterly Journal of Economics*, 84 (August) 488–500.

Alexakis, P. (1981) On the Formation of the European Monetary Union. Unpublished Ph.D. Dissertation, University of Stirling.

Ando, A. and Modigliani, F. (1965) The Relative Stability of Monetary Velocity and the Investment Multiplier. *American Economic Review*, 55(September), 693–728.

Andrews, P. W. S. (1949) *Manufacturing Business*. London: Macmillan.

Arrow, K. J. and Hahn, F. H. (1971) *General Competitive Analysis*. Edinburgh: Oliver & Boyd.

Artis, M. J. (1978) Fiscal Policy and Crowding Out. In M. V. Posner (ed.), *Demand Management*. London: Heinemann.

Artis, M. J. and Nobay, A. R. (1969) Two Aspects of the Monetary Debate. *National Institute Economic Review*, no. 49 (August), pp. 33–51.

Baltensperger, E. (1980) Alternative Approaches to the Theory of the Banking Firm. *Journal of Monetary Economics*, 6 (January), 1–38.

Bank of England (1975) The Capital and Liquidity Adequacy of Banks. *Bank of England Quarterly Bulletin*, 15 (September), 240–3.

Barro, R. J. and Grossman, H. I. (1976) *Money, Employment and Inflation*. Cambridge: Cambridge University Press.

Baumol, W. J. (1952) The Transactions Demand for Cash: An Inventory Theoretic Approach. *Quarterly Journal of Economics*, 66 (November), 545–56.

Baxter, J. L. (1980) A General Model of Wage Determination. *Yorkshire Bulletin of Economic Research*, 32 (May), 3–17.

Binhammer, H. H. (1968) *Money, Banking and the Canadian Financial System*. Toronto: Methuen.

Bird, P. J. W. N. (1981) An Investigation of the Role of Speculation in the 1972–5 Commodity Price Boom. Unpublished Ph.D Dissertation, University of Cambridge.

Black, H. (1975) The Relative Importance of Determinants of the Money Supply, *Journal of Monetary Economics*, 1 (April), 251–64.

Blinder, A. S. and Solow, R. M. (eds) (1974) *The Economics of Public Finance*: Washington, DC: The Brookings Imstitution.

Brunner, K. and Meltzer, A. H. (1963) The Place of Financial Intermediaries in the Transmission of Monetary Policy. *American Economic Review*, 53 (May), 372–82.

Cagan, P. (1965) *Determinants and Effects of Changes in the Stock of Money 1875–1960*. New York: National Bureau of Economic Research.

Cameron, R. (1967) *Banking in the Early Stages of Industrialisation: A Study in Comparative Economic History*. Oxford: Oxford University Press.

Carter, H. and Partington, I. (1979) *Applied Economics in Banking and Finance*. Oxford: Oxford University Press.

Checkland, S. G. (1975) *Scottish Banking: A History, 1695–1973*. Glasgow: Collins.

Chick, V. (1977) *The Theory of Monetary Policy* (rev. edn). Oxford: Basil Blackwell.

Clower, R. W. (1965) The Keynesian Counter-Revolution: a Theoretical Appraisal. In F. H. Hahn and F. Brechling (eds), *The Theory of Interest Rates*, London: Macmillan.

Clower, R. W. (1967) A Reconsideration of the Microfoundations of Monetary Theory, *Western Economic Journal*, 6, (December), 1–9.

Coddington, A. (1976) Keynesian Economics: The Search for First Principles. *Journal of Economic Literature*, 14 (December), 1258–73.

Cramp, A. B. (1970) Does Money Matter? *Lloyds Bank Review*, no. 98 (October), pp. 23–37.

Cramp, A. B. (1971) *Monetary Management*. London: George Allen & Unwin.

Davidson, P. (1978a) *Money and the Real World* (2nd ed). London: Macmillan.

Davidson, P. (1978b) Why Money Matters: Lessons from a Half-Century of Monetary Theory, *Journal of Post Keynesian Economics*, 1 (Fall), 46–70.

De Cecco, M. (1979) Origins of the Post-War Payments System. *Cambridge Journal of Economics*, 3 (March), 49–61.

De Prano, M. and Mayer, T. (1965) Tests of the Relative Importance Autonomous Expenditures and Money, *American Economic Review*, 55, (September), 728–52.

Dow, A. C. (1980) *Monetarism and Inflation*. University of Stirling: Department of Economics Teaching Paper, June.

Dow, S. C. (1980) Methodological Morality in the Cambridge Controversies. *Journal of Post Keynesian Economics*, 2 (Spring), 368–80.

Dow, S. C. (1981) Weintraub and Wiles: The Methodological Basis of Policy Conflict. *Journal of Post Keynesian Economics*, 3, (Spring), 325–39.

Dow, S. C. and Earl, P. E. (1981) Methodology and Orthodox Monetary Policy. Paper presented at the Cambridge Journal of Economics Conference on the New Orthodoxy in Economics, Sidney Sussex College, Cambridge, 22–25 June.

Drake, P. J. (1980) *Money, Finance and Development*. Oxford: Martin Robertson.

Earl, P. E. (1980) A Behavioural View of Economists' Behaviour and the Lack of Success of Behavioural Economics. University of Stirling Discussion Papers in Economics, Finance, and Investment, no. 85.

Earl, P. E. and Glaister, K. W. (1979) Wage Stickiness from the Demand Side. University of Stirling Discussion Papers in Economics, Finance, and Investment, no. 78.

Earl, P. E. and Glaister, K. W. (1980) Can the Unemployed Price Themselves Into Jobs? Stirling, Mimeo.

Eatwell, J. L. (1979) *Theories of Value, Output and Employment*. Woolwich: Thames Papers in Political Economy, no. 15.

Evans, G. (1980) A Bottleneck Theory of the Cross-Sectional Variance of Inflation. University of Stirling Discussion Papers in Economics, Finance, and Investment, no. 82.

Fisher, D. (1980) *Monetary Theory and the Demand for Money*. Oxford: Martin Robertson.

Fisher, I. (1911) *The Purchasing Power of Money*. New York: Macmillan.

Flannery, M. L. and Jaffee, D. M. (1973) *The Economic Implications of an Electronic Monetary Transfer System*. Lexington, Mass: Lexington Books.

Frenkel, J. A. and Johnson, H. G. (eds) (1976) *The Monetary Approach to the Balance of Payments*. London: Allen & Unwin.

Friedman, M. (1953) The Methodology of Positive Economics. In Milton Friedman, (ed.), *Essays in Positive Economics*. Chicago: University of Chicago Press.

Friedman, M. (1957) *A Theory of the Consumption Function*. Princeton: Princeton University Press.

Friedman, M. (1962) *Capitalism and Freedom*. Chicago: University of Chicago Press.

Friedman, M. (1968) The Role of Monetary Policy. *American Economic Review*, 58 (March), 1–17.

Friedman, M. (1970) A Theoretical Framework for Monetary Analysis. *Journal of Political Economy*, 78 (March/April), 193–238.

Friedman, M. (1974) *Monetary Correction*. London: Institute of Economic Affairs, Occasional Paper 41.

Friedman, M. and Meiselman, D. (1963) The Relative Stability of Monetary Velocity and the Investment Multiplier in the United States, 1897–1958. In E. Cary Brown *et al.* (eds), *Stabilization Policies: Commission on Money and Credit*. Englewood Cliffs, New Jersey: Prentice-Hall.

Friedman, M. and Schwartz, A. (1963) *A Monetary History of the United States: 1867–1960*. Princeton: Princeton University Press.

Fry, M. (1978) Money and Capital or Financial Deepening in Economic Development? *Journal of Money, Credit and Banking*, 10 (November), 464–75.

Galbraith, J. K. (1961) *The Great Crash*. Harmondsworth: Penguin.

Galbraith, J. K. (1975) *Money: Whence it Came, Where it Went*. Harmondsworth: Penguin.

Garegnani, P. (1979) Notes on Consumption, Investment and Effective Demand: II, *Cambridge Journal of Economics* 3 (March), 63–82.

Goldfeld, S. M. (1976) The Case of the Missing Money. *Brookings Papers on Economic Activity*, 3, 683–730.

Goldsmith, R. W. (1969) *Financial Structure and Development*. New York: Yale University Press.

Goodhart, C. A. E. (1975) *Money, Information and Uncertainty*. London: Macmillan.

Gordon, R. J. (1979) *Macroeconomics*. Boston: Little, Brown.

Greene, M. (1981) Will Technology Undermine Today's Monetary Control Techniques? *The Banker*, 131 (August), 29–32.

Gurley, J. G. and Shaw, E. S. (1955) Financial Aspects of Economic Development, *American Economic Review*, 45 (September), 515–38.

Gurley, J. G. and Shaw, E. S. (1960) *Money in a Theory of Finance*. Washington, DC: Brookings Institution.

Gurley, J. G. and Shaw, E. S. (1967) Financial Structure and Development. *Economic Development and Cultural Change*, 15 (April), 257–68.

Hahn, F. H. (1977) Keynesian Economics and General Equilibrium Theory: Reflections on Some Current Debates. In G. C. Harcourt (ed.), *The Microfoundations of Macroeconomics*. London: Macmillan.

Harcourt, G. C. (1972) *Some Cambridge Controversies in the Theory of Capital*. Cambridge: Cambridge University Press.

Hayek, F. A. (1972) *A Tiger by the Tail: The Keynesian Legacy of Inflation*. London: Institute of Economic Affairs.

Hester, D. D. (1964) Keynes and the Quantity Theory: A Comment on Friedman–Meiselman CMC Paper. *Review of Economics and Statistics*, 46 (November), 364–8.

Hicks, J. R. (1937) Mr Keynes and the 'Classics'; A Suggested Reinterpretation. *Econometrica*, 5 (April), 147–59.

Hirschman, A. O. (1963) *Journeys Towards Progress: Studies of Policy-Making in Latin America*. New York: Twentieth Century Fund.

Hirschman, A. O. (1970) *Exit, Voice, and Loyalty: Responses to Decline in Firms, Organizations, and States*. Cambridge, Mass: Harvard University Press.

Hogendorn, J. S. and Gemery, H. A. (1981) Abolition and the Impact on Monies Imported to West Africa. In D. Eltis and J. Walvin (eds), *The Slave Trade and Abolition*. Madison: University of Wisconsin Press.

Hutchison, T. W. (1977) *Keynes Versus the 'Keynesians'—?: An Essay on the Thinking of J. M. Keynes and the Accuracy of Interpretation by his Followers*. London: Institute of Economic Affairs.

Irwin, H. S. (1937) The Nature of Risk Assumption in the Trading on Organized Exchanges. *American Economic Review*, **27** (June), 267–78.

Johnson, M. (1970) The Cowrie Currencies of West Africa, parts 1 and 2, *Journal of African History*, 11, 17–49 and 331–53.

Kahn, R. F. and Posner, M. V. (1977) Inflation, Unemployment and Growth. *National Westminster Bank Review*, November, pp. 28–37.

Kaldor, N. (1970) The New Monetarism. *Lloyds Bank Review*, no. 97 (July), pp. 1–18.

Katona, G. (1960) *The Powerful Consumer: Psychological Studies of the American Economy*. New York: McGraw-Hill.

Katona, G. (1976) Consumer Investment Versus Business Investment. *Challenge*. January/February.

Katouzian, H. (1980) *Ideology and Method in Economics*. London: Macmillan.

Keynes, J. M. (1936) *The General Theory of Employment, Interest and Money*. London: Macmillan.

Keynes, J. M. (1937a) The General Theory of Employment. *Quarterly Journal of Economics*, **51**, 209–23.

Keynes, J. M. (1937b) The 'Ex Ante' Theory of the Rate of Interest. *Economic Journal*, **47** (December), 663–9.

Keynes, J. M. (1940) *How To Pay For The War: A Radical Plan for the Chancellor of the Exchequer*. London: Macmillan.

Khatkhate, D. R. (1980) False Issues in the Debate on Interest Rate Policies in Less Developed Countries. *Banca Nazionale del Lavoro Quarterly Review*, **133** (June), 205–24.

Kindleberger, C. P. (1974) The Formation of Financial Centres: A Study in Comparative Economic History. *Princeton Studies in International Finance*, no. 36.

Kindleberger, C. P. (1978) *Manias, Panics and Crashes*. London: Macmillan.

Kouri, P. J. K. (1975) The Hypothesis of Offsetting Capital Flows: A Case Study of Germany. *Journal of Monetary Economics*, **1** (January), 21–39.

Laidler, D. E. W. (1975) *Essays on Money and Inflation*. Manchester: Manchester University Press.

Laidler, D. E. W. (1977) *The Demand for Money: Theories and Evidence* (2nd edn). New York: Harper & Row.

Lakatos, I. (1970) Falsification and the Methodology of Scientific Research Programme. In I. Lakatos and A. Musgrave (eds), *Criticism and the Growth of Knowledge*. London: Cambridge University Press.

Leijonhufvud, A. (1967) Keynes and the Keynesians: a Suggested Interpretation. *American Economic Review*, 57 (May), 401–10.
Leijonhufvud, A. (1968) *On Keynesian Economics and the Economics of Keynes*. New York: Oxford University Press.
Leijonhufvud, A. (1969) *Keynes and the Classics*. London: Institute of Economic Affairs.
Leijonhufvud, A. (1973) Effective Demand Failures. *Swedish Journal of Economics*, 75, 27–48.

McKenzie, G. W. (1976) *The Economics of the Euro-Currency System*. London: Macmillan.
McKinnon, R. I. (1973) *Money and Capital in Economic Development*. Washington, DC: Brookings Institution.
Magdoff, H. (1969) *The Age of Imperialism: The Economics of US Foreign Policy*. New York: Monthly Review Press.
Malinvaud, E. (1977) *The Theory of Unemployment Reconsidered*. Oxford: Basil Blackwell.
Matthews, R. C. O. and Reddaway, W. B. (1980) Can Mrs Thatcher Do It? *Midland Bank Review*, Autumn.
Minsky, H. P. (1975) *John Maynard Keynes*. New York: Columbia University Press (London: Macmillan, 1976).
Modigliani, F. (1944) Liquidity Preference and the Theory of Interest and Money. *Econometrica*, 12 (January), 45–88.
Myrdal, F. (1957) *Economic Theory and Underdeveloped Regions*. London: Duckworth.

Nadler, P. S. (1979) *Commercial Banking in the Economy*. New York: Random House.
Naylor, T. (1975) *The History of Canadian Business 1867–1914: The Banks and Finance Capital*. Toronto: James Lorimer & Co.
Neild, R. R. (1963) *Pricing and Employment in the Trade Cycle: a Study of British Manufacturing Industry 1950–1961*. London: Cambridge University Press.
Niehans, J. and Hewson, J. (1976) The Eurodollar Market and Monetary Theory. *Journal and Money, Credit and Banking*, 8 (February), 1–27.

Penrose, E. T. (1959) *The Theory of the Growth of the Firm*. Oxford: Basil Blackwell (2nd edn, 1980).
Penrose, E. T. (1971) *The Growth of Firms, Middle East Oil, and Other Essays*. London: Frank Cass.
Pesek, B. P. and Saving, T. R. (1967) *Money, Wealth and Economic Theory*. New York: Collier-Macmillan.
Pigou, A. C. (1941) *Employment and Equilibrium*. London: Macmillan.
Polak, J. J. (1957) Monetary Analysis of Income Information and Balance of Payments Problems. *IMF Staff Papers*, 6 (November), 1–50.

Polak, J. J. and Boissoneault, L. (1960) Monetary Analysis of Income and Imports and its Statistical Operation. *IMF Staff Papers*, 7 (April), 349–415.

Poole, W. (1970) Optimal Choice of Monetary Policy Instruments in a Simple Stochastic Macro Model. *Quarterly Journal of Economics*, 84 (May), 197–216.

Poole, W. and Kornblith, E. B. F. (1973) The Friedman–Meiselman CMC Paper: New Evidence on an Old Controversy. *American Economic Review*, 63 (December), 908–17.

Porter, R. D., Simpson, T. D. and Mauskopf, E. (1979) Financial Innovation and Monetary Aggregates. *Brookings Papers on Economic Activity*, 1, 213–29.

Radcliffe Report (1959) *The Committee on the Working of the Monetary System, Report*, Cmnd. 827. London: HMSO.

Revell, J. (1973) *The British Financial System*. London: Macmillan.

Richardson, G. B. (1953) Imperfect Knowledge and Economic Efficiency. *Oxford Economic Papers*, 5 (June), 136–56.

Richardson, G. B. (1960) *Information and Investment*. Oxford: Oxford University Press.

Richardson, G. B. (1964) The Limits to a Firm's Rate of Growth. *Oxford Economic Papers*, 16 (March), 9–23.

Robertson, D. H. (1956) *Economic Commentaries*. London: Macmillan.

Roe, A. R.(1973) The Case for Flow of Funds and National Balance Sheet Analysis. *Economic Journal*, 83 (June), 339–420.

Salter, W. E. G. (1966) *Productivity and Technical Change* (2nd edn). Cambridge: Cambridge University Press.

Savin, N. E. (1978) Friedman–Meiselman Revisited: A Study in Autocorrelation. *Economic Inquiry*, 16 (January), 37–52.

Shackle, G. L. S. (1974) *Keynesian Kaleidics*. Edinburgh: Edinburgh University Press.

Shaw, E. S. (1973) *Financial Deepening in Economic Development*. New York: Oxford University Press.

Sheppard, D. K. (1971) *The Growth and Role of UK Financial Institutions 1880–1962*. London: Methuen.

Silber, W. L. (1969) Portfolio Substitutability, Regulations, and Monetary Policy. *Quarterly Journal of Economics*, 83 (May), 197–219.

Simon, H. A. (1969) *The Sciences of the Artificial*. Cambridge, Mass: Harvard University Press.

Singh, A. (1977) UK Industry and the World Economy: A Case of De-Industrialisation? *Cambridge Journal of Economics*, 1 (June), 113–26.

Smith, A. (1970) *The Wealth of Nations*, ed. by A. Skinner. Harmondsworth: Penguin.

Smith, R. P. (1975) *Consumer Demand for Cars in the USA.* Cambridge University Department of Applied Economics, Occasional Paper 44. London: Cambridge University Press.
Solow, R. M. and Kareken, J. (1963) Lags in Monetary Policy. In E. Cary Brown *et al* (eds), *Stabilization Policies: Commission on Money and Credit.* Englewood Cliffs, New Jersey: Prentice-Hall.
Spero, J. E. (1980) *The Failure of the Franklin National Bank: Challenge to the International Banking System.* New York: Columbia University Press.
Steinbruner, J. D. (1974) *The Cybernetic Theory of Decision.* Princeton: Princeton University Press (paperback edn, 1976).

Tobin, J. (1958) Liquidity Preference as Behaviour Towards Risk. *Review of Economic Studies,* 25 (February), 65–86.
Tobin, J. (1963) Commercial Banks as Creators of 'Money'. In D. Carson (ed.), *Banking and Monetary Studies,* pp. 408–19. Homewood, Illinois: Richard D. Irwin Inc.
Tobin, J. and Brainard, W. C. (1963) Financial Intermediaries and the Effectiveness of Monetary Controls. *American Economic Review,* 53 (May), 383–400.
Townshend, H. (1937) Liquidity Premium and the Theory of Value. *Economic Journal,* 47 (March), 157–69.
Trevithick, J. A. (1976) Money Wage Inflexibility and the Keynesian Labour Supply Function. *Economic Journal,* 86 (June), 327–32.
Trevithick, J. A. (1978) Recent Developments in the Theory of Employment. *Scottish Journal of Political Economy,* 25 (February), 107–18.
Triffin, R. (1964) The Myth and Realities of the So-Called Gold Standard. *The Evolution of the International Monetary System: Historical Reappraisal and Future Perspectives,* pp. 2–20. Princeton: Princeton University Press.

UK (1976) *The Licensing and Supervision of Deposit-Taking Institutions.* (White Paper) Cmnd. 6584, August. London: HMSO.
UK (1980) *Monetary Control* (Green Paper). Cmnd. 7858, March. London: HMSO.

West, R. C. (1977) *Banking Reform and the Federal Reserve 1863–1923.* Ithaca: Cornell University Press.
Whittington, G. and Meeks, G. (1976) *The Financing of Quoted Companies in the United Kingdom: Background Paper No. 1 for the Royal Commission on Income and Wealth.* London: HMSO.
Wilson, T. (1979) Crowding Out: The Real Issues. *Banca Nazionale Del Lavoro Quarterly Review,* no. 130 (September), pp. 227–42.
Worswick, G. D. N. (ed.) (1973) *The Concept and Measurement of Involuntary Unemployment.* London: George Allen & Unwin.

Index